Scott Seely
Eric A. Smith
Deon Schaffer

Creating and Consuming Web Services in Visual Basic

Addison-Wesley

Boston • San Francisco • New York • Toronto • Montreal
London • Munich • Paris • Madrid
Capetown • Sydney • Tokyo • Singapore • Mexico City

Creating and Consuming Web Services in Visual Basic

Many of the designations used by manufacturers and sellers to distinguish their products are claimed as trademarks. Where those designations appear in this book, and Addison-Wesley were aware of a trademark claim, the designations have been printed in initial capital letters or in all capitals.

The author and publisher have taken care in the preparation of this book, but make no expressed or implied warranty of any kind and assume no responsibility for errors or omissions. No liability is assumed for incidental or consequential damages in connection with or arising out of the use of the information or programs contained herein.

The publisher offers discounts on this book when ordered in quantity for special sales.

For more information, please contact:

Pearson Education Corporate Sales Division
201 W. 103rd Street
Indianapolis, IN 46290
(800) 428-5331
corpsales@pearsoned.com

Visit AW on the Web: www.awl.com/cseng/

International Standard Book Number: 0-672-32156-4

Library of Congress Catalog Card Number: 2001086076

Printed in the United States of America

First Printing: May 2002

05   04   03   02   4   3   2   1

Trademarks

Warning and Disclaimer

Acquisitions Editor
Sondra Scott

Development Editor
Laurie McGuire

Managing Editor
Charlotte Clapp

Project Editors
Tony Reitz
Linda Seifert

Copy Editor
Pat Kinyon

Indexer
Eric Schroeder

Proofreader
Andrea Dugan

Technical Editors
Ken Cox
Jawahar Puvvala

Team Coordinator
Lynne Williams

Media Developer
Dan Scherf

Interior Designer
Gary Adair

Contents at a Glance

Table of Contents

Foreword

Looking back at the last 30 years of human-computer interaction, a number of key milestones stand out prominently: the shift from the mainframe computing to the PC, the introduction of the graphical user interface, the move from 16- to 32-bit processors, and most recently, the pervasiveness of the Internet and the Web. Each of these landmarks represents a fundamental turning point in the relationship between human and machine. They also served to address some of the most pressing industry challenges of the time, from providing a viable platform for consumer-based computing to satisfying the need for richer, graphical user interaction to enabling ubiquitous application deployment and access.

Now, as businesses seek to address the ongoing fundamental challenges of software integration, a new technology called XML Web services is promising to once again fundamentally transform and enhance the way consumers and businesses interact with computers. The core concept behind these Web services is relatively straightfor-ward[md]components that are accessible using standardized Internet protocols. Yet their potential to affect the industry is both far-reaching and profound. Similar to computing revolutions of the past, XML Web services represents a new paradigm around which the entire computing industry is converging. Partners and competitors alike are quickly recognizing the value of XML Web services as a universal compo-nent architecture[md]one that spans programming languages, networks, and even platforms.

But why this sudden move to a new software integration paradigm when technolo-gies such as DCOM and CORBA already exist? Although they provide a viable option for integration of systems residing in a uniform corporate Intranet, they lack the capability to adapt to the loosely coupled, heterogeneous environment of the Internet. As this became evident to more and more businesses that required integra-tion not only within the firewall, but also with diverse business partners and customers, it became clear that the path to success lay not in tightly-coupled, propri-etary systems, but in the adoption of integration technologies based on open stan-dards. This is the fundamental differentiator and the key to the success of Web services.

For developers, Web services present a nearly limitless world of new opportunities. Because of the fundamental issues they address, Web services are pertinent to the entire spectrum of today's software, from rich Windows applications, to thin-client Web applications to the emerging market of mobile device software. For Visual Basic developers, Web services represent a new era in component creation and reuse. From day one, Visual Basic developers have been avid consumers of preexisting compo-nents. With XML Web services, the ability to consume components is vastly expanded to the Internet, across firewalls and even to other operating systems. And with Visual Basic .NET, the ability to call this remote functionality is as easy as setting a reference to an existing COM component in VB 6.0. Building XML Web services in Visual Basic .NET is just as effortless. In fact, if you've ever written a class in Visual Basic 6, you're well on your way to creating Web services that can be deployed locally, on your corporate Intranet, or on the Internet itself.

In Creating and Consuming Web Services in Visual Basic, the authors cover the basics of XML Web service construction and consumption as well as numerous advanced topics associated with Web-service development. Their practical approach to describing the concepts of Web services will have you up and running in the first chapter. From there, you'll discover and implement Web services that address pertinent issues of security, state management, and asynchronous calls as well as the ever-important bottom line: how Visual Basic .NET and XML Web services can save your business money, promote integration with business partners and customers, and reduce your project's time to market.

As we enter a new era in component development and reuse, Visual Basic .NET and XML Web services empower us as VB developers to continue to be on the cutting edge of application development. And with this book, you've already taken the first step to understanding and implementing these crucial components that will take our Visual Basic applications to the next level.

Ari Bixhorn
Product Manager
Visual Basic .NET
Microsoft Corporation

About the Authors

Scott Seely works for Microsoft. He is a member of the MSDN Architectural Samples team bringing you content in the form of the Favorites Web Service and Web Service How-To (if the content was on interop with other toolkits, Scott probably wrote it) and as coauthor of the "At Your Service" *Voices* column on msdn.microsoft.com. He has authored two other books for Prentice Hall-PTR: *Windows Shell Programming* and *SOAP: Cross Platform Web Service Development Using XML*. When not thinking about Web Services, Scott likes to go hiking or on bike rides with his family.

Eric A. Smith works as an independent consultant, author, and trainer in the Indianapolis area. He is also the owner of Northstar Computer Systems (www.northcomp.com), a value-added reseller and Web hosting company. His company was one of the first to offer commercial .NET hosting services to its clients. Eric has written or contributed to 12 books covering Microsoft technologies, including *ASP.NET at Work: 10 Enterprise Projects* (Wiley). He can be reached at eric@northcomp.com.

Deon Schaffer has been developing with Visual Basic and other Microsoft technologies for more than seven years. For several years now, Deon's focus has been on designing and developing Windows DNA applications. Recently, he has concentrated specifically on Microsoft's .NET initiative.

Deon has a Bachelor's degree in Industrial Engineering with a major in Information Systems Engineering from the Ben-Gurion University in Be'er Sheva, Israel. He is also a Microsoft Certified Solutions Developer(MCSD). Deon is a senior consultant at Information Strategies in Washington, DC. He can be reached at Deon_Schaffer@hotmail.com.

About the Technical Editors

Ken Cox is a technical writer and Web developer in Toronto. A Microsoft Most Valuable Professional (MVP), Ken is a frequent contributor to computer books and magazines dealing with Microsoft technologies, especially ASP.NET. Before turning his interests to computers and things high-tech, Ken had a successful career as a broadcast journalist in Toronto and Quebec City. Contact Ken at `kjopc@hotmail.com`.

Jawahar Puvvala currently works as a senior developer. He has a great deal of experience in Microsoft and Java technology and has designed and developed several enterprise level systems. J.P. has two Master's degrees (Hong Kong University of Science and Technology and Florida Institute of Technology) and holds MCSD, MCSE, and MCDBA certifications. He has published several conference and journal papers.

Dedication

To Jean. Thanks for always believing in me.

—Scott

For Lauren and Jodi

—Eric

*To my wife, Oshrat, for all her support and patience, and to our
daughter, Zoe Amit, who was born during the writing of this book.*

—Deon

Acknowledgments

I have to start out by thanking my wife, Jean, and my children for their patience
while Daddy wrote another book. I don't think that they were ready for this so soon.
Fortunately, this is a team effort, and I had help from some great coauthors. Because
of them, I don't feel quite so burned out this time around.

I would like to thank Tim Moore at Prentice Hall for giving me an excuse to learn
about SOAP, starting with his little note back in December of 1999 saying "So, what
do you think?". By getting really involved with the protocol, I have had an opportunity to meet many great people (you know who you are) and do great things
(working at Microsoft ROCKS!).

I'd like to thank Kent Sharkey and Michael Edwards for talking me into going to
Microsoft to help shape how people use XML Web Services (the broader term
describing SOAP and its related technologies). By working there, I've had an opportunity to work and cooperate with others active in shaping where Web Services are
taking us. This includes folks outside Microsoft. I really feel that this is a community
effort and that it is working very well.

Thanks to Kenn Scribner and Mark Stiver for introducing me to the good folks at
Sams Publishing. I told the Sams people that I never want to write a book on my
own again (I've done so twice already), but that I would gladly be part of a larger
team. They said "cool" and provided a good opportunity to help out within a few
weeks of my opening my mouth. In case you are curious why I am thanking Sams
Publishing in a book published by Addison-Wesley, some of the team working on the
book was reorganized into Addison-Wesley from Sams early in 2002. Many of their
titles went with them, including this one. As a result, the team has never changed,
just the name of the imprint.

While reviewing the Scribner and Stiver book, *Applied SOAP: Implementing .NET XML Web Services*, I got to work with Laurie McGuire. I was excited to hear that Laurie would be the development editor on this text as well. Laurie never leaves me waiting for material and is patient when I slip delivery by a day or two. Finally, I want to thank Linda Engelman for passing my name to Sondra Scott. Sondra really believed in this book and thought it should be written. I hope she is happy about what we all created. I know that I am.

—Scott

First of all, I give God the glory for giving me the strength to get this book done. My wife and daughter were understanding, as usual, with Daddy having to lock himself in his office every so often. Sondra Scott and Laurie McGuire were understanding and helpful in getting the manuscript into shape. Scott Seely provided good guidance on the chapters that I contributed. Thanks to all!

—Eric

Introduction

One of the more confusing items about Web Services regards defining exactly what and why they are. Let's begin with why they exist.

Web Services exist to make it easier to integrate applications. Existing technologies include Java RMI, CORBA, and DCOM. All of these technologies work over networked environments and allow for application integration. This application integration is possible if all the components are reachable over a LAN. However, when going out to the public Internet, these networked applications start to break down. Another problem is that none of these technologies work well for cross platform, cross language integration. Often, working with one of these technologies ties you to a particular language, operating system, or toolkit that must be uniform across the solution. In today's world, the odds of having all systems being written in the same language or using the same operating system and interconnection libraries is fairly small. Add to this a desire to connect these applications across large distances using the Internet and you will find that almost all of these technologies come up short. The necessity of addressing these shortcomings gave birth to Web Services. So, what are they?

A Web Service is a programmatic interface that is accessible via the Internet. As such, it must rely on standardized protocols. You may be aware of the various technologies surrounding Web Services. SOAP (an abbreviation that does not really mean anything anymore), Web Services Description Language (WSDL), and Universal Description Discovery and Integration (UDDI) are just a few of the technologies that are a part of Web Services. To make Internet accessibility a reality, SOAP v1.1 and v1.2 rely on existing, widely deployed technologies. The de facto minimum requirements for Web Service interaction state that the platform, whether client or server, must understand the following standards:

- Hypertext Transfer Protocol (HTTP)
- Transmission Control Protocol/Internet Protocol (TCP/IP)
- eXtensible Markup Language (XML)
- XML Schema Definition (XSD)

Due to the wide adoption of the Internet and XML, it is extremely difficult to find an operating system or programming language that does not have some support for these standards. Because the interest in Web Services is building to a fever pitch, vendors and individuals are rallying to make additional Web Service–specific tools available. While not a silver bullet for interoperability woes, talking to other languages and platforms just got a lot easier to do.

For many people, the promise of interoperability drew them into learning more about Web Services. As a Visual Basic developer, this promise may have caused you to buy this book. One question probably remains: How real is this promise of inter-operability? For any two implementations to work together, they typically have to agree on two items: what the WSDL for a particular interface looks like and how to represent the SOAP message for any given operation in XML. To this end, the many serious development teams and individuals are working together to make sure they all agree.

At XMethods, `http://www.xmethods.com/ilab`, you can see a list of all the participants. This page also describes what it means to pass or fail the set of tests, as well as the tests themselves. If an implementation is not a part of this effort, you should steer clear of it. Yes, the Microsoft implementations are active in this process.

Applications of Web Services

Before going too far into this book, you should understand some of the reasons for using a Web Service:

- *Interface between languages where a binary interface does not exist or is inappropriate to use*—For example, you may want a Perl script to be able to talk to a Visual Basic interface.

- *Interface in between systems*—For example, you may want to make a business application on a mainframe accessible to boxes scattered throughout the business.

- *You need to allow a wide, unknown array of clients to access your application*—This is a common requirement in larger applications assembled using "best of breed" components.

- *You are exposing the functionality as a service for a fee*—In this case, instead of inventing your own protocol, use what Web Services provide to you. Examples include stock trading services and access to research databases, among other things.

When creating a Web Service, make sure that the various APIs are stateless. If you must maintain a pseudo-state, that state information should be obtainable from data passed in the SOAP messages. For example, a Web Service may require that users be validated. To do so, they log in and receive an authentication token. Other Web Service calls will require that the token appear somewhere within the SOAP message. With this, you have state (the user is "logged in") and this state is maintained over transient connections. Maintaining state this way helps with scalability and will be covered in Chapter 6, "Security Issues with Web Services."

What You Will Need

While you could run most of these examples using the free Microsoft .NET Framework SDK, you will get the greatest benefit and productivity by using Visual Studio .NET. This book assumes that the reader has Visual Studio .NET installed. This book will still be valuable to users with only the SDK, but many things will be harder to do.

You should also have a copy of the Microsoft SOAP Toolkit v2 installed on your machine. Yes, install this even if all you do is program .NET applications. The toolkit comes with an application called MSSOAPT.EXE. This application allows you to review the SOAP messages going between the SOAP endpoints.

The machine that you are developing on must have Internet Information Server (IIS) installed. Without it, you will not be able to run the examples in the book or develop Web Services on your local machine. This is only available on Windows NT 4.0, Windows 2000, and Windows XP. The good news is that all versions of these operating systems can host IIS. On the Professional versions of XP and 2000, you need to explicitly install IIS. You can do this through the Add/Remove Programs Control Panel applet. Refer to your Windows documentation for instructions. NT 4.0 Workstation can host IIS 4.0. This is available through the Windows NT 4.0 Option Pack.

Finally, it would help to have a good book on Visual Basic .NET handy. *Learn Visual Basic .NET in 21 Days* by Kent Sharkey and Duncan MacKenzie is one text that would work nicely. Their book serves as an overview of the language.

Who Is This Book For?

Because Web Service development with Visual Basic will attract Internet-savvy developers, Visual Basic application developers, and hobbyists, a wide range of people will be picking up this text and reading it. You do not necessarily need a lot of experience with the latest version of Visual Basic. That said, you should know that the language has changed a bit and has become more flexible. If you have not made yourself familiar with the changes, you should plan on updating your knowledge on Visual Basic .NET specifics along with this book.

You probably bought this book for one of two reasons:

- You want to learn how to write code that uses Web Services just to keep up to date.

- You just found out that you need to expose your application to outside applications and you need to learn this stuff as fast as possible.

With these goals in mind, this book is organized into the following parts:

- *Part I: The Basics*—Part I gets you programming right away. Almost everyone should, at a minimum, skim all of Part I before proceeding through other chapters.

  Keep in mind that the examples presented in Chapters 1, "Create Your First Web Service," and 2, "Consuming Your First Web Service," are appropriate for only one reason—they teach the concepts without burying you in special techniques. You would never offer these to internal applications or external partners, but they are very useful for getting you started learning the basics of Web Services. In subsequent chapters, you will tackle practical and realistic examples.

- *Part II: Going Deeper*—Part II covers some of the more advanced Web Service topics. In it, we examine securing a Web Service and tradeoffs you can make to maximize the scalability, reliability, and manageability of a Web Service. With some of the Web Services, you will have a need to maintain some kind of state in between Web Service calls. Different techniques for maintaining that state are useful depending on the circumstances. This section closes out with a look at Web Service enabling existing applications written using Visual Studio 6.0 and the Microsoft Web Services Toolkit.

- *Part III: Solving Real-World Problems*—Part III examines the uses of Web Services in real world situations. Web Services can be used to enable integration between business partners and customers. Within your own business, you can use Web Services to tie your heterogeneous computing environment together. The section closes out with a look at how this investment in Web Services can help improve your business's bottom line.

Now, let's jump right in and learn how to write Web Services!

PART I

The Basics

This section allows you to jump right in by creating and using a very simple Web Service. Then, you'll take a look at features such as SOAP, WSDL, UDDI, how they work and how you can take advantage of them through the XML and Web Service-specific attributes in .NET. You conclude your study of the basics by learning how to find and fix any bugs in the Web Services you create and consume.

IN THIS PART

1

Create Your First Web Service

If you have never written a Visual Basic .NET Web Service before, you are in the right place. You may be under the impression that Web Services are hard to write and deploy. With many toolkits, that impression is 100% correct. Fortunately, .NET was designed with Web Services in mind, making their coding and deployment an easy task. As someone who has used several of the more popular toolkits out there, I can honestly say that .NET is by far the easiest to use.

In this chapter, we are going to develop a Web Service that exposes a set of operations that demonstrate what .NET can do for you without you knowing a thing about what is going on under the covers. The demonstration will showcase the following items:

- A "Hello World" operation that shows the basics

- Returning a simple structure

- Returning an array of simple data types

- Returning an array of complex data types

The reason we are focusing on returning the items instead of passing them as arguments is simple—.NET will allow me to show you the results of the operations through Internet Explorer. To do so, all I have to do is make sure that none of the operations takes a complex type as an argument. In Chapter 2, "Consuming Your Web Service," we will look at how easy it is to write a client for this Web Service.

Let's dig in!

The "Hello World" Operation

Before you get the idea that "Hello World" is just a silly little example, consider that "Hello World" can do a great job diagnosing some basic problems. If a machine has an endpoint that returns a simple string when called correctly, programs using that code can perform simple tests to see if they can connect to the server.

The good news for us is that the wizards inside Visual Basic .NET will write this operation for us. To get there, we need to go through the Visual Studio IDE and create a new project. To do so, perform the following steps:

1. Open up Visual Studio .NET.

2. Select File, New Project.

3. Select the following items in the New Project dialog ((as shown in Figure 1.1):

   - Project Types: Visual Basic Projects

   - Templates: ASP.NET Web Service

   - Name: **Chapter1**

   - Location: **http://localhost**

4. Click OK.

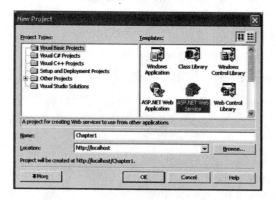

FIGURE 1.1   Creating a Visual Basic .NET Web Service project.

At this point, the IDE will create the Web Application on your local machine and generate the files needed for your Web Service. A skeleton class for a Web Service will be created as well. This class is always named Service1. Few people actually want a class named like this. To get a class with a meaningful name, you have two options— rename everything or delete Service1.asmx from the project and create a new class with a better name. Deleting the existing class has the added advantage that you will not miss some tiny detail. To delete Service1.asmx from the project, simply right-click the filename and select Delete. When the IDE warns you that the file will be permanently deleted, press OK. Now, let's add a new, better-named class to the project.

1. In the IDE, select Project, Add Web Service.

2. In the Add New Item dialog, name the Web Service **FirstService.asmx** (see Figure 1.2).

3. Click Open.

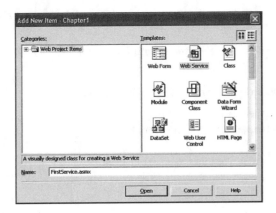

FIGURE 1.2   Adding a Visual Basic .NET Web Service Class.

You should now be looking at a screen similar to the one shown in Figure 1.3. From here, click the text Click Here to Switch to Code View. The wizard generated the sample in Listing 1.1 just for you.

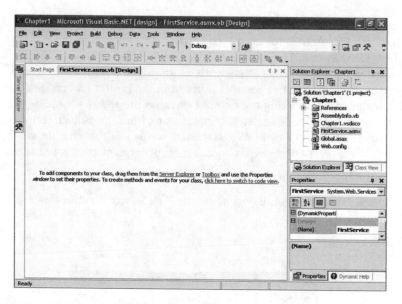

FIGURE 1.3   IDE immediately after adding a new .NET Web Service Class.

LISTING 1.1   Wizard-Generated Code for Web Service

```
Public Class FirstService
    Inherits System.Web.Services.WebService

#Region " Web Services Designer Generated Code "

    Public Sub New()
        MyBase.New()

        'This call is required by the Web Services Designer.
        InitializeComponent()

        'Add your own initialization code after the InitializeComponent() call

    End Sub

    'Required by the Web Services Designer
    Private components As System.ComponentModel.Container
```

LISTING 1.1   Continued

```
    'NOTE: The following procedure is required by the Web Services Designer
    'It can be modified using the Web Services Designer.
    'Do not modify it using the code editor.
<System.Diagnostics.DebuggerStepThrough()> _
    Private Sub InitializeComponent()
        components = New System.ComponentModel.Container()
    End Sub

    Protected Overloads Overrides Sub Dispose(ByVal disposing As Boolean)
        'CODEGEN: This procedure is required by the Web Services Designer
        'Do not modify it using the code editor.
    End Sub

#End Region

    ' WEB SERVICE EXAMPLE
    ' The HelloWorld() example service returns the string Hello World.
    ' To build, uncomment the following lines then save and build the project.
    ' To test this web service, ensure that the .asmx file is the start page
    ' and press F5.
    '
    '<WebMethod()> Public Function HelloWorld() As String
    '    HelloWorld = "Hello World"
    'End Function

End Class
```

To enable the HelloWorld function, simply uncomment three lines of code.

```
<WebMethod()> Public Function HelloWorld() As String
    HelloWorld = "Hello World"
End Function
```

If you have not used Visual Basic .NET before, the statement before the keyword Public may look a bit odd. The value in angle brackets (< >) is an attribute. The languages shipping with .NET all allow for the use of attributes before class declarations, member variables, or methods. The attributes are specific to the data immediately following them. Instead of creating extra executable code, attributes provide metadata for the functions. When the Common Language Runtime (CLR) encounters that metadata, it may execute code or generate some other behavior. We will cover the attributes specific to Web Services in Chapter 4, "Using Attributes to Shape WSDL and XML."

When the CLR sees the attribute <WebMethod()> when loading a class through an
.asmx file, it knows to expose the method as a part of a Web Service. Web Services
themselves only need to derive from the base class System.Web.Services.WebService
to be able to access the ASP.NET Session and Application objects. You could just as
easily not derive from System.Web.Services.WebService and still have a fully func-
tional Web Service.

To build the project, go to the Build menu and select the Build option. To see if
everything worked, open Internet Explorer and navigate to http://localhost/
Chapter1/FirstService.asmx. After doing this, you should be presented with the
screen shown in Figure 1.4. The page contains a warning that we will explore shortly.

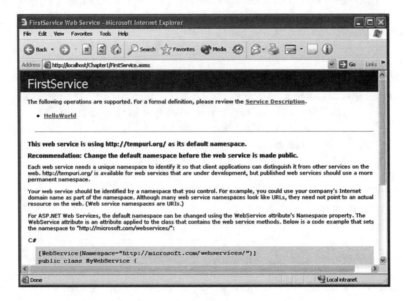

FIGURE 1.4   What ASP.NET presents for a .asmx page.

To get the screen shown in Figure 1.4 and any other links we might follow from this
page, we had to do no work. Instead, ASP.NET generates the pages for us by using
the .NET reflection APIs. We will cover how this all works in Chapter 4. Just know
that .NET makes your life very easy.

On the generated page, you will see a link to the HelloWorld operation. If you follow
that link, you will be presented with a page that allows you to call the function and
that outlines how to call the function using SOAP, HTTP/GET, and HTTP/POST. You see
the general format of the message exchange—what to send and what to expect in
return. This is another helpful piece of documentation that ASP.NET writes for you
(see Figure 1.5). This page also allows you to call the Web Service by clicking the
Invoke button.

FIGURE 1.5 Documentation ASP.NET generates for a Web method.

When you press Invoke, Internet Explorer will not use SOAP to call the underlying function. Instead, it will call the Web Service using HTTP GET.

The actual exchange will look like the following:

Request:

```
GET /Chapter1/FirstService.asmx/HelloWorld? HTTP/1.1
Host: localhost
```

Response:

```
HTTP/1.1 200 OK
Content-Type: text/xml; charset=utf-8
Content-Length: length

<?xml version="1.0" encoding="utf-8"?>
<string xmlns="http://tempuri.org/">string</string>
```

Clicking Invoke, we get the following response:

```
<?xml version="1.0" encoding="utf-8"?>
<string xmlns="http://tempuri.org/">Hello World</string>
```

For most of this book, we will only work with SOAP requests and responses. A SOAP Request/Response typically has this format:

```
<Envelope>
    <Header></Header>
    <Body>[interesting stuff here]</Body>
</Envelope>
```

But, Web Services can exist outside of the SOAP protocol. You can also send XML in a regular HTTP GET or POST request and return raw XML from that same request. When you do this, you are using Web Services in their simplest forms. To create the fancier, more powerful messages, only SOAP will work.

You will see a lot of messages in this chapter and the next. The idea is for you to become comfortable reading the messages. Outside of some special properties of the SOAP Envelope, your messages will be primarily Body content. That content is regular XML and only loosely related to SOAP. This book assumes you are already familiar with XML and that is why we start out with the simplest Web Service messages possible: HTTP GET/POST.

Other Files in the Project

Before we run headlong into the remaining examples, let's take a moment and see what other files got included in the project and where they sit on your hard drive. Looking at the Solution Explorer pane in Figure 1.3, you see the following files in your project:

- `AssemblyInfo.vb`   Contains version information related to the Visual Basic project.

- `[Project Name].vsdisco`   Contains the dynamic discovery information for this Web Service. The ASP.NET runtime uses this to discover and list all the Web Services hosted on a particular machine.

- `Global.asax`   Use this class to add handlers called by the ASP `Application` and `Session` objects. Web Services must derive from `System.Web.Services.WebService` to get access to these objects.

- `Web.config`   Configuration information related to the Web application. You can use this file to specify database connection strings, security settings, globalization settings, and other application-specific items.

By the time you are done reading this book, you will see the importance of `Web.config` because we will use it frequently. .NET uses config files extensively. These files are meant to replace static Registry settings. As an added bonus, they allow you to specify data that influences program behavior in an easy-to-use format. You can experiment with security, change databases, or edit application-specific settings without rebuilding the program. For example, let's say that we wanted to change the default string that our HelloWorld returned. To do this, we would open up Web.config and add the following section as a child element of the configuration root element:

```
<appSettings>
    <add key="ReturnString" value="I love config files!" />
</appSettings>
```

You should know that the elements not in quotes must appear as is. The add element has two attributes—key and value. When accessing application settings, you access them by key to get the associated value. Each key must be unique. After this XML is entered into Web.config, modify HelloWorld to read the ReturnString value from the configuration file.

```
<WebMethod()> Public Function HelloWorld() As String
    HelloWorld = System.Configuration.ConfigurationSettings. _
        AppSettings.Get("ReturnString")
End Function
```

Now, when you invoke HelloWorld via the ASP.NET–generated interface, it returns the following:

```
<?xml version="1.0" encoding="utf-8"?>
<string xmlns="http://tempuri.org/">I love config files!</string>
```

And yes, if you change the value attribute while the program is running, the program will get the new data the next time it goes to look. In the Web.config file, you will spend more time modifying appSettings than doing anything else. The first time you go into Web.config, the appSettings element does not exist. After you add it, if you need additional key/value pairs stored, just add them to the one appSettings element. For example, to add another element, the appSettings section would expand as follows:

```
<appSettings>
    <add key="ReturnString" value="I love config files!" />
    <add key="AnotherKey" value="Another Value" />
</appSettings>
```

Let's continue the example by having it handle a class object.

Passing Complex Types

ASP.NET makes it exceptionally easy to pass complex types as Web Service arguments and return values. If the complex type is passed as a method argument, ASP.NET will only be able to support SOAP messaging. This is because no definition exists to describe how to pass complex types as arguments via HTTP/GET or HTTP/POST. You can return complex types via these methods. So that we can see the immediate results of our coding via Internet Explorer, we will return the type.

Many people who learn of this functionality are often surprised to find out that when a value is passed via a Web Service, only the publicly visible fields are serialized. The receiver of the object has no access to any methods that the object may expose. Instead, the recipient of the object must already know what to do with the object when it is received. If you need to pass objects with methods intact, do not use Web Services. The Common Language Runtime (CLR) within .NET provides mechanisms when object identity and object value must be preserved. Web Services can only preserve the public object values.

To keep things simple, we will create a class called Person. Person will contain a Name object and a date for the person's birthday. Listing 1.2 shows a pair of classes that form a complex type. Name contains three strings and is itself a complex type. Person makes it a little more interesting for serialization because it must also serialize a Name inside.

LISTING 1.2   Source for Name and Person Objects

```
Public Class Name
    Public First As String
    Public Middle As String
    Public Last As String
End Class

Public Class Person
    Public theName As Name
    Public birthDay As Date

    Public Sub New()
        theName = New Name()
    End Sub
End Class
```

So far, so good. Now, we need to add a Web Method to the `FirstExample` object that returns a `Person`, as shown in the following code:

```
<WebMethod()> Public Function GetPerson() As Person
    GetPerson = New Person()
    GetPerson.birthDay = System.DateTime.Parse("April 5, 1972")
    GetPerson.theName.First = "Scott"
    GetPerson.theName.Middle = "Christopher"
    GetPerson.theName.Last = "Seely"
End Function
```

To test things out, we navigate over to `http://localhost/Chapter1/FirstService.asmx` and click `GetPerson`. Here, we see that the request and response via Internet Explorer will be fairly plain:

Request:

```
GET /Chapter1/FirstService.asmx/GetPerson? HTTP/1.1
Host: localhost
```

Response:

```
HTTP/1.1 200 OK
Content-Type: text/xml; charset=utf-8
Content-Length: length

<?xml version="1.0" encoding="utf-8"?>
<Person xmlns="http://tempuri.org/">
  <theName>
    <First>string</First>
    <Middle>string</Middle>
    <Last>string</Last>
  </theName>
  <birthDay>dateTime</birthDay>
</Person>
```

When we invoke the method, the Web Service responds as expected with the following:

```
<?xml version="1.0" encoding="utf-8"?>
<Person xmlns:xsi="http://www.w3.org/2001/XMLSchema-instance"
    xmlns:xsd="http://www.w3.org/2001/XMLSchema"
    xmlns="http://tempuri.org/">
  <theName>
    <First>Scott</First>
    <Middle>Christopher</Middle>
```

```
        <Last>Seely</Last>
    </theName>
    <birthDay>1972-04-05T00:00:00.0000000-07:00</birthDay>
</Person>
```

As you can see, the `Person` element came across with two sub-elements—`theName` and `birthDay`. The amazing part here is that no object-specific code had to be written to write it out as XML.

Returning Arrays of Simple Types

ASP.NET treats arrays of simple types as a list of items. Like everything we have seen so far, developers have little to think about other than stating that an array is being passed in or returned. To demonstrate the power here, we will write a Web Method in Listing 1.3 that returns an array of random numbers. As arguments, it will take the number of items to be returned as well as the smallest and largest permissible values to be returned.

Listing 1.3   Source for the `FirstService.GetRandomNumbers` Function

```
<WebMethod()> Public Function GetRandomNumbers( _
    ByVal arraySize As Long, ByVal min As Long, _
    ByVal max As Long) As Long()

    Dim retval(arraySize - 1) As Long
    Dim rnd As New System.Random()
    Dim index As Long
    For index = 0 To retval.Length - 1
        retval(index) = rnd.Next(min, max)
    Next
    GetRandomNumbers = retval
End Function
```

The code creates an array of size `arraySize` and a random number generator. Using the random number generator, the code loops through all the elements assigning them different values, and then returns those values to the caller. The `Next` function takes two values and returns a random number within that range. The return value from this function will be as small as the minimum value but never as large as the maximum. In mathematical terms, `Next` returns a value in the range (`min`, `max`). When testing this function from Internet Explorer, we will continue to use HTTP/GET. The message exchange will look something like the following:

Request:

```
GET /Chapter1/FirstService.asmx/GetRandomNumbers?
➥arraySize=string&min=string&max=string HTTP/1.1
Host: localhost
```

Response:

```
HTTP/1.1 200 OK
Content-Type: text/xml; charset=utf-8
Content-Length: length

<?xml version="1.0" encoding="utf-8"?>
<ArrayOfLong xmlns="http://tempuri.org/">
  <long>long</long>
  <long>long</long>
</ArrayOfLong>
```

To get five values between –1000 and 1000, I would fill in the generated form as shown in Figure 1.6. The outgoing request is then formatted within the URL as `http://localhost/Chapter1/FirstService.asmx/GetRandomNumbers?arraySize=5&m in=-1000&max=1000`. This request returns the XML shown in Listing 1.4.

LISTING 1.4   Returned XML for call to GetRandomNumber

```
<?xml version="1.0" encoding="utf-8"?>
<ArrayOfLong
  xmlns:xsi="http://www.w3.org/2001/XMLSchema-instance"
  xmlns:xsd="http://www.w3.org/2001/XMLSchema"
  xmlns="http://tempuri.org/">
  <long>-593</long>
  <long>203</long>
  <long>-158</long>
  <long>799</long>
  <long>20</long>
  <long>-930</long>
</ArrayOfLong>
```

Simple arrays get passed around all the time. It may be a list of temperatures, dates, strings, or something else. Arrays of structured data are equally common.

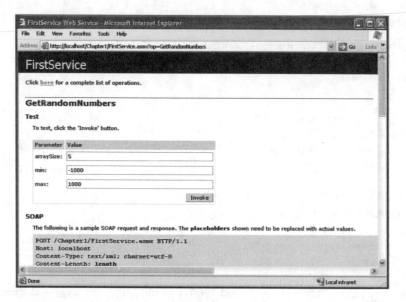

FIGURE 1.6   Using the ASP.NET–generated Web page to call GetRandomNumbers.

Returning Arrays of Structures

Many times, applications need to return arrays of structured data. Frequently, this data is stored in a database or on a device and needs to be transmitted en masse. For example, when requesting the details of a purchase order, it makes sense to return the lines and delineate the parts of the line. A line item might contain the following details:

- Part number

- Part name

- Part description

- Quantity ordered

- Price per part

As we saw with the GetPerson example, a bit of structured data can contain other structures. Likewise, arrays can appear anywhere within the data. Arrays are very powerful and are often quite handy. Fortunately, .NET handles these well too. To keep things simple, we will not introduce any new classes for this example (see Listing 1.5). Instead, we will take an example that returns an array of names. This example will return a list of all the authors (contributing authors included) involved with this book.

Listing 1.5   Source for the `FirstService.GetAuthorNames` Function

```
<WebMethod()> Public Function GetAuthorNames() As Name()
    Dim firstNames() As String = {"Scott", "Michael", "Jeffrey", "Deon"}
    Dim lastNames() As String = {"Seely", "Carnell", "Huntsman", "Schaffer"}

    ' Array will be dimensioned 0 to firstNames.Length - 1. The
    ' assumption here is that firstNames.Length == lastNames.Length
    Dim retval(firstNames.Length - 1) As Name
    Dim index As Long
    ' Instantiate the four names
    For index = 0 To retval.Length - 1
        retval(index) = New Name()
        retval(index).First = firstNames(index)
        retval(index).Middle = ""
        retval(index).Last = lastNames(index)
    Next

    GetAuthorNames = retval
End Function
```

To make things very simple, all the first names are stored in one array and the last names in another. Then, as the code loops through initializing the individual array elements, it also sets the values for the `Name.First`, `Name.Middle`, and `Name.Last`. Again, we will test this Web Method using the HTTP/GET interface. The message exchange will look like the following:

Request:

```
GET /Chapter1/FirstService.asmx/GetAuthorNames? HTTP/1.1
Host: localhost
```

Response:

```
<?xml version="1.0" encoding="utf-8"?>
<ArrayOfName xmlns="http://tempuri.org/">
  <Name>
    <First>string</First>
    <Middle>string</Middle>
    <Last>string</Last>
  </Name>
  <Name>
    <First>string</First>
```

```
      <Middle>string</Middle>
      <Last>string</Last>
    </Name>
</ArrayOfName>
```

When choosing the Invoke button on the generated Web page, the names are returned with the following XML:

```
<?xml version="1.0" encoding="utf-8"?>
<ArrayOfName
  xmlns:xsi="http://www.w3.org/2001/XMLSchema-instance"
  xmlns:xsd="http://www.w3.org/2001/XMLSchema"
  xmlns="http://tempuri.org/">
  <Name>
    <First>Scott</First>
    <Middle />
    <Last>Seely</Last>
  </Name>
  <Name>
    <First>Michael</First>
    <Middle />
    <Last>Carnell</Last>
  </Name>
  <Name>
    <First>Jeffrey</First>
    <Middle />
    <Last>Huntsman</Last>
  </Name>
  <Name>
    <First>Deon</First>
    <Middle />
    <Last>Schaffer</Last>
  </Name>
</ArrayOfName>
```

Once again, the serialization is done without any effort on the developer's part.

Summary

Visual Basic, working together with the .NET runtime, gives developers the ability to easily create Web Services with little or no knowledge of XML, SOAP, or the underlying machinery. Because you will rarely have to concern yourself with the particulars, you can concentrate on developing good, solid code. You can easily pass around simple and complex types, as well as arrays.

In this chapter, we tested the various functions by using the HTTP/GET interface. Web Services can typically be accessed via HTTP/GET, HTTP/POST, and SOAP. The rest of the book will concentrate on talking to Web Services using SOAP. The messages are slightly different from what we showed here. We will look at the SOAP messages being exchanged between the client and server. As a Web Service programmer, you will find it helpful to become very familiar with what these messages look like. Chapter 3, "SOAP, WSDL, and UDDI Explained," will cover the SOAP protocol in detail.

2

Consuming Your First Web Service

In the previous chapter, we created a Web Service that showed the variety of things you could do. The next thing we need to cover is consuming that Web Service. It might have many different types of clients. Anything that can talk to a Web Service might come calling. The following are just a few examples of the entities that might call your Web Service:

- Command-line interface (CLI) applications
- Graphical user interface (GUI) applications
- Web applications
- Other Web Services

When using Visual Basic .NET, the code you write to talk to a Web Service does not vary based on the client type. To emphasize that point, we will build a simple example for each of the four different Web Service clients just mentioned. Each example will only access one of the methods the Web Service exposes. To test your understanding of the subject matter, I encourage you to work along with the examples. After you complete the chapter, modify the individual example applications to access Web Methods not used by that example.

We will begin by looking at how you attach a Web reference. Regardless of application type, you always attach a Web reference the same way.

Attaching a Web Reference

Visual Studio .NET has a special name for the machinery that hooks up a Web Service client to the server—Web reference. A Web reference consists of the WSDL (Web Services Description Language) and any related disco files. It also includes the automatically generated code that the client uses to call the Web Service. We call this generated code the *proxy*.

> **NOTE**
>
> What is a disco file? It's a term for the Web Service discovery files. A given Web Service application may have multiple Web Services running within the same .NET binary. The disco file enumerates the services available within that binary by listing the paths to the WSDL files. Within .NET, that typically maps to a listing of all the .asmx files in the directory with the string "?WSDL" appended to the end of the filename.

When we hook up a Web Service, we can do so two ways—through command-line tools or through the Visual Studio IDE. In this text, we will concentrate on using the Visual Studio IDE. If you want to use the command-line tool WSDL.EXE, please refer to the Framework SDK documentation.

So that you can follow along with these instructions, create a simple Visual Basic application in the Visual Studio IDE. The application type does not matter much, but to keep things simple, I recommend creating a Console Application. Let's attach to the Chapter1 Web Service using the IDE by following these steps:

1. Select Project, Add Web Reference.

2. In the Add Web Reference dialog, go to the Address combo box and type **http://localhost/Chapter1/chapter1.vsdisco** (see Figure 2.1).

3. Click Add Reference.

> **NOTE**
>
> Besides using the IDE, there are other ways to add references to Web Services. When you first open the Add Web Reference dialog, the opening screen (shown in Figure 2.2) shows that you have the option to view Web references that reside on the Local Web Server.
>
> You can also add a Web reference by browsing straight to the WSDL file of the Web Service. To get the WSDL file for the Chapter1 Web Service, the URL would be http://localhost/Chapter1/FirstService.asmx?WSDL. In this case, you would still click Add reference to create the proxy.

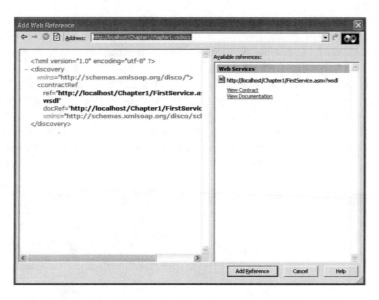

FIGURE 2.1   Adding a Web reference through the Visual Studio .NET IDE.

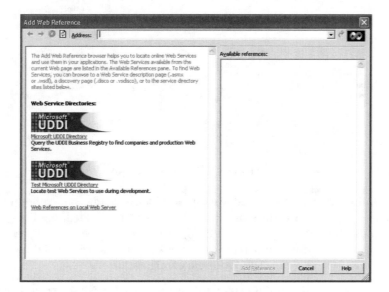

FIGURE 2.2   The startup view of the Add Web Reference dialog.

At this point, the Web reference has been added to the project and is contained in the `localhost` namespace. . When the IDE creates the proxy, the IDE automatically places the proxy in a separate namespace. The namespace comes from the start of the URL that helped grab the namespace in the first place. If you do not like the IDE chosen namespace, you can easily change the namespace. Just go to the Solution Explorer pane within the IDE, navigate to the Web references node, and right-click the Web reference you want to change. In our case, we right-click on the node underneath the Web Reference named `localhost` and select Rename from the pop-up menu (see Figure 2.3). Rename `localhost` to something slightly more meaningful: `Chapter1`.

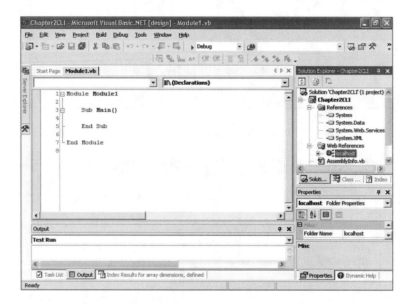

FIGURE 2.3   Manipulating the namespace associated with a Web reference.

Now that this has been completed, we can also look at doing some other interesting things. In Chapter 1, "Create Your First Web Service," I indicated that the application configuration file would be something with which you should get very familiar. We are going to continue our education by looking at how we can get our Web Service to read the endpoint URL from the configuration file.

In the IDE, go to the Solution Explorer pane and click the Chapter1 node underneath the Web References node. In the Properties pane, you should see the list of properties for the Web reference (see Figure 2.4). One of the properties is URL Behavior. This item can be static or dynamic. Static behavior means that the URL never changes and is stored in the proxy object base on the endpoint listed in the WSDL file. If the endpoint changes and you want to avoid rebuilding the application every time the Web Service does move, you can tell the application to look for the endpoint URL in the application configuration file by setting the URL Behavior to Dynamic. Under the covers, what is happening?

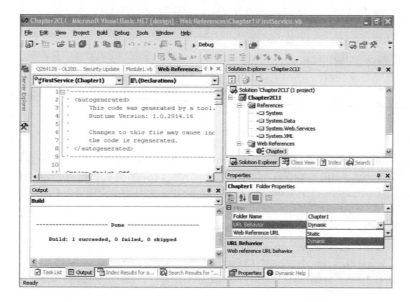

FIGURE 2.4   Changing the URL Behavior property related to a Web reference.

To answer that question, we need to look at the proxy that the IDE generates for us. That proxy is located in a subdirectory of the main project. On my machine, this is located in `My Documents\Visual Studio Projects\Chapter2CLI\Web References\ Chapter1\FirstService.vb`. When the URL Behavior property is set to Static, the constructor of the proxy looks like the following:

```
<System.Diagnostics.DebuggerStepThroughAttribute()> _
Public Sub New()
    MyBase.New()
    Me.Url = "http://localhost/Chapter1/FirstService.asmx"
End Sub
```

When the URL Behavior property is set to Dynamic, the constructor of the proxy changes to the code shown in Listing 2.1.

LISTING 2.1   Proxy Constructor with URL Behavior Set to Dynamic

```
<System.Diagnostics.DebuggerStepThroughAttribute()> _
Public Sub New()
    MyBase.New()
    Dim urlSetting As String = _
        System.Configuration.ConfigurationSettings.AppSettings( _
            "Chapter2CLI.Chapter1.FirstService")
    If (Not (urlSetting) Is Nothing) Then
        Me.Url = String.Concat(urlSetting, "")
    Else
        Me.Url = "http://localhost/Chapter1/FirstService.asmx"
    End If
End Sub
```

As you can see, the code for the Dynamic URL behavior is a little different. The
Dynamic lookup still defaults to the URL listed in the WSDL file. For reference,
Listing 2.2 shows the service section of the FirstService.asmx?WSDL file.

LISTING 2.2   Service declaration From the FirstService.asmx?WSDL Listing

```
<service name="FirstService">
  <port name="FirstServiceSoap" binding="s0:FirstServiceSoap">
    <soap:address location="http://localhost/Chapter1/FirstService.asmx" />
  </port>
  <port name="FirstServiceHttpGet" binding="s0:FirstServiceHttpGet">
    <http:address location="http://localhost/Chapter1/FirstService.asmx" />
  </port>
  <port name="FirstServiceHttpPost" binding="s0:FirstServiceHttpPost">
    <http:address location="http://localhost/Chapter1/FirstService.asmx" />
  </port>
</service>
```

The proxy is a SOAP proxy, so it references the port named FirstServiceSoap and
getting the endpoint from the soap:address element. The dynamic setting allows
me to change this up a bit and access the Web Service using a URL defined in
the application configuration file in an appSetting key named Chapter2CLI.
Chapter1.FirstService. Because I used the IDE, this key has already been placed
in the app.config file. I can change this URL to hit my local machine by its name,
scottnb, instead of by localhost. The appSettings section now looks like the following:

```
<appSettings>
    <add key="Chapter2CLI.Chapter1.FirstService"
        value="http://scottnb/Chapter1/FirstService.asmx"/>
</appSettings>
```

Command-Line Interface Applications

The simplest user interface is the command-line application. It uses the console for its input and output. While not visually appealing, it often provides a fast and simple way to accomplish tasks. For our CLI application, we will have it call the HelloWorld Web Method and print the results. As you will recall, HelloWorld was modified in Chapter 1 to read its value from the Web.config file associated with the Web Service.

The first things we need to do are open up Visual Studio and create a new project. In Visual Studio, you will see CLI applications called console applications. Perform the following steps to create the console application:

1. Select File, Project, New Project.

2. Select the following items in the New Project dialog:

    a. Project Type: Visual Basic Projects

    b. Templates: Console Application

    c. Name: Chapter2CLI

Figure 2.5 shows what the dialog should look like.

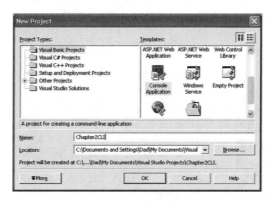

FIGURE 2.5   Setting up the *Chapter2CLI* application.

At this point, you have a skeleton for a console application. The IDE should have an opened file called Module1.vb. Our next task is to hook in the Chapter1 Web Service. To do this, add a Web reference to http://localhost/Chapter1/Chapter1.vsdisco and rename the namespace from localhost to Chapter1.

Your next step is to edit the Main subroutine. It will call HelloWorld, print the result to the console, and then exit. The edited code looks as follows:

```
Sub Main()
    Dim svc As New Chapter1.FirstService()
    System.Console.WriteLine(svc.HelloWorld())
End Sub
```

It does not get any easier than this. Figure 2.6 shows the output of this application.

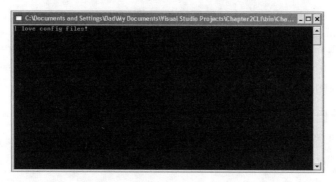

FIGURE 2.6   Running *Chapter2CLI*.

I also promised you that we would look at the SOAP message exchange that occurs under the covers. The following is the request and response that occurred for our CLI application:

Request:

```
<?xml version="1.0" encoding="utf-8"?>
<soap:Envelope
  xmlns:soap="http://schemas.xmlsoap.org/soap/envelope/"
  xmlns:xsi="http://www.w3.org/2001/XMLSchema-instance"
  xmlns:xsd="http://www.w3.org/2001/XMLSchema">
  <soap:Body>
    <HelloWorld xmlns="http://tempuri.org/" />
  </soap:Body>
</soap:Envelope>
```

Response:

```
<?xml version="1.0" encoding="utf-8"?>
<soap:Envelope
  xmlns:soap="http://schemas.xmlsoap.org/soap/envelope/"
  xmlns:xsi="http://www.w3.org/2001/XMLSchema-instance"
  xmlns:xsd="http://www.w3.org/2001/XMLSchema">
```

```
<soap:Body>
  <HelloWorldResponse xmlns="http://tempuri.org/">
    <HelloWorldResult>I love config files!</HelloWorldResult>
  </HelloWorldResponse>
</soap:Body>
</soap:Envelope>
```

Let's move on to the next application.

Graphical User Interface (GUI) Applications

GUI applications are known as Windows applications in Visual Studio .NET. The big advantage of a GUI is that you can show much more data to the user at once. In addition to text, you can harness the full power of graphics to compartmentalize data or translate that information into whatever makes the most sense. By now, most developers are familiar with the advantages of a GUI—easy menu navigation, event-driven programming, richer user interaction models, and so on. Because all of these advantages exist, it only makes sense to be able to access Web Service here as well. This time around, we will access the FirstService.GetRandomNumbers Web Method. To begin, we must first create a Windows Application project. Perform the following steps to create the Windows application:

1. Select File, Project, New Project.

2. Select the following items in the New Project dialog:

   a. Project Type: Visual Basic Projects

   b. Templates: Windows Application

   c. Name: Chapter2GUI

This time around we have the skeleton for a GUI application. The IDE displays a blank form, Form1. On this form, we want to place controls for the following items:

- A place for the user to enter the number of random numbers he or she wants.

- A place for the user to enter the number of minimum value of the random numbers.

- A place for the user to enter the number of maximum value of the random numbers.

- A place to display the results to the user.

Figure 2.7 shows my proposed layout of the form.

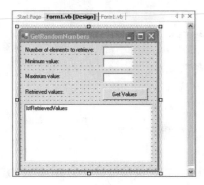

FIGURE 2.7   Layout of the *Chapter2GUI* main form.

After placing the controls on the form, I changed their names to make their data association clear. Our next step is to generate the proxy for the FirstService Web Service. Add a Web reference to http://localhost/Chapter1/Chapter1.vsdisco and rename the namespace from localhost to Chapter1. With this, we are almost done. We just have to write the code that executes when the Get Values button is clicked. The fastest and easiest way to do this is to double-click the Get Values button in the form designer. This will create the skeleton for the click event handler and bring up the code view.

Within the code, we want to make sure that all of the client input is valid. If all of the input is valid, we will call the Web Service and display the output. Listing 2.3 shows the full source for click handler:

LISTING 2.3   btnGetValues Click Event Handler

```
Private Sub btnGetValues_Click(ByVal sender As System.Object, _
    ByVal e As System.EventArgs) Handles btnGetValues.Click

    Dim minValue As Long
    Dim maxValue As Long
    Dim numElements As Long
    Dim elements() As Long
    Dim rndValue As Long

    'Read in the user data and validate the input

    ' Validate the number of elements value
    If (Me.txtNumElements.Text.Length = 0) Then
        MsgBox("You must enter the number of elements")
        Me.txtNumElements.Select()
        Exit Sub
```

LISTING 2.3   Continued

```
ElseIf Not (IsNumeric(Me.txtNumElements.Text)) Then
    MsgBox("The number of elements must be a number")
    Me.txtNumElements.Select()
    Exit Sub
End If


' Validate the minimum value
If (Me.txtMinValue.Text.Length = 0) Then
    MsgBox("You must enter a minimum value")
    Me.txtMinValue.Select()
    Exit Sub
ElseIf Not (IsNumeric(Me.txtMinValue.Text)) Then
    MsgBox("The minimum value must be a number")
    Me.txtMinValue.Select()
    Exit Sub
End If


' Validate the maximum value
If (Me.txtMaxValue.Text.Length = 0) Then
    MsgBox("You must enter a maximum value")
    Me.txtMaxValue.Select()
    Exit Sub
ElseIf Not (IsNumeric(Me.txtMaxValue.Text)) Then
    MsgBox("The maximum value must be a number")
    Me.txtMaxValue.Select()
    Exit Sub
End If


' Read in the values since they are all numbers
numElements = System.Convert.ToInt32(Me.txtNumElements.Text)
minValue = System.Convert.ToInt32(Me.txtMinValue.Text)
maxValue = System.Convert.ToInt32(Me.txtMaxValue.Text)


' Now for a little more validation

' Make sure that the number of elements is a positive number
If (numElements < 1) Then
    MsgBox("The number of elements must be greater than 0")
    Me.txtNumElements.Select()
    Exit Sub
End If
```

LISTING 2.3   Continued

```
' Make sure that the minimum value is less than the maximum
' value.
If (minValue >= maxValue) Then
    MsgBox("The minimum value must be less than the" & _
        " maximum value")
    Me.txtMinValue.Select()
    Exit Sub
End If


' Everything must be valid. Call the web service
Dim svc As New Chapter1.FirstService()
Try
    elements = svc.GetRandomNumbers(numElements, _
        minValue, maxValue)
    If (elements.Length > 0) Then

        ' Clear out the listbox
        Me.lstRetrievedValues.Items.Clear()

        'Add the elements to the list box
        For Each rndValue In elements
            Me.lstRetrievedValues.Items.Add(rndValue.ToString())
        Next

    End If
Catch ex As Exception
    MsgBox(ex.ToString())
Finally
    svc.Dispose()
End Try

End Sub
```

Most of the code in here is fairly straightforward. It checks what the user typed in for the various values and lets him or her know if anything is wrong. The Web Service-specific code does not occur until the last few lines of code.

The first thing you might notice is that the call to GetRandomNumbers is enclosed in a Try...Catch...Finally block. This is a brand new construct in Visual Basic .NET and is meant to supercede the On Error Goto syntax of its predecessors. All calls to Web Services can throw exceptions. Sometimes, it will be because of a connection failure, bad input, a SOAP Fault generated by the server, or some other item. Because an exception might leave the proxy with an open connection, it is very important to wrap the SOAP call in a `Try...Catch...Finally` block. The `Finally` part of the block should call the proxy's `Dispose` function. Doing so will release any resources and close the connection to the server. You will note that we did not do this in the CLI example. Now might be a good time to go back to that example and properly handle the call to the Web Service.

With this code in place, let's experiment with the application itself. Build the application (go to the Build menu and select Build). Then, select Debug, Start. With the application running, experiment and see how it works. Figure 2.8 shows the results of one run on my machine.

FIGURE 2.8   `Chapter2GUI` at work.

Before going on to the next example, we will also look at what the SOAP message exchange looked like. You may want to compare this with the request and response done with the `HTTP/GET` Web request listed in Chapter 1. The differences are minimal at best.

Request:

```
<?xml version="1.0" encoding="utf-8"?>
<soap:Envelope
  xmlns:soap="http://schemas.xmlsoap.org/soap/envelope/"
  xmlns:xsi="http://www.w3.org/2001/XMLSchema-instance"
  xmlns:xsd="http://www.w3.org/2001/XMLSchema">
  <soap:Body>
    <GetRandomNumbers xmlns="http://tempuri.org/">
      <arraySize>10</arraySize>
      <min>1</min>
      <max>10</max>
    </GetRandomNumbers>
  </soap:Body>
</soap:Envelope>
```

Response:

```
<?xml version="1.0" encoding="utf-8"?>
<soap:Envelope
  xmlns:soap="http://schemas.xmlsoap.org/soap/envelope/"
  xmlns:xsi="http://www.w3.org/2001/XMLSchema-instance"
  xmlns:xsd="http://www.w3.org/2001/XMLSchema">
  <soap:Body>
    <GetRandomNumbersResponse xmlns="http://tempuri.org/">
      <GetRandomNumbersResult>
        <long>6</long>
        <long>10</long>
        <long>9</long>
        <long>7</long>
        <long>8</long>
        <long>1</long>
        <long>10</long>
        <long>10</long>
        <long>6</long>
        <long>2</long>
      </GetRandomNumbersResult>
    </GetRandomNumbersResponse>
  </soap:Body>
</soap:Envelope>
```

Enough work on the desktop. Let's try out some Web-based access next.

Web Applications

You should be seeing a pattern by now. No matter the medium used to access a Web Service, the actions you perform to call the Web Service do not change. The only thing that changes is the way you get your input or display the results.

For this particular example, we will get the list of authors of this book and display the names in a table. Once again, we will create a new project.

1. Select File, Project, New Project.

2. Select the following items in the New Project dialog:

    a. Project Type: Visual Basic Projects

    b. Templates: ASP.NET Web Application

    c. Name: Chapter2WEB

At this point, you should be looking at the design view of `WebForm1.aspx`. On this screen, we will place a simple caption and a table. Set up the table to have one row and two columns. That row has a heading. The code will grow the table as appropriate. Figure 2.9 shows one way to display this.

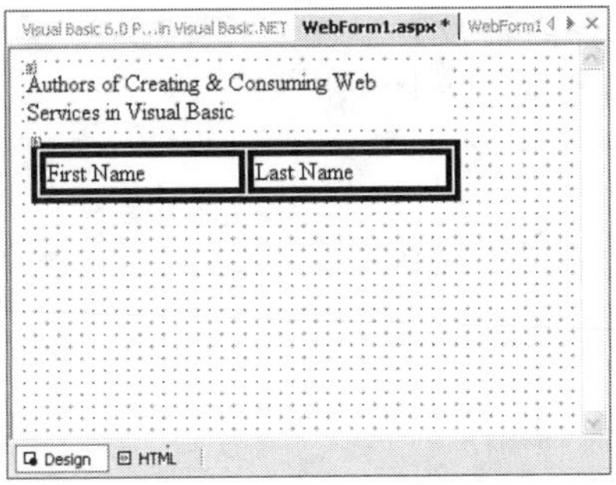

FIGURE 2.9   Layout for `WebForm1.aspx`.

After the Web form is configured, you need to add a Web reference to `http://localhost/Chapter1/Chapter1.vsdisco` and rename the namespace from `localhost` to `Chapter1`. With the proxy in place, we only need to add the author names to the table. To do this, open up the Solution Explorer pane and right-click `WebForm1.aspx`. Select View Code from the pop-up menu. We are now going to edit the `Page_Load` event handler to call to the `FirstService.GetAuthorNames` Web Method and add the author names to the table. Listing 2.4 shows the code.

LISTING 2.4   WebForm1 Page_Load Event Handler

```
Private Sub Page_Load(ByVal sender As System.Object, _
    ByVal e As System.EventArgs) Handles MyBase.Load

    'Put user code to initialize the page here
    Dim svc As New Chapter1.FirstService()
    Dim aName As Chapter1.Name
    Dim authorNames() As Chapter1.Name
    Dim tr As TableRow
    Dim fName As TableCell
    Dim lName As TableCell

    Try
        ' Get the names of the authors
        authorNames = svc.GetAuthorNames()
```

LISTING 2.4   Continued

```
    ' For every name in the array,
    ' create a new table row and two
    ' cells for that row.
    ' Set the text and add the row to
    ' the table.
    For Each aName In authorNames
        tr = New TableRow()
        fName = New TableCell()
        lName = New TableCell()
        fName.Text = aName.First
        lName.Text = aName.Last
        tr.Cells.Add(fName)
        tr.Cells.Add(lName)
        Me.authorTable.Rows.Add(tr)
    Next
Catch ex As Exception
    Response.Write(ex.ToString())
Finally
    ' Clean up after the service.
    svc.Dispose()
End Try
End Sub
```

Again, you see nothing terribly fancy here. Perhaps the most interesting bit of code here is that this uses the actual compiled source code instead of script to create the Web page. Depending on the number of items returned by the GetAuthorNames call, the code adds an appropriate number of rows to the table. This allows for some flexibility when filling in the table. If an author joins or leaves the authoring team, this code does not need to be modified. The correct number of rows will always be present. When viewing the page, we get a list of all four authors, just as expected. Figure 2.10 shows the results.

We will finish up this section with a quick look at the SOAP request and response. You may want to compare the results here against those in Chapter 1, which was done using HTTP/GET instead of SOAP.

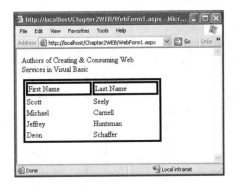

FIGURE 2.10   Live view of `WebForm1.aspx`.

Request:

```
<?xml version="1.0" encoding="utf-8"?>
<soap:Envelope
  xmlns:soap="http://schemas.xmlsoap.org/soap/envelope/"
  xmlns:xsi="http://www.w3.org/2001/XMLSchema-instance"
  xmlns:xsd="http://www.w3.org/2001/XMLSchema">
  <soap:Body>
    <GetAuthorNames xmlns="http://tempuri.org/" />
  </soap:Body>
</soap:Envelope>
```

Response:

```
<?xml version="1.0" encoding="utf-8"?>
<soap:Envelope
  xmlns:soap="http://schemas.xmlsoap.org/soap/envelope/"
  xmlns:xsi="http://www.w3.org/2001/XMLSchema-instance"
  xmlns:xsd="http://www.w3.org/2001/XMLSchema">
  <soap:Body>
    <GetAuthorNamesResponse xmlns="http://tempuri.org/">
      <GetAuthorNamesResult>
        <Name>
          <First>Scott</First>
          <Middle />
          <Last>Seely</Last>
        </Name>
```

```
    <Name>
      <First>Michael</First>
      <Middle />
      <Last>Carnell</Last>
    </Name>
    <Name>
      <First>Jeffrey</First>
      <Middle />
      <Last>Huntsman</Last>
    </Name>
    <Name>
      <First>Deon</First>
      <Middle />
      <Last>Schaffer</Last>
    </Name>
   </GetAuthorNamesResult>
  </GetAuthorNamesResponse>
 </soap:Body>
</soap:Envelope>
```

We will finish this chapter. by looking at a Web Service that uses another Web Service.

Web Services Calling Other Web Services

You might sometimes find it useful to have a Web Service you write call other Web Services. There are many reasons to have Web Services talk to each other. SOAP can be used as a cross-language and/or cross-platform communication mechanism. Your data center might be designed to use Web Services to improve the ability to upgrade or change hardware without significant changes to applications that talk to that hardware. You may also have partners or customers whose applications use your Web Services to coordinate activities, update data, and, in general, automate a large amount of work.

For a simple demonstration, we are going to write a Web Service that calls the FirstService.GetPerson Web Method. It will examine the data and return the number of days that person has been alive at the time the method was called.

The first thing we need to do is create another ASP.NET Web Service. You did this once already in Chapter 1. This time, name the project Chapter2WS. When the wizard is done creating everything for you, add a Web Reference to http://localhost/Chapter1/Chapter1.vsdisco and rename the namespace from localhost to Chapter1.

Finally, open up `Service1.asmx.vb` (the code view for `Service1.asmx`) and add a new Web Method named `GetDaysAlive`. This function should return a long value. Listing 2.5 shows the code.

LISTING 2.5   GetDaysAlive Web Method

```
<WebMethod()> Public Function GetDaysAlive() As Long
    Dim svc As New Chapter1.FirstService()
    Dim aPerson As Chapter1.Person
    Dim ts As TimeSpan

    GetDaysAlive = -1
    Try
        aPerson = svc.GetPerson()

        ' Get the difference between now and the
        ' person's birthday.
        ts = DateTime.Now.Subtract(aPerson.birthDay)
        GetDaysAlive = ts.Days
    Catch ex As Exception
        ' Let the caller know something bad happened
        Dim aFault As New SoapException( _
            "Call to next Web Service failed", _
            SoapException.ClientFaultCode)
        ' Need to call Dispose since we are throwing again
        ' out of this catch block.
        svc.Dispose()
        Throw aFault
    End Try

    svc.Dispose()
End Function
```

We will let ASP.NET write the user interface for this one. Navigating to `http://localhost/Chapter2WS/Service1.asmx?op=GetDaysAlive` on our machine, we see that the `HTTP/GET` response and request pair will look pretty simple. By sending a request to `http://localhost/Chapter2WS/Service1.asmx/GetDaysAlive?`, we can expect to get back a single `long` value. Executing this code on September 3, 2001, I got the following response when clicking the Invoke button on the ASP.NET–generated Web page:

```
<?xml version="1.0" encoding="utf-8"?>
<long xmlns="http://tempuri.org/">10743</long>
```

To make sure this number looks right, we should look at the SOAP request/response pair sent by the Chapter2WS Web Service.

Request:

```xml
<?xml version="1.0" encoding="utf-8"?>
<soap:Envelope
  xmlns:soap="http://schemas.xmlsoap.org/soap/envelope/"
  xmlns:xsi="http://www.w3.org/2001/XMLSchema-instance"
  xmlns:xsd="http://www.w3.org/2001/XMLSchema">
  <soap:Body>
    <GetPerson xmlns="http://tempuri.org/" />
  </soap:Body>
</soap:Envelope>
```

Response:

```xml
<?xml version="1.0" encoding="utf-8"?>
<soap:Envelope
  xmlns:soap="http://schemas.xmlsoap.org/soap/envelope/"
  xmlns:xsi="http://www.w3.org/2001/XMLSchema-instance"
  xmlns:xsd="http://www.w3.org/2001/XMLSchema">
  <soap:Body>
    <GetPersonResponse xmlns="http://tempuri.org/">
      <GetPersonResult>
        <theName>
          <First>Scott</First>
          <Middle>Christopher</Middle>
          <Last>Seely</Last>
        </theName>
        <birthDay>1972-04-05T00:00:00.0000000-07:00</birthDay>
      </GetPersonResult>
    </GetPersonResponse>
  </soap:Body>
</soap:Envelope>
```

Given that I am claiming to be approximately 29.5 years old, that would mean that the number returned should be something less than 365.25 * 29.5, which is equal to 10774.875. 10743 is about 32 days under that number. Given that, I would need that many days to actually be 29.5 years old, it looks like the Web Method is working correctly.

Summary

In this chapter, we took a look at the many different ways that you could use a Web Service. Whether building an application that runs on the desktop or on the Internet, you can use a Web Service. The skills you need to access that Web Service transfer between environments quite easily. From my perspective, that is the strongest feature of the .NET implementation of Web Services and the related protocols.

Chapter 1 showed you that Web Services can ride along without SOAP. This time, we took a look at traditional Web Services by calling the Web Methods using SOAP and by looking at the message exchange.

3

SOAP, WSDL, and UDDI Explained

If you are going to do any Web Service development, you need to have a basic understanding of what is going on under the covers. Because the underlying technology uses plain text to communicate, you do not need any fancy tools to view and makes sense of what is going back and forth. You do, however, need to understand how the messages are defined and what the different parts mean. Web Services use three different specifications to do different things. These specifications are

- *SOAP*—The XML-based protocol specification

- *Web Services Description Language (WSDL)*—Defines the Web Service interface

- *Universal Description, Discovery, and Integration (UDDI)*—A Web Service that serves as a way to advertise and discover Web Services

These three items combine to form what you can think of as the first version of Web Services. Here, you have the foundation on which to build more complex items. SOAP specifies the general message format. WSDL states what messages a particular SOAP server accepts and describes the format of the messages and the types contained by those messages. UDDI functions as a registry for Web Services and is a Web Service in its own right.

In this chapter, you will explore these three topics so that you are familiar with the terminology and elements used by these three complementary technologies. By the end of the chapter, you should be relatively comfortable reading SOAP messages and WSDL files. Additionally, you will be able to dig into a UDDI registry and discover specific Web Services.

SOAP

SOAP was originally an acronym for Simple Object Access Protocol. That stood well through version 1.1 of the protocol itself. Many companies contributed to the wording in that specification—IBM, Microsoft, DevelopMentor, Ariba, Compaq, Hewlett Packard, Commerce One, IONA, Lotus, and SAP AG. Soon after that release, Web Service adoption began in earnest. More and more people saw that something originally developed for simple object access and remote procedure calls could be used as a general purpose messaging system. Using SOAP, you can exchange any data that can be expressed in XML.

> **NOTE**
>
> At the time of this writing, SOAP v1.2 standardization is nearing completion as the specification moves through the World Wide Web Consortium (W3C). SOAP is no longer an acronym. Instead, the letters simply represent the name of the messaging protocol. Why? A lot of time and effort went into making developers aware of SOAP. The people involved in standardization see no benefits in giving the protocol a better acronym and have decided to just make SOAP the name of the protocol. If you already invested a lot of time in learning SOAP v1.1, that investment has paid off. The latest version of the protocol has only three really big changes:
>
> * SOAPAction is deprecated.
> * The versioning scheme has changed.
> * The mustUnderstand attribute has been more clearly defined.

A SOAP message has the following major elements:

* Envelope   Contains the SOAP message
* Header   Contains message metadata, such as authentication information
* Body   Contains the main data being sent in the message
* Fault   Communicates any errors that occurred while processing the SOAP message

You will examine these elements within the context of a typical SOAP message being sent over HTTP, as shown in Listing 3.1.

LISTING 3.1   Complete HTTP Exchange for a SOAP Message

Request:

```
POST /CHapter6CustomAuthen/Authenticate.asmx HTTP/1.1

User-Agent: Mozilla/4.0 (compatible; MSIE 6.0;
    ➥MS Web Services Client Protocol 1.0.3328.2)
```

LISTING 3.1 Continued

```
Content-Type: text/xml; charset=utf-8
SOAPAction: "http://www.samspublishing.com/ch6ex1/HelloWorld"
Content-Length: 709
Expect: 100-continue
Host: localhost

<?xml version="1.0" encoding="utf-8"?>
<soap:Envelope xmlns:soap="http://schemas.xmlsoap.org/soap/envelope/"
    xmlns:soapenc="http://schemas.xmlsoap.org/soap/encoding/"
    xmlns:tns="http://www.samspublishing.com/ch6ex1"
    xmlns:types="http://www.samspublishing.com/ch6ex1/encodedTypes"
    xmlns:xsi="http://www.w3.org/2001/XMLSchema-instance"
    xmlns:xsd="http://www.w3.org/2001/XMLSchema">
    <soap:Header>
        <tns:TokenHeader id="id1"
            soap:mustUnderstand="1"
            soap:actor="http://schemas.xmlsoap.org/soap/actor/next">
            <theToken xsi:type="xsd:string">this_is_the_token</theToken>
        </tns:TokenHeader>
    </soap:Header>
    <soap:Body
      ➥soap:encodingStyle="http://schemas.xmlsoap.org/soap/encoding/">
        <tns:HelloWorld />
    </soap:Body>
</soap:Envelope>
```

Response:

```
HTTP/1.1 200 OK
Server: Microsoft-IIS/5.1
Date: Sun, 07 Oct 2001 00:54:45 GMT
Cache-Control: private, max-age=0
Content-Type: text/xml; charset=utf-8
Content-Length: 591

<?xml version="1.0" encoding="utf-8"?>
<soap:Envelope
    xmlns:soap="http://schemas.xmlsoap.org/soap/envelope/"
    xmlns:soapenc="http://schemas.xmlsoap.org/soap/encoding/"
    xmlns:tns="http://www.samspublishing.com/ch6ex1"
```

```
    xmlns:types="http://www.samspublishing.com/ch6ex1"
    xmlns:xsi="http://www.w3.org/2001/XMLSchema-instance"
    xmlns:xsd="http://www.w3.org/2001/XMLSchema">
    <soap:Body soap:encodingStyle="http://schemas.xmlsoap.org/soap/encoding/">
        <types:HelloWorldResponse>
            <HelloWorldResult xsi:type="xsd:string"
                >Hello World!</HelloWorldResult>
        </types:HelloWorldResponse>
    </soap:Body>
</soap:Envelope>
```

In the rest of this section, you will examine the message and explain all of its various parts.

SOAPAction

The first SOAP-specific item you see in the header section of the HTTP request is the `SOAPAction` HTTP header. This header was originally included to indicate the intent of the SOAP message. The thinking went that by using this header, network administrators could grant or deny access to certain callers. SOAP v1.2 has a better solution—let the URL indicate the intent. The URL of the SOAP endpoint can be formed to contain the same amount of meaning as the `SOAPAction` header. As an added benefit, most networking hardware and software already have mechanisms in place to deal with URL based filtering.

Envelope

All SOAP messages have an `Envelope` element as the document root. The namespace used to qualify this element also serves to indicate the SOAP version. Version 1.1 SOAP messages use the `http://schemas.xmlsoap.org/soap/envelope/` namespace. When version 1.2 of the SOAP specification rolls out in the middle of 2002, it will have a different namespace. The working draft of the specification states that the namespace is `http://www.w3.org/2001/09/soap-envelope`. When the recommendation is passed, the version will most likely be `http://www.w3.org/2002/soap-envelope`.

Other than supplying versioning information, most SOAP envelopes also contain XML Namespace declarations that may be used in the rest of the message. You will often see namespace declarations that define the version of XSD being used to communicate type information. Those namespaces are as follows:

- XSD Instance data: `http://www.w3.org/2001/XMLSchema-instance`

- XSD Schema data: `http://www.w3.org/2001/XMLSchema`

The ASP .NET implementation always includes a definition for the XSD namespaces, even if they are not used by the message.

Header

The Header is used to communicate "out of band" data. Typically, you will see the Header used to include information about the caller's identity, any transactions the message might be involved in, or information that various intermediaries might need. A number of specifications use the SOAP Header for their information.

A client can put any number of elements within the Header. Each element that is an immediate child of the Header can use two attributes: mustUnderstand and actor. mustUnderstand indicates whether a recipient of the message must understand the particular Header element. If it does not understand the Header element, the server must return a MustUnderstand Fault. In SOAP v1.1, mustUnderstand uses the value 0 to tell the server that it does not need to handle the particular Header element to process the message and 1 to tell the server that it must understand the element. In SOAP v1.2, the values true and false are also allowed because mustUnderstand is defined as a Boolean. An XSD Boolean type allows the values 1 or true and 0 or false.

Body

The Body element typically contains the main information being sent by the SOAP message. Within this element, almost anything goes. When doing remote procedure calls over SOAP, the main element in the message is typically the name of the method being called. Normally, the response to that message is named MethodNameResponse. Within that element, you will find parameters and, optionally, type information. The type information helps to deserialize the message into the correct types when the message format is unknown. Because most toolkits rely on WSDL documents, the client and server know the types of the elements and their names long before any message exchanges occur.

When used to send information, the SOAP Body can declare that the data uses a specific encoding style. This is specified by using the encodingStyle attribute. If you are using the encoding style supported by the SOAP specification, you will see the encodingStyle attribute set to the http://schemas.xmlsoap.org/soap/encoding/ URI. The final version of the SOAP v1.2 recommendation will probably specify the SOAP encoding style URI as http://www.w3.org/2002/soap-encoding. What does this encoding style mean to you? It means that every element in the message has its type specified as an XSD instance data type.

You can also use SOAP to send XML documents to a recipient. In this case, the Body just contains the document and the SOAP protocol serves as a way to get the document to an endpoint that can understand it.

Fault

As with all applications, errors can and will happen in SOAP. SOAP uses the `Fault` element to communicate those errors. When a SOAP `Fault` is present, it must appear in the SOAP `Body`. This is true if a `Header` element is not understood or if the `Body` has something messed up. `Fault` elements have the following sub-elements:

- `faultcode`   States why the fault occurred. It is meant to be used by other machines to algorithmically determine what went wrong. This element is required.

- `faultstring`   Provides a human readable explanation of the faultcode. This element is required.

- `faultactor`   This element indicates the URI of the entity that encountered the error. It is optional when the entity discovering the error is the ultimate endpoint, and it is required when the SOAP error is discovered by an interme-diate processor. SOAP allows for multiple entities to handle fulfillment of a message.

- `detail`   This must be present when the error resides in the `Body` element. It cannot be used to carry information about errors in `Header` entries. Error details regarding `Header` entries must be carried in the `Header`.

The `faultcode` might contain one of the following values:

- `VersionMismatch`   The version of the SOAP envelope is not understood by this endpoint.

- `MustUnderstand`   The `Header` contains an element marked as `mustUnderstand` that the endpoint does not understand.

- `Client`   An error exists in the message and that error originated with the client. Sending the message again will result in another failure.

- `Server`   An error occurred on the server side of the message exchange. The client should expect to see the message succeed if the message is sent again after a short delay.

All of the `faultcode` elements can be expanded on using a dot notation. For example, to tell the client that an error exists in the expected type for the `arg1` element expressed by the `doIt` method, the `faultcode` could be expressed as `Client.doIt.arg1`.

SOAP v1.2 adds one more `faultcode` to the mixture—`DataEncodingUnknown`. If the message specifies the `encodingStyle` attribute on the `Body` or on a `Header` element and that encoding style is not supported by the endpoint, the endpoint will return a `DataEncodingUnknown faultcode`. (In SOAP v1.1, the endpoint would return a `Client` fault.)

NOTE

The term *endpoint* can be used in discussions about SOAP to refer to the computer and related software that handle a given SOAP message. The endpoint can be reached through a particular URL. For example, you can describe a typical .NET Web Service endpoint in the following manner:

- Intel Pentium IV
- ASP.NET-based Web Service
- Web Service written using Visual Basic .NET.

At least, this definition works fine when I talk to others. I can ask things like "What's the endpoint running?" and get the information that I want in return.

Another common usage of endpoint by Web Service developers is to refer to the value of the endpoint as described in the SOAP extensibility element located within the service element of a given WSDL file.

WSDL

The Web Services Description Language (WSDL) allows servers to describe a SOAP endpoint. The file describes the types passed back and forth, the messages in which those types are used, and the collection of messages used by various operations. The file also describes what protocols are used to communicate when using the supported operations.

WSDL provides for extra elements within any WSDL document called *extensibility elements*. Extensibility elements are used to map the semantics of a particular protocol into the WSDL document. Because of this, you can map any protocol into a WSDL document. You can use WSDL to describe any message exchange mechanism. The only requirement is that both the sender and receiver have to understand how those extensibility elements were mapped into WSDL. For use with .NET, you will only see extensibility elements used for SOAP, HTTP GET, and HTTP POST. What does this mean in practical terms?

WSDL is just another interface definition language. The notable difference is that it describes the interface using a standardized XML schema. The authors of the specification recognize that the concepts behind Web Service messaging transcend things already done over many different protocols. E-mail, whose protocols are POP3 and SMTP, allows for message exchanges via mailboxes. Microsoft Message Queue (MSMQ) allows for message exchanges via queues hosted on machines. COM and

CORBA specify message exchanges over particular binary protocols. The content of the message does not change depending on the underlying protocol. The thing that does change is how the content is exchanged and communicated. The extensibility elements of WSDL let me do things such as define that when I pass the integer value 4, in a SOAP message it will be expressed as `<someElement>4</someElement>`, and in a binary format it will be the third byte of the message and represented as 0100 (binary). To date, the only widely accepted extensibility elements relate to SOAP on HTTP. However, if you can get another party to agree to what your set of extensibility elements means, you can define mappings onto any format you choose.

In this section, you will learn about the parts of a WSDL document as well as the SOAP and HTTP bindings.

Document Parts

A WSDL document is made up of several different elements. Each of these elements has a specific purpose and a defined set of attributes. Listing 3.2 contains a sample document that you may want to refer to while reading over the description of the elements contained within a WSDL document. The major elements in the WSDL document are as follows:

- `definitions`   Root element of all WSDL documents. Typically, this element also declares the namespaces used within the document.

- `types`   An XML Schema document specifying the types used by the messages defined in the document. This element typically occurs once within a WSDL document.

- `message`   This element can occur zero or more times within the WSDL document.

- `portType`   Defines a collection of `operation` elements. The `operation` elements in turn define the `input` and or `output` message that define the operation.

- `binding`   Defines the semantics of an `operation` with respect to a specific protocol. WSDL specifies bindings for SOAP, HTTP GET and POST, and MIME.

- `service`   Used to tell a client of the Web Service where to communicate with the Web Service. Typically, a `service` maps a set of `bindings` that all map to the same `portType` and states the URL to use to access the Web Service.

- `documentation`   This element can exist anywhere within the WSDL document. It allows the WSDL author to add extra information for human readers about the particular WSDL element.

WSDL documents allow for the importing of other parts, including XSD and fragments of other WSDL documents. Those document fragments might contain message definitions as well as `portType` and binding data. WSDL also allows for the addition of content specific to the protocol being used to carry the data. This content, called extensibility elements, could be used to define ways to carry data over binary protocols, such as binary RPC, via e-mail or other methods. Because of this, extensibility elements are typically protocol specific. In this chapter, you will only look at the elements specific to SOAP that are defined in the WSDL 1.1 specification. Other extensibility elements have been defined for other transports (HTTP GET and POST) and other uses of SOAP. For example, Microsoft's .NET My Services uses extensibility elements to add routing and other information to the WSDL document. In general, a WSDL document will have the layout shown in Listing 3.2.

LISTING 3.2   Pseudo-XML Document Describing the General Layout of a WSDL Document

```
<wsdl:definitions>

    <import namespace="some-uri" location="some-uri" /> {1 or more}

    <wsdl:documentation></wsdl:documentation> {0 or 1}

    <wsdl:types> {0 or 1}
        <wsdl:documentation></wsdl:documentation> {0 or 1}
        <xsd:schema></xsd:schema> {0 or more}
        <-- extensibility element --> {0 or more}
    </wsdl:types>

    <wsdl:message> {0 or more}
        <wsdl:documentation></wsdl:documentation> {0 or 1}
        <part name="nmtoken" element="qname" type="qname" />
            {0 or more}
    </wsdl:message>

    <wsdl:portType>
        <wsdl:documentation></wsdl:documentation> {0 or 1}
        <wsdl:operation> {0 or more}
            <wsdl:documentation></wsdl:documentation> {0 or 1}
            <wsdl:input name="nmtoken"? message="qname"> {0 or 1}
                <wsdl:documentation></wsdl:documentation> {0 or 1}
            </wsdl:input>
            <wsdl:output name="nmtoken"? message="qname"> {0 or 1}
                <wsdl:documentation></wsdl:documentation> {0 or 1}
```

LISTING 3.2 Continued

```
            </wsdl:output>
            <wsdl:fault name="nmtoken"? message="qname"> {0 or 1}
                <wsdl:documentation></wsdl:documentation> {0 or 1}
            </wsdl:fault>
        </wsdl:operation>
    </wsdl:portType>

    <wsdl:binding name="token" type="qname"> {0 or more}
        <wsdl:documentation></wsdl:documentation> {0 or 1}
        <-- extensibility element --> {0 or more}
        <wsdl:operation name="nmtoken"> {0 or more}
            <wsdl:documentation></wsdl:documentation> {0 or 1}
            <-- extensibility element --> {0 or more}
            <wsdl:input> {0 or 1}
                <wsdl:documentation></wsdl:documentation> {0 or 1}
                <-- extensibility element --> {0 or more}
            </wsdl:input>
            <wsdl:output> {0 or 1}
                <wsdl:documentation></wsdl:documentation> {0 or 1}
                <-- extensibility element --> {0 or more}
            </wsdl:output>
            <wsdl:fault> {0 or 1}
                <wsdl:documentation></wsdl:documentation> {0 or 1}
                <-- extensibility element --> {0 or more}
            </wsdl:fault>
        </wsdl:operation>
    </wsdl:binding>

    <wsdl:service name="nmtoken"> {0 or more}
        <wsdl:documentation></wsdl:documentation> {0 or 1}
        <wsdl:port> {0 or more}
            <wsdl:documentation></wsdl:documentation> {0 or 1}
            <-- extensibility element --> {0 or more}
        </wsdl:port>
        <-- extensibility element --> {0 or more}
    </wsdl:service>

    <-- extensibility element --> {0 or more}
</wsdl:definitions>
```

As you can see, documentation and extensibility elements can appear almost anywhere within the document.

Supported Message Patterns

WSDL supports the definition of four different message patterns:

- *Request/Response*—This is typical procedure call semantics. You send out a message and expect the result to be returned in a response to that message.

- *Solicit/Response*—In this case, the roles of server and client are reversed. The server asks a client for data, and the client provides it. You would use this mechanism for things such as a Web Service that reports on overall system health or any other service where it would be useful to aggregate data from several other machines.

- *One-way*—The client sends a message to the server and does not wait for a response. This can be used when the message itself has a limited period of usefulness. For example, a client may regularly report status or event information to a main server. The client does not want any data back, it just wants to send the data.

- *Notification*—The server sends a message to a client and does not wait for a response. This might happen when a server is informing interested clients that a particular event occurred. When the clients start up, they may notify the server that they want to hear about certain system events. When those events happen, the server sends a notification to the client.

With these message patterns, you can use Web Services to create complex behaviors and interactions.

SOAP Extensibility Elements

Looking at Listing 3.2, you will note that WSDL does not allow for extensibility elements in the message or portType definitions. Extensibility elements are used to describe how a particular portType is bound to a specific protocol and how to describe the method of accessing that portType via service. Because of this, these mappings typically are called *bindings*. The WSDL 1.1 specification defines a set of elements specific to SOAP that allow the WSDL document to communicate the following information:

- The method of message exchange for the portType.

- The SOAPAction element for a given operation on the portType.

- Any Header types, Header fault, and Body information for input and output messages.

- Any fault information for `Fault` messages.

- The location of the SOAP endpoint (defined in the service element).

Listing 3.3 shows the SOAP-specific extensibility elements with respect to their locations within a WSDL document. Elements shown as *a|b* means that either value *a* or value *b* can exist for the attribute, but not both.

LISTING 3.3   Pseudo-WSDL File Showing only the Parts that Contain the SOAP-Specific Extensibility Elements

```
<wsdl:definitions>
    <wsdl:binding>
        <soap:binding style="rpc|document" transport="uri">
        <wsdl:operation>
            <soap:operation soapAction="uri"
                style="rpc|document"> {0 or 1}
            <wsdl:input>
                <soap:body parts="nmtokens" use="literal|encoded"
                    encodingStyle="uri-list" namespace="uri">
                <soap:header message="qname" part="nmtoken"
                    use="literal|encoded"
                    encodingStyle="uri-list"
                    namespace="uri"> {0 or more}
                    <soap:headerfault message="qname"
                        part="nmtoken" use="literal|encoded"
                        encodingStyle="uri-list"
                        namespace="uri" /> {0 or more}
                <soap:header>
            </wsdl:input>
            <wsdl:output>
                <soap:body parts="nmtokens" use="literal|encoded"
                    encodingStyle="uri-list" namespace="uri">
                <soap:header message="qname" part="nmtoken"
                    use="literal|encoded" encodingStyle="uri-list"
                    namespace="uri"> {0 or more}
                    <soap:headerfault message="qname" part="nmtoken"
                        use="literal|encoded"
                        encodingStyle="uri-list"
                        namespace="uri"/>{0 or more}
                <soap:header>
            </wsdl:output>
            <wsdl:fault> {0 or 1}
```

LISTING 3.3   Continued

```
            <soap:fault name="nmtoken" use="literal|encoded"
                encodingStyle="uri-list" namespace="uri">
        </wsdl:fault>
    </wsdl:operation>
</wsdl:binding>

<wsdl:service>
    <wsdl:port>
        <soap:address location="uri"/>
    </wsdl:port>
</wsdl:service>
</definitions>
```

To understand what the various SOAP extensibility elements mean, the next sections cover them individually. In Chapter 4, "Using Attributes to Shape the WSDL and XML," you will see how to manipulate an actual WSDL document using these elements.

soap:binding
This element describes the style of the set of operations being sent back and forth and the transport being used to send them. The style attribute can have one of two values—rpc or document. The rpc setting indicates that the messages contain parameters and return values. When set to document, the WSDL document indicates that this Web Service exchanges XML documents. When the style attribute is omitted, it is assumed to be document.

The transport attribute holds a URI referring to the network method being used to carry the message. Currently, the only value defined in the WSDL specification is http://schemas.xmlsoap.org/soap/http, which maps to HTTP. Other values can be defined for transports, such as SMTP or FTP.

soap:operation
The SOAP operation extensibility element provides a means for the WSDL to describe individual SOAP methods. The style attribute can have a value of rpc or document, just like the soap:binding element. The meanings of rpc and document are the same and provide a way to override what was stated for the binding as a whole. If the binding is set to document, all operations default to document unless otherwise defined. The same is true for the rpc style.

This element also allows the user to define the SOAPAction related to each operation through the `soapAction` attribute. This attribute is only useful for SOAP v1.1. SOAP v1.2 currently intends to drop this attribute. The URI should be used as it appears in the document. Readers of the URI should not try to read this as a relative URI.

soap:body and soap:fault

These elements convey the same meaning. The `soap:body` and `soap:fault` extensibility elements refers to content found in the SOAP `Body` and SOAP `Fault` elements, respectively. This element defines how the `Body` will be presented within the `input` or `output` of the `operation`. The `parts` attribute, if included, indicates which parts show up somewhere within the SOAP `Body` element. Other parts may appear elsewhere with multipart/related MIME binding. When the attribute does not appear, all parts defined by the message are assumed to be included in the SOAP `Body`.

The use attribute can have the value of `literal` or `encoded`. When set to `literal`, the `encodingStyle` attribute can be set to indicate how the concrete format of the message was derived. Typically, you will not see the `encodingStyle` set for literal encoding. Why? Because literal encoding indicates that the writer of the message should already know the message data being sent. As such, the type information is not embedded in the message, and the reader is expected to know how to transform the data into the correct types.

When the encoding style is set to encoded, the `encodingStyle` needs to be set to describe the types of encoding used on the elements. The encoding styles are separated by spaces and ordered from most restrictive to least restrictive. Typically, this means that the actual SOAP message will contain attributes on each element that map to values defined in the types section of the WSDL document or map to XML schema types. The `namespace` attribute only applies to types not defined by the abstract types.

soap:header and soap:headerfault

The `soap:header` and `soap:headerfault` extensibility elements and their attributes have the same meaning as the `soap:body` and `soap:fault` extensibility elements. They also contain one additional attribute—message. The message attribute maps to one of the message elements defined earlier in the WSDL document. You can have multiple, optional `Header` elements used with any given operation. Each headerfault maps back to a specific fault that can occur when the SOAP `Header` cannot be evaluated.

soap:address

This element allows the WSDL document to indicate where ports supporting a particular binding are found. The `location` attribute indicates the URL used to access the SOAP Web Service. When using the HTTP transport, this will be an HTTP address.

UDDI

The Universal Description, Discovery, and Integration (UDDI) specification defines how to register business data as well as to advertise the existence and location of XML Web Services. As a developer and user of Web Services, you will typically interact with UDDI by either registering your Web Service with UDDI or by looking for Web Services that serve particular needs. When using UDDI, you need to have a good understanding of how to discover what you are looking for. This section will cover the basic concepts you need to understand to publish and discover Web Services.

After reading this overview, you may be interested in the detailed usage of the UDDI Web Service. Microsoft provides an SDK for .NET clients to use when accessing UDDI. This and other resources are listed in Appendix A, "Additional Resources."

tModels

A tModel, or type model, describes an XML Web Service in detail. Typically, this is a WSDL file that may or may not omit the service element. In UDDI, one organization may register a tModel and several may implement it. For example, the insurance industry may define the semantics for processing health insurance claims using Web Services. An organization representing the insurance industry may register that tModel but not provide the implementations. Instead, the member organizations would provide implementations. Businesses and other organizations that want to be able to access those implementations would provide the clients.

All tModels registered in UDDI get an automatically generated globally unique ID (GUID). If you know the ID of the tModel you want to use in your client application, and if one implementation is as good as another, you can write a generic client that connects to any number of endpoints. As long as they support the tModel, you should be able to connect to the endpoint, regardless of what language it is written in or the platform on which it relies.

Registering with UDDI

When registering with a UDDI Registry, you have two choices—use a user interface or the UDDI SOAP interface. Both the IBM and Microsoft registries have a Web-based user interface. Figure 3.1 shows Microsoft's UDDI administrative user interface.

You can visit this site at `http://uddi.microsoft.com`. The user interface walks you through various steps. You can register your business and declare the types of industries you are involved in and where the business or servers are located. When registering a tModel, you can apply the same information to it. For example, you can declare that you have an XML Web Service that is hosted in Redmond, Washington,

USA, and London, England that services the lumber industry and has a WSDL definition. UDDI provides quite a set of capabilities. In Chapter 4, you will take a look at
some of the UDDI capabilities built into Visual Studio .NET.

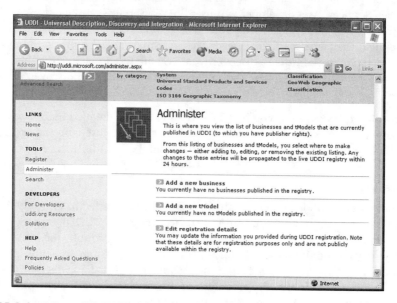

FIGURE 3.1   Microsoft's UDDI administrative user interface.

One thing you may not realize is that UDDI is itself an XML Web Service with a
SOAP binding. This SOAP interface allows you to programmatically access UDDI
registries as well. Using these APIs, you can create applications that publish Web
Service details without any human intervention.

By listing your XML Web Service with either Microsoft or IBM (at no cost, by the
way), you get some nice advertising benefits. For one, potential users can more
easily find the XML Web Service. Another benefit is that the two UDDI registries
share information. Every night, Microsoft and IBM share the changes that happened
during the day to their registries. If you publish your XML Web Service on Microsoft
today, it will be listed on IBM by tomorrow.

Figure 3.2 shows the details of the scottseely.com registration. When I published this
business in the Microsoft UDDI registry, that night synchronization brought the
content over to IBM.

One final advantage of registering your Web Service is that it gives your customers a
way to find the service again if you ever move it to a different server. By updating
the location of the server in the UDDI registry, a client can find the endpoint via a
simple query.

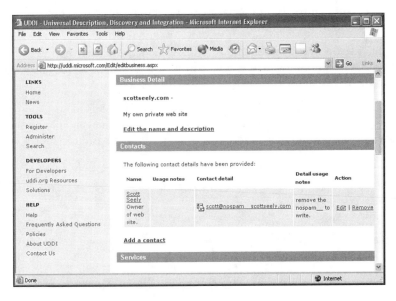

FIGURE 3.2   scottseely.com registration at http://uddi.microsoft.com.

Query Patterns

The UDDI specification identifies three different ways that users will use the registry to find the services in which they are interested:

- Browse pattern
- Drill-down pattern
- Invocation pattern

These three patterns all work together to help the user find the business or Web Service they are seeking. After discussing the particular pattern, we will look at how the Microsoft UDDI site implements the pattern to help us discover a Web Service. As a goal, let's look for a Web Service that provides a "quote of the day."

Browse Pattern

Users employ the browse pattern to help find the group that most likely contains the Web Service or business for which they are looking. The data in UDDI can be organized hierarchically, depending on what makes sense for the users. The browse pattern assumes that a user will search for a set of criteria and then sort through those criteria manually. UDDI has a set of find_*xxx* APIs that allow users to browse through the data. For example, the find_business API will return a list of businesses based on the name of the business. Likewise, the `find_service` API will return a list services related to a specific business.

When one of these APIs is called and it returns the list, the user then needs to inspect the list and decide which elements hold any interest. At this point, the user drills into the information using the next pattern—drill-down.

Because the browse API does allow for searching, I will go over to `http://microsoft.uddi.com` and go to the search page. From there, I will search all the tModel names for the text "quote of the day." The page and the layout of that search is shown in Figure 3.3.

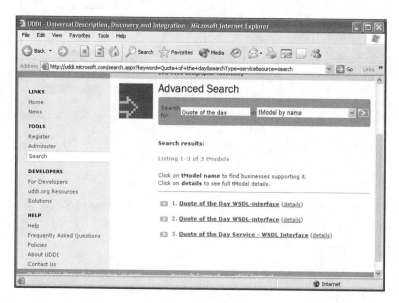

FIGURE 3.3   Results of searching for "quote of the day."

Drill-Down Pattern

The get_*xxx* APIs handle the inspection of listed items generated by the browse pattern. For example, a user can get information about a business of interest by calling `get_businessDetail`. If the information about the business looks correct, the user may ask the UDDI registry for a list of all the Web Services that business exposes and then dig into a few of those Web Services. That is, the user will drill down until he or she finds something interesting, browse the contents, and then drill-down some more. This pattern continues until the user either finds what he or she is looking for or discovers that the item does not exist in the UDDI store.

After the user has selected a Web Service, he or she may need to make arrangements with the provider of that Web Service to access it. This may mean acquiring a license, signing a contract, or doing nothing. The user will then create a proxy that can access the Web Service, test the application that uses the proxy, and distribute the application. After the application is deployed, the user will need a way to find the endpoint should the owner of the Web Service ever decide to move the servers. To handle the potential movement of the server, the UDDI specification recommends the use of the invocation pattern.

Going back to the search for a quote of the day Web Service, I did find three potential candidates. Now, I need to drill down into the results and see if any of them meet my needs. To go straight to the details of each Web Service, I click the Details link. This brings up the data in Figure 3.4. I can drill down deeper and check out the WSDL from the page as well as any other links the owner of the Web Service has provided.

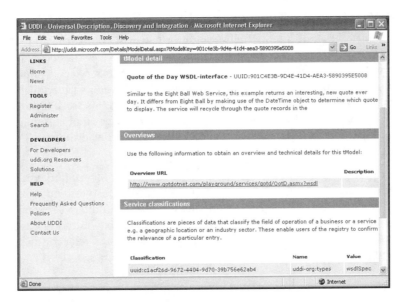

FIGURE 3.4   Drilling into the first result of the search.

Invocation Pattern

The invocation pattern spells out how a Web Service client should use UDDI to keep the endpoint up to date. A client application will use data cached from the UDDI registry. When using Visual Studio, the user's application caches this information when creating the initial proxy. The client will then proceed to use that cached information until a Web Service call fails. If the call fails because the client cannot connect to the endpoint, the client goes to the UDDI registry and posts an inquiry to find the endpoint of the Web Service. The client then takes the information regarding the location of the endpoint and tries to make a new call. If the call succeeds, the client saves the new location and uses it until another failure happens. If the call fails again, the client can look for another service implementing the tModel, or it can fail completely and post a notification for a human operator to respond to.

A Visual Basic .NET client application would keep everything up to date by caching the ID for the endpoint. The proxy code would then be modified to handle instances where the service could not even be contacted. In those cases, the client would requery the UDDI registry using the Microsoft UDDI SDK. If the endpoint's URL had changed, the client application would update the endpoint and update the stored URL.

Summary

In this chapter, you took a fairly high-level overview of SOAP, WSDL, and UDDI. These three technologies are part of the foundation of SOAP. By understanding how they all work, you will be able to develop high-quality Web Services. Coupled with some prior experience reading XML, this chapter provides you with enough information to understand a WSDL file and what a compliant SOAP message for a given WSDL file should look like. When developing SOAP messages that communicate with non-Microsoft toolkits, you will have to know how to read the raw XML messages going between endpoints.

You will rarely program directly against a UDDI data store. More often, you will use the user interface provide by the registrar to register your business and Web Services. This task is made easier through tools provided by Visual Studio .NET. You will learn more about lookup and registration of Web Services in Visual Studio in Chapter 4. For more information on the material covered in this chapter, refer to the resources in Appendix A.

4

Shaping the WSDL, XML, and SOAP Message

So far, we have covered how to write a basic server and client, and covered the basics behind SOAP, WSDL, and UDDI. To write self-documenting WSDL files, state the exact form your objects will take and publish that data to the Internet, you will need a bit more knowledge of what tools are available.

.NET includes a number of attributes that let you control every aspect of your WSDL file. Because your messages must follow the interfaces and types that appear in your WSDL file, you also end up modeling the way that messages appear on the wire. If you need to augment the attributes provided by .NET, you can write your own. This can allow you to do something as simple as writing the message out to a log file. Attributes can also be used to modify the SOAP message itself. You could encrypt individual elements, handle specific headers, or anything else that you want. Custom attributes give you all the access you will need for your own objects.

An important thing to know about attributes is that an attribute class always ends with the text `Attribute`. Visual Studio .NET uses this fact to allow for a shorthand that omits this part of the attribute classname. The exception to this rule is any attribute whose classname contains the word `Attribute` twice in a row. For example, the class to set the name of an XML attribute is called `XmlAttributeAttribute`. The naming rules state that the attribute name has to be spelled out in full within the code. You can use shorthand in all other situations. This chapter avoids using the shorthand. I only explain this confusing bit because you will see examples in other venues that use the shorthand instead of the complete name.

The .NET Framework SDK comes with a tool called WSDL.EXE. While this tool is commonly used to create proxies based on a WSDL file, it can also create stub implementations of a server that implements the WSDL. This can allow you to define the interface of a Web Service in WSDL before implementing it. You can also create implementations for other, existing WSDL files.

At the end of the chapter, we will take a look at how to use the UDDI support included in Visual Studio .NET to register your Web Services. As you can tell, this chapter covers a lot of somewhat unrelated topics. I believe that you do need to know about these topics sooner rather than later. Understanding how they all fit together will allow you to create more effective Web Services.

Before proceeding, make sure to grab the code from the companion Web site. This is one chapter that should be read with these files handy so that you can follow along and experiment as the chapter moves along.

Shaping the WSDL File

In this section, we will take a simple, unadorned WSDL file. Through the use of attributes, we will change the file in every way we possibly can. By doing this, you will see the many ways a SOAP message can be shaped. Each change will be explained so that you understand what was done and what the effects were. ASP.NET will generate the WSDL for us in every instance. For the example, we will look at a simple Web Method that takes a number and returns a structure that supposedly relates to that number. In reality, everything will be hard coded. That's okay. The purpose of this section is to show what happens outside the body of the implementation, not inside it. You will want to follow along with the modifications on your own. The project file, Ch4WSDL, contains the starting point for the discussion and can be obtained from the companion Web site for this book. We will start with the code in Listing 4.1. The name of the file is service1.asmx.vb.

LISTING 4.1   The Class We Will Be Modifying in service1.asmx.vb

```
Imports System.Web.Services

Public Enum CDType
    Mini
    Normal
End Enum

Public Class AudioCD
    Public Name As String
```

LISTING 4.1   Continued

```
    Public NumTracks As Long
    Public YearPublished As Long
    Public Artist As String
    Public TheType As CDType
End Class

<WebService(Namespace:="http://tempuri.org/")> _
Public Class Service1
    Inherits System.Web.Services.WebService

    <WebMethod()> _
    Public Function GetCD(ByVal CD_ID As Long) As AudioCD
        GetCD = New AudioCD()
        GetCD.Artist = "The Pixies"
        GetCD.NumTracks = 15
        GetCD.YearPublished = 1991
        GetCD.Name = "Trompe le Monde"
    End Function

    <WebMethod()> _
    Public Sub DoSomething(ByVal someArgument As String)
        ' This subroutine does nothing, and that's OK.
    End Sub
End Class
```

The web.config file has been modified so that it will only support SOAP (that is, it has no HTTP POST/GET functionality). To do this, the following lines were added to the web.config file inside the configuration/system.web tag.

```
<webServices>
    <protocols>
        <remove name="HttpPost" />
        <remove name="HttpGet" />
    </protocols>
</webServices>
```

Now, when we go to get the WSDL from the Web Service by navigating to http://localhost/ch4wsdl/service1.asmx?WSDL we will have a WSDL that only supports SOAP. This particular version, shown in Listing 4.2, has no extra documentation or decoration and shows what ASP.NET generates without any prompting.

LISTING 4.2   The Default WSDL for the Ch4WSDL Web Service, Viewable at
`http://localhost/Ch4WSDL/Service1.asmx?WSDL`

```
 1:  <?xml version="1.0" encoding="utf-8"?>
 2:  <definitions
 3:      xmlns:http="http://schemas.xmlsoap.org/wsdl/http/"
 4:      xmlns:soap="http://schemas.xmlsoap.org/wsdl/soap/"
 5:      xmlns:s="http://www.w3.org/2001/XMLSchema"
 6:      xmlns:s0="http://tempuri.org/"
 7:      xmlns:soapenc="http://schemas.xmlsoap.org/soap/encoding/"
 8:      xmlns:tm="http://microsoft.com/wsdl/mime/textMatching/"
 9:      xmlns:mime="http://schemas.xmlsoap.org/wsdl/mime/"
10:      targetNamespace="http://tempuri.org/"
11:      xmlns="http://schemas.xmlsoap.org/wsdl/">
12:    <types>
13:      <s:schema elementFormDefault="qualified"
14:          targetNamespace="http://tempuri.org/">
15:        <s:element name="GetCD">
16:          <s:complexType>
17:            <s:sequence>
18:              <s:element minOccurs="1" maxOccurs="1"
19:                  name="CD_ID" type="s:long" />
20:            </s:sequence>
21:          </s:complexType>
22:        </s:element>
23:        <s:element name="GetCDResponse">
24:          <s:complexType>
25:            <s:sequence>
26:              <s:element minOccurs="0" maxOccurs="1"
27:                  name="GetCDResult" type="s0:AudioCD" />
28:            </s:sequence>
29:          </s:complexType>
30:        </s:element>
31:        <s:complexType name="AudioCD">
32:          <s:sequence>
33:            <s:element minOccurs="0" maxOccurs="1"
34:              name="Name" type="s:string" />
35:            <s:element minOccurs="1" maxOccurs="1"
36:              name="NumTracks" type="s:long" />
37:            <s:element minOccurs="1" maxOccurs="1"
38:              name="YearPublished" type="s:long" />
39:            <s:element minOccurs="0" maxOccurs="1"
40:              name="Artist" type="s:string" />
```

LISTING 4.2   Continued

```
41:              <s:element minOccurs="1" maxOccurs="1"
42:                name="TheType" type="s0:CDType" />
43:            </s:sequence>
44:          </s:complexType>
45:          <s:simpleType name="CDType">
46:            <s:restriction base="s:string">
47:              <s:enumeration value="Mini" />
48:              <s:enumeration value="Normal" />
49:            </s:restriction>
50:          </s:simpleType>
51:          <s:element name="DoSomething">
52:            <s:complexType>
53:              <s:sequence>
54:                <s:element minOccurs="0" maxOccurs="1"
55:                    name="someArgument" type="s:string" />
56:              </s:sequence>
57:            </s:complexType>
58:          </s:element>
59:          <s:element name="DoSomethingResponse">
60:            <s:complexType />
61:          </s:element>
62:        </s:schema>
63:      </types>
64:      <message name="GetCDSoapIn">
65:        <part name="parameters" element="s0:GetCD" />
66:      </message>
67:      <message name="GetCDSoapOut">
68:        <part name="parameters" element="s0:GetCDResponse" />
69:      </message>
70:      <message name="DoSomethingSoapIn">
71:        <part name="parameters" element="s0:DoSomething" />
72:      </message>
73:      <message name="DoSomethingSoapOut">
74:        <part name="parameters" element="s0:DoSomethingResponse" />
75:      </message>
76:      <portType name="Service1Soap">
77:        <operation name="GetCD">
78:          <input message="s0:GetCDSoapIn" />
79:          <output message="s0:GetCDSoapOut" />
80:        </operation>
81:        <operation name="DoSomething">
```

LISTING 4.2   Continued

```
82:          <input message="s0:DoSomethingSoapIn" />
83:          <output message="s0:DoSomethingSoapOut" />
84:       </operation>
85:    </portType>
86:    <binding name="Service1Soap" type="s0:Service1Soap">
87:       <soap:binding transport="http://schemas.xmlsoap.org/soap/http"
88:          style="document" />
89:       <operation name="GetCD">
90:         <soap:operation soapAction="http://tempuri.org/GetCD"
91:           style="document" />
92:         <input>
93:           <soap:body use="literal" />
94:         </input>
95:         <output>
96:           <soap:body use="literal" />
97:         </output>
98:       </operation>
99:       <operation name="DoSomething">
100:        <soap:operation soapAction="http://tempuri.org/DoSomething"
101:          style="document" />
102:        <input>
103:          <soap:body use="literal" />
104:        </input>
105:        <output>
106:          <soap:body use="literal" />
107:        </output>
108:       </operation>
109:    </binding>
110:    <service name="Service1">
111:      <port name="Service1Soap" binding="s0:Service1Soap">
112:        <soap:address location="http://localhost/ch4wsdl/service1.asmx" />
113:      </port>
114:    </service>
115: </definitions>
```

I promise, we won't be looking at the WSDL file in its entirety again. We're going to do a top down approach and cover each of the elements in the following order:

- definitions
- types

- messages

- portType

- binding

- service

Each of these sections will also cover how you would modify the parts inside of it. Because the definitions element contains all of the others, I will not cover definitions the same way.

One attribute that does not fit neatly into this discussion is the effect of declaring that a particular Web Service is either RPC/encoded or document/literal. A Web Service that is RPC/encoded exists primarily for easy setup of remote procedure call SOAP messages. The intention of RPC/encoded is to make it possible for a receiver of the SOAP message to reconstruct any data without prior knowledge of the data format. Document/literal SOAP messages are sent with the assumption that the message recipient will know how to interpret the message ahead of time. With WSDL becoming more prevalent for defining message formats, RPC/encoded messaging is becoming less useful as time goes on.

The WSDL file shown in Listing 4.2 shows a document/literal Web Service. By default, all Web Services have the System.Web.Services.Protocols.SoapDocumentService attribute applied to them. You get the same code if you add this attribute yourself. To enable RPC/encoded access to the Web Service, you just apply the System.Web.Services.Protocols.SoapRpcService attribute to the Web Service class. This does change the WSDL quite a bit. Listing 4.3 shows the WSDL for the updated service. The changes from line 1 of the code are visible in the following lines for the WSDL: 37, 40, 43, 58, 61, 63–64, 67–68, 73, 75–76, and 79–80. Also, the [method name]Request/Response elements from the types section are completely missing.

LISTING 4.3 Applying the SoapRpcService (Line 1) to the Web Service Class
(service2.asmx.vb)

```
1:  <System.Web.Services.Protocols.SoapRpcService()> _
2:  Public Class Service1
3:  Inherits System.Web.Services.WebService
4:
5:      <WebMethod()> _
6:      Public Function GetCD(ByVal CD_ID As Long) As AudioCD
7:          GetCD = New AudioCD()
8:          GetCD.Artist = "The Pixies"
9:          GetCD.NumTracks = 15
```

LISTING 4.3   Continued

```
10:          GetCD.YearPublished = 1991
11:          GetCD.Name = "Trompe le Monde"
12:      End Function
13:
14:      <WebMethod()> _
15:      Public Sub DoSomething(ByVal someArgument As String)
16:          ' This subroutine does nothing, and that's OK.
17:      End Sub
18:  End Class
```

Effect on WSDL, viewable at `http://localhost/Ch4WSDL/Service2.asmx?WSDL`.

```
1:  <?xml version="1.0" encoding="utf-8"?>
2:  <definitions
3:      xmlns:http="http://schemas.xmlsoap.org/wsdl/http/"
4:      xmlns:soap="http://schemas.xmlsoap.org/wsdl/soap/"
5:      xmlns:s="http://www.w3.org/2001/XMLSchema"
6:      xmlns:s0="http://tempuri.org/"
7:      xmlns:soapenc="http://schemas.xmlsoap.org/soap/encoding/"
8:      xmlns:tm="http://microsoft.com/wsdl/mime/textMatching/"
9:      xmlns:mime="http://schemas.xmlsoap.org/wsdl/mime/"
10:     targetNamespace="http://tempuri.org/"
11:     xmlns="http://schemas.xmlsoap.org/wsdl/">
12:   <types>
13:     <s:schema targetNamespace="http://tempuri.org/">
14:       <s:complexType name="AudioCD">
15:         <s:sequence>
16:           <s:element minOccurs="1" maxOccurs="1"
17:             name="Name" type="s:string" />
18:           <s:element minOccurs="1" maxOccurs="1"
19:             name="NumTracks" type="s:long" />
20:           <s:element minOccurs="1" maxOccurs="1"
21:             name="YearPublished" type="s:long" />
22:           <s:element minOccurs="1" maxOccurs="1"
23:             name="Artist" type="s:string" />
24:           <s:element minOccurs="1" maxOccurs="1"
25:             name="TheType" type="s0:CDType" />
26:         </s:sequence>
27:       </s:complexType>
```

```
28:          <s:simpleType name="CDType">
29:            <s:restriction base="s:string">
30:              <s:enumeration value="Mini" />
31:              <s:enumeration value="Normal" />
32:            </s:restriction>
33:          </s:simpleType>
34:        </s:schema>
35:      </types>
36:      <message name="GetCDSoapIn">
37:        <part name="CD_ID" type="s:long" />
38:      </message>
39:      <message name="GetCDSoapOut">
40:        <part name="GetCDResult" type="s0:AudioCD" />
41:      </message>
42:      <message name="DoSomethingSoapIn">
43:        <part name="someArgument" type="s:string" />
44:      </message>
45:      <message name="DoSomethingSoapOut" />
46:      <portType name="Service1Soap">
47:        <operation name="GetCD">
48:          <input message="s0:GetCDSoapIn" />
49:          <output message="s0:GetCDSoapOut" />
50:        </operation>
51:        <operation name="DoSomething">
52:          <input message="s0:DoSomethingSoapIn" />
53:          <output message="s0:DoSomethingSoapOut" />
54:        </operation>
55:      </portType>
56:      <binding name="Service1Soap" type="s0:Service1Soap">
57:        <soap:binding transport="http://schemas.xmlsoap.org/soap/http"
58:            style="rpc" />
59:        <operation name="GetCD">
60:          <soap:operation soapAction="http://tempuri.org/GetCD"
61:            style="rpc" />
62:          <input>
63:            <soap:body use="encoded" namespace="http://tempuri.org/"
64:                encodingStyle="http://schemas.xmlsoap.org/soap/encoding/" />
65:          </input>
66:          <output>
67:            <soap:body use="encoded" namespace="http://tempuri.org/"
68:                encodingStyle="http://schemas.xmlsoap.org/soap/encoding/" />
```

```
69:        </output>
70:      </operation>
71:      <operation name="DoSomething">
72:        <soap:operation soapAction="http://tempuri.org/DoSomething"
73:          style="rpc" />
74:        <input>
75:          <soap:body use="encoded" namespace="http://tempuri.org/"
76:              encodingStyle="http://schemas.xmlsoap.org/soap/encoding/" />
77:        </input>
78:        <output>
79:          <soap:body use="encoded" namespace="http://tempuri.org/"
80:              encodingStyle="http://schemas.xmlsoap.org/soap/encoding/" />
81:        </output>
82:      </operation>
83:    </binding>
84:    <service name="Service1">
85:      <port name="Service1Soap" binding="s0:Service1Soap">
86:        <soap:address location="http://localhost/ch4wsdl/service1.asmx" />
87:      </port>
88:    </service>
89:  </definitions>
```

The big difference between the RPC/encoded version and the document/literal version is that the types and resulting messages are different. The document/literal version wraps the types in a request or response-related message. The RPC/encoded version simply passes the specialized data type. This change cascades down into the `message`, `portType`, and `binding` definitions. The RPC/encoded option gives a SOAP endpoint the ability to figure out the object graph without any prior knowledge of any type information. Document/literal typically requires prior knowledge of the document layout. In general, document/literal encoding gives the most flexibility.

definitions

Through the use of .NET attributes you can set the name for two of the XML attributes in the `definitions` element—`xmlns:s0` and `targetNamespace`. Changes to these namespaces will cascade throughout the WSDL file. The text `tempuri.org` will be replaced with the new namespace name. How do you do this? The `WebService` attribute has a member, `Namespace`, that affects the definitions element. `Namespace` defines the default root namespace associated with any messages or XSD documents. This will also be used to define any `targetNamespace` items for the document. As an example, let's set the `Namespace` member. Listing 4.4 shows the changes to the code as well as the effect on the WSDL file. The change is reflected on the following lines within the WSDL: 1–2, 6, and 13.

LISTING 4.4   Applying the `WebService` Attribute on a Class (`service3.asmx.vb`)

```
<WebService( _
    Namespace:="http://www.samspublishing.com/VBWS/Ch4WSDL/")> _
Public Class Service1
```

Effect on WSDL, viewable at `http://localhost/Ch4WSDL/Service3.asmx?WSDL`.

```
 1:  <definitions xmlns:s0="http://www.samspublishing.com/VBWS/Ch4WSDL/"
 2:      targetNamespace="http://www.samspublishing.com/VBWS/Ch4WSDL/"
 3:      <!--other attributes deleted--> >
 4:      <types>
 5:          <s:schema elementFormDefault="qualified"
 6:              targetNamespace="http://www.samspublishing.com/VBWS/Ch4WSDL/">
 7:              <!--types deleted-->
 8:          </s:schema>
 9:      </types>
10:      <binding name="Service1Soap" type="s0:Service1Soap">
11:          <operation name="GetCD">
12:              <soap:operation soapAction=
13:                  "http://www.samspublishing.com/VBWS/Ch4WSDL/GetCD"
14:                  style="document" />
15:              <!--input and output deleted-->
16:          </operation>
17:      </binding>
18:      <!--service deleted-->
19:  </definitions>
```

The `WebService` attribute allows for changes to the `service` and `binding` elements as
well. We will look at those changes toward the end of this section.

types

Stepping through the WSDL file, the next element up for modification is the `types`
section. You modify the `types` by setting attributes on the class definition itself. You
can set the following information for any given type:

- `targetNamespace` for the type. By default, the type will share the
  `targetNamespace` stated by the `WebService` attribute for the Web Service using
  the type.

- Declare what the name of the type is when serialized as XML. The default
  name matches the classname.

- Specify whether the item is serialized as an element or as an attribute. By default, members will get serialized as elements.

- Specify the name of the element when serialized as SOAP.

To change the target namespace and the name of the type, you use the `System.Xml.Serialization.XmlTypeAttribute` class. To set the namespace, you set the value of the `Namespace` property. The `TypeName` property will set the name of the type. The `XmlTypeAttribute` class has a third property, `IncludeInSchema`. If you set this property to `false`, the WSDL cannot be generated for any Web Service that uses that type as an argument or return value. Why? Setting that property to `false` says "do not generate schema for this type." If .NET cannot create schema, it cannot generate the file that tells others how to use the type.

When the WSDL file needs to include a type that lives outside the default `targetNamespace`, it creates an extra schema element for that new type inside the types element. Any schemas using that element will import the new namespace into their own namespace. Listing 4.5 shows the code being applied to the `AudioCD` class and `CDType` enumeration, as well as the fragment of the WSDL file this change effects. Specifically, the following lines in the WSDL shown in Listing 4.5 have changed: 4–7, 12, 18–20, and 30–31.

LISTING 4.5   Setting the `targetNamespace` and Type Name for a Class
(`service4.asmx.vb`)

```
 1:  <System.Xml.Serialization.XmlType( _
 2:       Namespace:="http://www.samspublishing.com/VBWS/CDType", _
 3:       TypeName:="CompactDiscType")> _
 4:  Public Enum CDType
 5:       Mini
 6:       Normal
 7:  End Enum
 8:
 9:  <System.Xml.Serialization.XmlType( _
10:       Namespace:="http://www.samspublishing.com/VBWS/CDType", _
11:       TypeName:="MyAudioCD")> _
12:  Public Class AudioCD
13:       Public Name As String
14:       Public NumTracks As Long
15:       Public YearPublished As Long
16:       Public Artist As String
17:       Public TheType As CDType
18:  End Class
```

Effect on WSDL, viewable at http://localhost/Ch4WSDL/Service4.asmx?WSDL.

```
 1:  <definitions xmlns:s1="http://www.samspublishing.com/VBWS/CDType"
 2:    <!--attributes deleted--> >
 3:   <types>
 4:     <s:schema elementFormDefault="qualified" targetNamespace=
 5:             "http://www.samspublishing.com/VBWS/Ch4WSDL/">
 6:       <s:import namespace=
 7:             "http://www.samspublishing.com/VBWS/CDType" />
 8:       <s:element name="GetCDResponse">
 9:         <s:complexType>
10:           <s:sequence>
11:             <s:element minOccurs="0" maxOccurs="1"
12:                 name="GetCDResult" type="s1:MyAudioCD" />
13:           </s:sequence>
14:         </s:complexType>
15:       </s:element>
16:       <!--types deleted-->
17:     </s:schema>
18:     <s:schema elementFormDefault="qualified"
19:         targetNamespace="http://www.samspublishing.com/VBWS/CDType">
20:       <s:complexType name="MyAudioCD">
21:         <s:sequence>
22:           <s:element minOccurs="0" maxOccurs="1"
23:               name="Name" type="s:string" />
24:           <s:element minOccurs="1" maxOccurs="1"
25:               name="NumTracks" type="s:long" />
26:           <s:element minOccurs="1" maxOccurs="1"
27:               name="YearPublished" type="s:long" />
28:           <s:element minOccurs="0" maxOccurs="1"
29:               name="Artist" type="s:string" />
30:           <s:element minOccurs="1" maxOccurs="1" name="TheType"
31:               type="s1:CompactDiscType" />
32:         </s:sequence>
33:       </s:complexType>
34:       <s:simpleType name="CompactDiscType">
35:         <s:restriction base="s:string">
36:           <s:enumeration value="Mini" />
37:           <s:enumeration value="Normal" />
38:         </s:restriction>
39:       </s:simpleType>
```

```
40:      </s:schema>
41:    </types>
42:  </definitions>
```

You can also change the layout of the individual elements within the type. Using the `System.Xml.Serialization.XmlElementAttribute` class, you can define how each element gets serialized. For example, you can allow for the items to be nil or not. The name used by XML serialization can also be changed from the default name. How do these changes manifest inside of the WSDL file? If you set the namespace for the given element and that namespace differs from the one used for serializing the class, a separate item will be generated in the WSDL. That element will be contained within a schema element for that namespace and will map the element name to the declared type. Listing 4.6 shows these changes, applied to the `AudioCD.Name` member variable, in action. The changes are reflected in the WSDL in the listing on lines 9, 12, and 17–20.

The declaration states that the name should be serialized with the name `CDName`. Our use of the `Form` property indicates that the `Name` element must be namespace qualified. When placing an element into another namespace, you cannot set the value to `System.Xml.Schema.XmlSchemaForm.Unqualified`. An unqualified element will not correctly serialize or deserialize. Furthermore, ASP.NET will generate an exception at runtime when it sees `System.Xml.Schema.XmlSchemaForm.Unqualified` chosen.

LISTING 4.6   Modifying the `AudioCD.Name` Member Variable (`service5.asmx.vb`)

```
1:  <System.Xml.Serialization.XmlElement( _
2:      Form:=System.Xml.Schema.XmlSchemaForm.Qualified, _
3:      ElementName:="CDName", _
4:      IsNullable:=False, _
5:      Namespace:="http://www.scottseely.com/newNS")> _
6:  Public Name As String
```

Effect on WSDL, viewable at `http://localhost/Ch4WSDL/Service5.asmx?WSDL`.

```
1:  <definitions
2:      xmlns:s2="http://www.scottseely.com/newNS"
3:      <!--attributes deleted-->>
4:    <types>
5:     <!--types deleted-->
6:     <s:schema elementFormDefault="qualified"
7:          targetNamespace="http://www.aw.com/VBWS/CDType">
8:       <s:import
9:          namespace="http://www.scottseely.com/newNS" />
```

```
10:        <s:complexType name="MyAudioCD">
11:          <s:sequence>
12:            <s:element minOccurs="0" maxOccurs="1" ref="s2:CDName" />
13:            <!--elements deleted-->
14:          </s:sequence>
15:        </s:complexType>
16:      </s:schema>
17:      <s:schema elementFormDefault="qualified"
18:          targetNamespace="http://www.scottseely.com/newNS">
19:        <s:element name="CDName" type="s:string" />
20:      </s:schema>
21:    </types>
22:    <!--lots more deleted-->
23: </definitions>
```

You can even decide to have a member variable get serialized as an attribute. Like an element, you can set the name, namespace, and require that the element is namespace qualified. This is all done through the `System.Xml.Serialization.XmlAttributeAttribute` class. Listing 4.7 contains a modification to the `AudioCD.NumTracks` member variable, as well as how these modifications affect the types declaration. The changes to the WSDL due to the changes in the code can be seen on the following lines: 9, 12, and 15–18.

LISTING 4.7   Using the `XmlAttributeAttribute` (service6.asmx.vb)

```
1: <System.Xml.Serialization.XmlAttributeAttribute( _
2:     Form:=System.Xml.Schema.XmlSchemaForm.Qualified, _
3:     AttributeName:="NumberOfTracks", _
4:     Namespace:="http://www.scottseely.com/AnotherNewNS")> _
5: Public NumTracks As Long
```

Effect on WSDL, viewable at `http://localhost/Ch4WSDL/Service6.asmx?WSDL`.

```
1: <definitions
2:     xmlns:s3="http://www.scottseely.com/AnotherNewNS"
3:     <!--attributes deleted-->>
4:    <types>
5:     <!--schema deleted-->
6:      <s:schema elementFormDefault="qualified"
7:          targetNamespace="http://www.samspublishing.com/VBWS/CDType">
8:        <s:import namespace="http://www.scottseely.com/newNS" />
9:        <s:import namespace="http://www.scottseely.com/AnotherNewNS" />
```

```
10:            <s:complexType name="MyAudioCD">
11:              <!--elements deleted-->
12:              <s:attribute ref="s3:NumberOfTracks" />
13:            </s:complexType>
14:          </s:schema>
15:          <s:schema elementFormDefault="qualified"
16:              targetNamespace="http://www.scottseely.com/AnotherNewNS">
17:            <s:attribute name="NumberOfTracks" type="s:long" />
18:          </s:schema>
19:        </types>
20:        <!--rest deleted-->
21:    </definitions>
```

Finally, you can also change the names of the enumerated values. For example, the internal names for the CD types may not be what you want the outside to use. To change the name to something else, use the System.Xml.Serialization.XmlEnumAttribute class. This class allows you to change the name of the enumeration by setting its Name property. Listing 4.8 shows how to map the internal type names to a string representing the diameter in millimeters of the CD media to which the type refers.

LISTING 4.8   Using the XmlEnumAttribute Class on an Enumeration (service7.asmx.vb)

```
1:  Public Enum CDType
2:        <System.Xml.Serialization.XmlEnum(Name:="80mm")> _
3:        Mini
4:
5:        <System.Xml.Serialization.XmlEnum(Name:="120mm")> _
6:        Normal
7:  End Enum
```

Effect on WSDL, viewable at http://localhost/Ch4WSDL/Service7.asmx?WSDL.

```
1:  <s:simpleType name="CDType">
2:        <s:restriction base="s:string">
3:            <s:enumeration value="80mm" />
4:            <s:enumeration value="120mm" />
5:        </s:restriction>
6:  </s:simpleType>
```

The preceding attributes work only when the Web Service is set up to transmit messages using document/literal. While this will certainly be the way most messages are serialized going forward, if you want to specify that the Web Service is RPC-based, you will need to do something else. RPC/encoded Web Services ignore the XML related attributes. Can you accomplish the same task another way? Yes, you can still send an XML document to a caller as a URL-encoded string. URL encoding makes the string "safe" for placing in a URL or as a string by encoding special characters such as <, >, and [.

For comparison to what these attributes do, compare the WSDL elements to the ones shown in Listing 4.4. This next example will show how to set the namespace for the class, as well as how to change the name of an individual element. For an RPC/encoded Web Service, the class namespace and type can be set by using the `System.Xml.Serialization.SoapTypeAttribute` class. In ASP.NET, you mark the Web Service class with the attribute `System.Web.Services.Protocols.SoapRpcServiceAttribute`. Just like the `XmlTypeAttribute` class, `SoapTypeAttribute` can set the type name for enumeration and class types. To change the element name, use `System.Xml.Serialization.SoapElementAttribute`. Use `System.Xml.Serialization.SoapEnum` to change the name of a value within an enumeration. Finally, you can also make it so that certain members will not even show up in the message by applying the `System.Xml.Serialization.SoapIgnoreAttribute` class to the member variable you do not want to see transmitted, in the listing this is the value NumTracks on lines 21 and 22 of the code. Listing 4.9 shows the code changes and the effects on the WSDL file. The changes are visible on the following lines: 9–10 and 21–22.

LISTING 4.9 Applying the `SoapTypeAttribute`, `SoapElementAttribute`, `SoapIgnoreAttribute`, and `SoapEnum` Classes to the AudioCD Class (`service8.asmx.vb`)

```
 1: <System.Xml.Serialization.SoapType( _
 2:     TypeName:="CompactDiscType", _
 3:     Namespace:="http://www.scottseely.com")> _
 4: Public Enum CDType
 5:     <System.Xml.Serialization.SoapEnum(Name:="80mm")> _
 6:     Mini
 7:
 8:     <System.Xml.Serialization.SoapEnum(Name:="120mm")> _
 9:     Normal
10: End Enum
11:
12: <System.Xml.Serialization.SoapType( _
13:     TypeName:="MyAudioCD", _
14:     Namespace:="http://www.scottseely.com")> _
```

LISTING 4.9   Continued

```
15:   Public Class AudioCD
16:       <System.Xml.Serialization.SoapElement( _
17:           ElementName:="CDName", _
18:           IsNullable:=True)> _
19:       Public Name As String
20:
21:       <System.Xml.Serialization.SoapIgnore()> _
22:       Public NumTracks As Long
23:       Public YearPublished As Long
24:       Public Artist As String
25:       Public TheType As CDType
26:   End Class
```

Effect on WSDL, viewable at `http://localhost/Ch4WSDL/Service8.asmx?WSDL`.

```
1:   <?xml version="1.0" encoding="utf-8" ?>
2:   <definitions
3:       xmlns:s0="http://www.scottseely.com"
4:       <!--attributes deleted-->>
5:       <types>
6:           <s:schema targetNamespace="http://www.scottseely.com">
7:               <s:complexType name="MyAudioCD">
8:                   <s:sequence>
9:                       <s:element minOccurs="1" maxOccurs="1"
10:                          name="CDName" type="s:string" />
11:                      <s:element minOccurs="1" maxOccurs="1"
12:                          name="YearPublished" type="s:long" />
13:                      <s:element minOccurs="1" maxOccurs="1"
14:                          name="Artist" type="s:string" />
15:                      <s:element minOccurs="1" maxOccurs="1"
16:                          name="TheType" type="s0:CompactDiscType" />
17:                   </s:sequence>
18:               </s:complexType>
19:               <s:simpleType name="CompactDiscType">
20:                   <s:restriction base="s:string">
21:                       <s:enumeration value="80mm" />
22:                       <s:enumeration value="120mm" />
23:                   </s:restriction>
24:               </s:simpleType>
```

```
25:            </s:schema>
26:          </types>
27:          <!--elements deleted-->
28:    </definitions>
```

This wraps up the information on how to shape the layout of elements within the types section of the WSDL file. When you do change the layout of your types, you need to remember that the attribute that applies to the type depends on the type of Web Service. If the Web Service is document/literal, the attributes starting with XML will apply. For RPC/encoded Web Services, use the attributes that start with SOAP.

message, portType, and binding

A lot of the things you do to a message element cascades to the portType and binding elements. As a result, something you do to change the message element will show up in the others. For this section, we will cover the attributes that effect these elements based on the scope of the change. Attributes that affect all three will be discussed first. Attributes that only affect one element or the other will then be discussed. Let's start by looking at the message element and how to mold it.

The message elements are used to define the various messages that flow between the client and the Web Service. By default, each message reflects the name of the function being called. If the function or subroutine is called foo, the request and response messages will be called fooSoapIn and fooSoapOut, respectively. Using the attributes provided by the ASP.NET runtime, you can rename the attributes and the part names and tell ASP.NET to generate messages for only an input/output combo, as well as just an input or just an output message.

To change the message name alone, you can use the System.Web.Services.WebMethodAttribute class. You have to use this attribute to expose the method as a part of the SOAP endpoint. This class has a property, MessageName, that will change the name of both the request and response messages. Listing 4.10 shows how to use this property and its effect on the WSDL file. The WSDL is changed on the following lines in listing 4.10: 7, 15, 18, 27–28, 30–31, 41–42, 50, 52, and 55.

LISTING 4.10   Using the WebMethodAttribute.MessageName Property (service9.asmx.vb)

```
<WebMethod(Messagename:="GetCompactDisc")> _
Public Function GetCD(ByVal CD_ID As Long) As AudioCD
```

Effect on WSDL, viewable at `http://localhost/Ch4WSDL/Service9.asmx?WSDL`.

```
 1:  <?xml version="1.0" encoding="utf-8"?>
 2:  <definitions
 3:      <!--attributes deleted-->>
 4:    <types>
 5:     <s:schema elementFormDefault="qualified"
 6:         targetNamespace="http://tempuri.org/">
 7:       <s:element name="GetCompactDisc">
 8:         <s:complexType>
 9:           <s:sequence>
10:             <s:element minOccurs="1" maxOccurs="1" name="CD_ID"
11:                 type="s:long" />
12:           </s:sequence>
13:         </s:complexType>
14:       </s:element>
15:       <s:element name="GetCompactDiscResponse">
16:         <s:complexType>
17:           <s:sequence>
18:             <s:element minOccurs="0" maxOccurs="1" name="GetCompactDiscResult"
19:                 type="s0:AudioCD" />
20:           </s:sequence>
21:         </s:complexType>
22:       </s:element>
23:
24:       <!--Elements deleted-->
25:     </s:schema>
26:   </types>
27:   <message name="GetCompactDiscSoapIn">
28:     <part name="parameters" element="s0:GetCompactDisc" />
29:   </message>
30:   <message name="GetCompactDiscSoapOut">
31:     <part name="parameters" element="s0:GetCompactDiscResponse" />
32:   </message>
33:   <message name="DoSomethingSoapIn">
34:     <part name="parameters" element="s0:DoSomething" />
35:   </message>
36:   <message name="DoSomethingSoapOut">
37:     <part name="parameters" element="s0:DoSomethingResponse" />
38:   </message>
```

```
39:    <portType name="Service1Soap">
40:      <operation name="GetCD">
41:        <input name="GetCompactDisc" message="s0:GetCompactDiscSoapIn" />
42:        <output name="GetCompactDisc" message="s0:GetCompactDiscSoapOut" />
43:      </operation>
44:      <!--operation deleted-->
45:    </portType>
46:    <binding name="Service1Soap" type="s0:Service1Soap">
47:      <soap:binding transport="http://schemas.xmlsoap.org/soap/http"
48:          style="document" />
49:      <operation name="GetCD">
50:        <soap:operation soapAction="http://tempuri.org/GetCompactDisc"
51:            style="document" />
52:        <input name="GetCompactDisc">
53:          <soap:body use="literal" />
54:        </input>
55:        <output name="GetCompactDisc">
56:          <soap:body use="literal" />
57:        </output>
58:      </operation>
59:      <!--operation deleted-->
60:    </binding>
61:    <!--service deleted-->
62: </definitions>
```

The effect on a RPC/encoded Web Service is almost the same. Another change to make to the Web Service is to turn off the output message from the DoSomething Web Method. This method returns nothing, so we might as well not force an empty response element. Like a lot of the attributes we will use in the remainder of this section, one exists for RPC/encoded and for document/literal Web Methods. All of the listings will use the document/literal version of the attribute. These names all begin with SoapDocument. Just substitute SoapRpc for SoapDocument to get the name of the RPC/encoded version of the attribute. To change the element to just an input method, use the OneWay property of the System.Web.Services.Protocols.SoapDocumentMethod attribute. Setting the OneWay property to true tells ASP.NET that the method does not return anything. Listing 4.11 shows it all. Within lines 17–19, notice that the output message is now gone. The same is true within the binding on lines 23–29.

LISTING 4.12   Stating that the Web Method Does Not Return Anything
(`service10.asmx.vb`)

```
1:  <WebMethod(), _
2:    System.Web.Services.Protocols.SoapDocumentMethod( _
3:          OneWay:=True)> _
4:  Public Sub DoSomething(ByVal someArgument As String)
```

Effect on WSDL, viewable at `http://localhost/Ch4WSDL/Service10.asmx?WSDL`.

```
1:  <?xml version="1.0" encoding="utf-8"?>
2:  <definitions
3:      <!--attributes deleted-->>
4:    <types>
5:      <s:schema elementFormDefault="qualified"
6:          targetNamespace="http://tempuri.org/">
7:          <!--DoSomethingResponse does not appear here anymore-->
8:      </s:schema>
9:    </types>
10:   <!--messages deleted-->
11:   <message name="DoSomethingSoapIn">
12:     <part name="parameters" element="s0:DoSomething" />
13:   </message>
14:   <!--DoSomethingSoapOut doesn't appear here anymore-->
15:   <portType name="Service1Soap">
16:     <!--operation GetCD deleted-->
17:     <operation name="DoSomething">
18:       <input message="s0:DoSomethingSoapIn" />
19:     </operation>
20:   </portType>
21:   <binding name="Service1Soap" type="s0:Service1Soap">
22:     <!--operation GetCD deleted-->
23:     <operation name="DoSomething">
24:       <soap:operation soapAction="http://tempuri.org/DoSomething"
25:         style="document" />
26:       <input>
27:         <soap:body use="literal" />
28:       </input>
29:     </operation>
30:   </binding>
31:   <!--service element deleted-->
32: </definitions>
```

You can modify more of the message as well. All this is possible using the SoapDocumentMethodAttribute class. You can change the names of the request and response messages using the RequestElementName, ResponseElementName, RequestNamespace, and ResponseNamespace attributes. You can set the value ASP.NET should expect for the SOAPAction HTTP header using the Action property. Finally, the Binding property lets you name the WSDL binding with which the operation belongs. To use the Binding property, you must define one or more bindings for the class. We will cover using this property a little later in the section. Because all of these items have fairly small effects, they are bundled into one example. Listing 4.12 shows some changes to the GetCD Web Method and how these changes affect the WSDL. The changes are visible on lines 2–3, 7–27, 32–37, 40–43, and 50–51 of the WDSL snippet.

LISTING 4.12   Applying (almost) Everything Else Available from the SoapDocumentMethodAttribute (service11.asmx.vb)

```
 1:  <WebMethod(), _
 2:      SoapDocumentMethodAttribute( _
 3:          RequestElementName:="GetTheCD", _
 4:          RequestNamespace:="http://scottseely.com/GetCDRequest", _
 5:          ResponseElementName:="IGotTheCD", _
 6:          ResponseNamespace:="http://scottseely.com/GetCDResponse")> _
 7:  Public Function GetCD(ByVal CD_ID As Long) As AudioCD
 8:      GetCD = New AudioCD()
 9:      GetCD.Artist = "The Pixies"
10:      GetCD.NumTracks = 15
11:      GetCD.YearPublished = 1991
12:      GetCD.Name = "Trompe le Monde"
13:  End Function
```

Effect on WSDL, viewable at http://localhost/Ch4WSDL/Service11.asmx?WSDL.

```
 1:  <definitions
 2:      xmlns:s1="http://scottseely.com/GetCDResponse"
 3:      xmlns:s0="http://scottseely.com/GetCDRequest"
 4:      xmlns:s2="http://tempuri.org/"
 5:      <!-- attributes deleted-->>
 6:      <types>
 7:          <s:schema elementFormDefault="qualified"
 8:              targetNamespace="http://scottseely.com/GetCDRequest">
 9:              <s:element name="GetTheCD">
```

```
10:                      <s:complexType>
11:                          <s:sequence>
12:                              <s:element minOccurs="1" maxOccurs="1"
13:                                  name="CD_ID" type="s:long" />
14:                          </s:sequence>
15:                      </s:complexType>
16:                  </s:element>
17:          </s:schema>
18:          <s:schema elementFormDefault="qualified"
19:              targetNamespace="http://scottseely.com/GetCDResponse">
20:              <s:element name="IGotTheCD">
21:                  <s:complexType>
22:                      <s:sequence>
23:                          <s:element minOccurs="0" maxOccurs="1"
24:                              name="GetCDResult" type="s1:AudioCD" />
25:                      </s:sequence>
26:                  </s:complexType>
27:              </s:element>
28:              <!-- types deleted-->
29:          </s:schema>
30:          <!-- schema deleted-->
31:      </types>
32:      <message name="GetCDSoapIn">
33:          <part name="parameters" element="s0:GetTheCD" />
34:      </message>
35:      <message name="GetCDSoapOut">
36:          <part name="parameters" element="s1:IGotTheCD" />
37:      </message>
38:      <!--message deleted-->
39:      <portType name="Service1Soap">
40:          <operation name="GetCD">
41:              <input message="s2:GetCDSoapIn" />
42:              <output message="s2:GetCDSoapOut" />
43:          </operation>
44:          <!--operation deleted-->
45:      </portType>
46:      <binding name="Service1Soap" type="s2:Service1Soap">
47:          <soap:binding
48:              transport="http://schemas.xmlsoap.org/soap/http"
49:              style="document" />
50:          <operation name="GetCD">
51:              <soap:operation soapAction="IAmGettingACD" style="document" />
```

```
52:                    <!--input/output deleted-->
53:               </operation>
54:               <!--operation deleted-->
55:          </binding>
56:          <!--service deleted-->
57:     </definitions>
```

The following item affects only the message element. The
`System.Xml.Serialization.SoapElementAttribute` class can be used to change the
name of the message parts when developing an RPC/encoded Web Service and Web
Method. Listing 4.13 shows the code and the changes to the `GetCD` Web Method.

LISTING 4.13   Changing the Name of a Part (`service12.asmx.vb`)

```
1:  Public Function GetCD( _
2:      <System.Xml.Serialization.SoapElement( _
3:            ElementName:="CompactDiscID") > _
4:        ByVal CD_ID As Long) As AudioCD
```

Effect on WSDL, viewable at `http://localhost/Ch4WSDL/Service12.asmx?WSDL`.

```
1:  <message name="GetCDSoapIn">
2:      <part name="CompactDiscID" type="s:long" />
3:  </message>
```

That's all you can do that involves the `message` element. The `WebMethodAttribute`
class offers one other property that is useful to us in terms of shaping the WSDL. The
`Description` property adds a documentation element to the operation element
within the `portType`. You can embed HTML within the operation. This allows you to
place links, format text, or do anything else that makes sense for the Web Service
documentation. The information you add here will show up in the auto-generated
ASP.NET pages for your Web Service. It appears immediately beneath the method
name on the main page and on the page that describes the message accepted by the
method itself. Listing 4.14 shows the code and the resulting WSDL. The change
shows up on lines 3–6 of the WSDL snippet. Figure 4.1 shows the effect to the page
for the method.

LISTING 4.14   Setting the Description for the Web Method (`service13.asmx.vb`)

```
1:  <WebMethod( _
2:      Description:="This is the description. It can contain " & _
3:          "<font color='red'><i>HTML</i></font> " & _
4:          "to enhance the auto-generated pages.")> _
5:  Public Function GetCD(ByVal CD_ID As Long) As AudioCD
```

Effect on WSDL, viewable at `http://localhost/Ch4WSDL/Service13.asmx?WSDL`.

```
 1:   <portType name="Service1Soap">
 2:       <operation name="GetCD">
 3:           <documentation>This is the description. It can contain
 4:               &lt;font color='red'&gt;&lt;i&gt;HTML
 5:               &lt;/i&gt;&lt;/font&gt; to enhance the
 6:               auto-generated pages.</documentation>
 7:           <input message="s0:GetCDSoapIn" />
 8:           <output message="s0:GetCDSoapOut" />
 9:       </operation>
10:       <operation name="DoSomething">
11:           <input message="s0:DoSomethingSoapIn" />
12:       </operation>
13:   </portType>
```

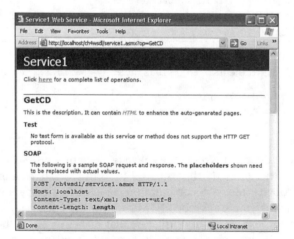

FIGURE 4.1   Displaying the documentation that was added via the
`WebMethodAttribute` class.

You can do some other interesting things to these parts of the WSDL file as well. We
will cover separating these pieces into distinct documents in the "Changing the
Location of WSDL Elements" section later in this chapter.

service

The only thing you can do that uniquely affects the `service` element is to add a
documentation element. The `System.Web.Services.WebServiceAttribute` class has a
description property. ASP.NET uses the value of this property to fill in the text

within the documentation element. Like other documentation elements, this element can contain embedded XML or HTML. Within the WSDL document, any special characters, such as < and > will be encoded as < and >. Listing 4.15 contains the code to add the documentation, as well as the changes to the WSDL, visible on lines 2-4. Figure 4.2 shows the effect on the ASP.NET-generated Web page.

LISTING 4.15   Adding Documentation to the `service` Element (`service14.asmx.vb`)

```
1:  <System.Web.Services.WebService( _
2:      Description:="This is some <b><font color='blue'>" & _
3:          "HTML-based</font></b> Web Service Documentation.")> _
4:  Public Class Service1
```

Effect on WSDL, viewable at `http://localhost/Ch4WSDL/Service14.asmx?WSDL`.

```
1:  <service name="Service1">
2:      <documentation>This is some &lt;b&gt;&lt;font color='blue'&gt;
3:          HTML-based&lt;/font&gt;&lt;/b&gt;
4:          Web Service Documentation.</documentation>
5:      <port name="Service1Soap" binding="s0:Service1Soap">
6:          <soap:address location=
7:              "http://localhost/ch4wsdl/service1.asmx" />
8:      </port>
9:  </service>
```

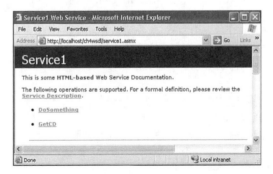

FIGURE 4.2   Viewing the HTML in the ASP.NET documentation page.

We are not done yet with ways to customize how things get laid out in the WSDL. We have two special topics left to cover—Header and binding information.

Using SOAP Headers

SOAP Headers do influence the layout of the WSDL in many of the same areas that the message itself influences the WSDL. Because SOAP Headers often are specially declared, we cover them separately and look at the various means of shaping them. In many ways, they are just like other classes that get serialized and deserialized. For example, the same attributes that manipulate the form of the header in XML and the WSDL are used on Header member variables. The name of the type when serialized is set the same as any other class. As a result, we will not cover those items again. Instead, we will focus on the things that are unique to a SOAP Header.

A SOAP Header can travel as a part of the request and or response. Depending on the use of the Header, the endpoint may need to be able to understand the Header to correctly process the message. Finally, some part of the class needs to read the Header and make it available to the endpoint. We will cover these items in this section.

To create a Header, create a class that derives from System.Web.Services.Protocols.SoapHeader. The Web Service class that uses the new class needs to contain an instance of that class as a member variable. After you have done that, you need to tie the Header to a particular Web Method. This is accomplished by using the System.Web.Services.Protocols.SoapHeaderAttribute class. This class has several properties that let you state which messages the Header travels (Direction), the name of the member variable associated with the Header (MemberName), and whether or not the Header is required (Required).

For an example, we can add a Header to be used by the DoSomething Web Method. We will make this Header required and state that it only comes in with the request. Listing 4.16 shows the declaration of the MyHeader class. The listing also shows how to use the class within the Web Service to use the Header. You will see that the code writes the information that comes with the SOAP message and writes the data out using the Trace class.

LISTING 4.16   Using a SOAP Header (service15.asmx.vb)

```
1:  Public Class MyHeader
2:      Inherits System.Web.Services.Protocols.SoapHeader
3:
4:      Public UserName As String
5:      Public CallTime As DateTime
6:  End Class
7:
8:  <System.Web.Services.WebService( )> _
9:  Public Class Service1
10:     Inherits System.Web.Services.WebService
11:
```

LISTING 4.16   Continued

```
12:      Public m_aHeader As New MyHeader()
13:
14:      <WebMethod(), _
15:      System.Web.Services.Protocols.SoapHeader("m_aHeader", _
16:          Required:=True, _
17:          Direction:= _
18:              System.Web.Services.Protocols.SoapHeaderDirection.In)> _
19:      Public Sub DoSomething(ByVal someArgument As String)
20:          Trace.WriteLine("UserName=" & m_aHeader.UserName)
21:          Trace.WriteLine("CallTime=" & m_aHeader.CallTime.ToString())
22:      End Sub
23:
24:  End Class
```

Yes, the GetCD Web Method was removed from the class so that only the parts pertaining to the SOAP Header were included. This change makes it easier to show the changes made to the Web Service. The biggest surprise to me was how the Header gets mapped to a member variable or property. ASP.NET uses reflection to find and set the value specified in the SoapHeaderAttribute. If the member variable or property is not public, ASP.NET will not generate a WSDL file or any other item related to the Web Service. Why? Code access will not let ASP.NET set the value when translating the SOAP message from XML to objects.

Listing 4.17 shows the changes to the WSDL file. First, a new type gets inserted into the types section in lines 7-15 that describes the Header. Second, the binding for the DoSomething operation includes a reference to the Header on lines 29-32, indicating that it is required for the SOAP call.

LISTING 4.17   Changes to the WSDL Document, Viewable at
http://localhost/Ch4WSDL/Service15.asmx?WSDL

```
1:   <?xml version="1.0" encoding="utf-8" ?>
2:   <definitions <!-- attributes deleted-->>
3:       <types>
4:           <s:schema elementFormDefault="qualified"
5:               targetNamespace="http://tempuri.org/">
6:               <!--elements deleted-->
7:               <s:element name="MyHeader" type="s0:MyHeader" />
8:               <s:complexType name="MyHeader">
9:                   <s:sequence>
10:                      <s:element minOccurs="0" maxOccurs="1"
```

LISTING 4.17   Continued

```
11:                      name="UserName" type="s:string" />
12:                   <s:element minOccurs="1" maxOccurs="1"
13:                      name="CallTime" type="s:dateTime" />
14:               </s:sequence>
15:            </s:complexType>
16:         </s:schema>
17:      </types>
18:      <!--messages and portType deleted-->
19:      <binding name="Service1Soap" type="s0:Service1Soap">
20:         <soap:binding
21:            transport="http://schemas.xmlsoap.org/soap/http"
22:            style="document" />
23:         <operation name="DoSomething">
24:            <soap:operation
25:               soapAction="http://tempuri.org/DoSomething"
26:               style="document" />
27:            <input>
28:               <soap:body use="literal" />
29:               <soap:header d5p1:required="true"
30:                  message="s0:DoSomethingMyHeader"
31:                  part="MyHeader" use="literal"
32:                  xmlns:d5p1="http://schemas.xmlsoap.org/wsdl/" />
33:            </input>
34:            <output>
35:               <soap:body use="literal" />
36:            </output>
37:         </operation>
38:      </binding>
39:      <!--service deleted-->
40: </definitions>
```

For most of the chapter, I have not written clients for the code because they simply are not interesting. Here, a client is called for no other reason than to show the Trace statements actually working. To get the Web Service set up correctly, you will need to edit the code included on the companion Web site. Remember, you are supposed to be following along with the book open somewhere near a PC for this chapter. (The sample client is included on the companion Web site as listed here.) Listing 4.18 shows that client and the resulting trace from the Web Service. It also shows the SOAP request sent to the service.

LISTING 4.18   Client Code for a Console Application that Uses the Header

```
1:  Sub Main()
2:      Dim svc As New localhost.Service1()
3:      svc.MyHeaderValue = New localhost.MyHeader()
4:      svc.MyHeaderValue.CallTime = DateTime.Now
5:      svc.MyHeaderValue.UserName = "Scott Seely"
6:      svc.MyHeaderValue.MustUnderstand = True
7:      svc.DoSomething("test")
8:  End Sub
```

Trace output (visible when debugging the Web Service).

```
UserName=Scott Seely
CallTime=1/1/2002 4:49:39 PM
```

The SOAP Request

```
1:  <?xml version="1.0" encoding="utf-8" ?>
2:  <soap:Envelope
3:      xmlns:soap="http://schemas.xmlsoap.org/soap/envelope/"
4:      xmlns:xsi="http://www.w3.org/2001/XMLSchema-instance"
5:      xmlns:xsd="http://www.w3.org/2001/XMLSchema">
6:      <soap:Header>
7:          <MyHeader soap:mustUnderstand="1"
8:              xmlns="http://tempuri.org/">
9:              <UserName>Scott Seely</UserName>
10:             <CallTime>2002-01-01T16:49:39.7752016-08:00</CallTime>
11:         </MyHeader>
12:     </soap:Header>
13:     <soap:Body>
14:         <DoSomething xmlns="http://tempuri.org/">
15:             <someArgument>test</someArgument>
16:         </DoSomething>
17:     </soap:Body>
18: </soap:Envelope>
```

Why did I set MustUnderstand to true? I did this because I know that the Header is required. Had this been a real Web Service, the client would want to make sure that any required elements are understood. Setting MustUnderstand to true is the only way for a client to make sure that this happens.

Changing the Location of WSDL Elements

When declaring a Web Service, you may want the generated WSDL file to contain only information related to the location endpoint. ASP.NET provides three options when distributing the parts of the WSDL file:

- Place all the information in one document.
- Place the schema in one document. In a second document place the portType, message, and binding data. A third document will contain the service information.
- Use the schema, portType, and binding information from a pre-existing WSDL.

By default, all elements will show up in one document. You can get this to happen by doing nothing. To split things up, you need to use a combination of the WebServiceBindingAttribute class and the SoapDocumentMethodAttribute or SoapRpcMethodAttribute class. Using just the WebServiceBindingAttribute class, you can change the name of the binding in the WSDL. This can be done using the Name property of the class. Set this value and the name of the binding changes. Listing 4.19 shows the code to set the value and the effect on the WSDL.

LISTING 4.19   Setting the Name of the Binding (service16.asmx.vb)

```
 1:  <WebServiceBinding(Name:="MyWebServiceBinding"), _
 2:       System.Web.Services.WebService()> _
 3:  Public Class Service1
 4:      Inherits System.Web.Services.WebService
 5:
 6:      <WebMethod(), _
 7:      System.Web.Services.Protocols.SoapDocumentMethod( _
 8:          Binding:="MyWebServiceBinding")> _
 9:      Public Sub DoSomething(ByVal someArgument As String)
10:          Trace.WriteLine("someArgument=" & someArgument)
11:      End Sub
12:
13:  End Class
```

Effect on WSDL, viewable at http://localhost/Ch4WSDL/Service16.asmx?WSDL.

```
 1:  <portType name="MyWebServiceBinding">
 2:      <!--internals deleted-->
 3:  </portType>
 4:  <binding name="MyWebServiceBinding" type="s0:MyWebServiceBinding">
```

```
5:      <!--internals deleted-->
6:  </binding>
7:  <service name="Service1">
8:      <port name="MyWebServiceBinding" binding="s0:MyWebServiceBinding">
9:          <!--internals deleted-->
10:     </port>
11: </service>
```

This is all good, but how do you split things up? UDDI and client creation actually can benefit when the Web Service definition exists independently of any endpoint data. For example, you can register the tModel information and then register a particular implementation as an implementation of that tModel with UDDI. Recall that a tModel is short for "type model" and contains all of the type information particular to a given Web Service. You can then register the fact that an implementation of that tModel exists at some endpoint.

So, how do you make ASP.NET separate everything out? Simply set the Namespace property on the WebServiceBindingAttribute class. By setting this attribute and leaving everything else in the class declaration the same, you will get three documents instead of one. You will get an XSD definition for any elements. The second document will contain everything except the type and endpoint information. The third document defines the service endpoint. Listing 4.20 shows the class declaration and the resulting WSDL.

LISTING 4.20 Simple Class Declaration That Causes Segmented WSDL (service17.asmx.vb)

```
1:  <WebServiceBinding(Name:="MyWebServiceBinding", _
2:      Namespace:="http://scottseely.com/MyWS"), _
3:      System.Web.Services.WebService()> _
4:  Public Class Service1
5:      Inherits System.Web.Services.WebService
6:
7:      <WebMethod(), _
8:      System.Web.Services.Protocols.SoapDocumentMethod( _
9:          Binding:="MyWebServiceBinding")> _
10:     Public Sub DoSomething(ByVal someArgument As String)
11:         Trace.WriteLine("someArgument=" & someArgument)
12:     End Sub
13:
14: End Class
```

Schema Definition, viewable at
http://localhost/Ch4WSDL/Service17.asmx?schema=schema1.

```
 1:  <?xml version="1.0" encoding="utf-8" ?>
 2:  <xs:schema xmlns:tns="http://scottseely.com/MyWS"
 3:      elementFormDefault="qualified"
 4:      targetNamespace="http://scottseely.com/MyWS"
 5:      id="schema1" xmlns:xs="http://www.w3.org/2001/XMLSchema">
 6:      <xs:element name="DoSomething">
 7:          <xs:complexType>
 8:              <xs:sequence>
 9:                  <xs:element minOccurs="0"
10:                      maxOccurs="1" name="someArgument"
11:                      type="xs:string" />
12:              </xs:sequence>
13:          </xs:complexType>
14:      </xs:element>
15:      <xs:element name="DoSomethingResponse">
16:          <xs:complexType />
17:      </xs:element>
18:  </xs:schema>
```

Web Service Definition Minus the `service` Element, viewable at
http://localhost/Ch4WSDL/Service17.asmx?wsdl=wsdl1.

```
 1:  <?xml version="1.0" encoding="utf-8" ?>
 2:  <definitions
 3:      xmlns:http="http://schemas.xmlsoap.org/wsdl/http/"
 4:      xmlns:soap="http://schemas.xmlsoap.org/wsdl/soap/"
 5:      xmlns:s="http://www.w3.org/2001/XMLSchema"
 6:      xmlns:soapenc="http://schemas.xmlsoap.org/soap/encoding/"
 7:      xmlns:i0="http://scottseely.com/MyWS"
 8:      xmlns:tm="http://microsoft.com/wsdl/mime/textMatching/"
 9:      xmlns:mime="http://schemas.xmlsoap.org/wsdl/mime/"
10:      targetNamespace="http://scottseely.com/MyWS"
11:      xmlns="http://schemas.xmlsoap.org/wsdl/">
12:      <import namespace="http://scottseely.com/MyWS"
13:          location=
14:              "http://localhost/Ch4WSDL/Service1.asmx?schema=schema1" />
15:      <types />
16:      <message name="DoSomethingSoapIn">
17:          <part name="parameters" element="i0:DoSomething" />
```

```
18:     </message>
19:     <message name="DoSomethingSoapOut">
20:         <part name="parameters" element="i0:DoSomethingResponse" />
21:     </message>
22:     <portType name="MyWebServiceBinding">
23:         <operation name="DoSomething">
24:             <input message="i0:DoSomethingSoapIn" />
25:             <output message="i0:DoSomethingSoapOut" />
26:         </operation>
27:     </portType>
28:     <binding name="MyWebServiceBinding" type="i0:MyWebServiceBinding">
29:         <soap:binding
30:             transport="http://schemas.xmlsoap.org/soap/http"
31:             style="document" />
32:         <operation name="DoSomething">
33:             <soap:operation
34:                 soapAction="http://tempuri.org/DoSomething"
35:                 style="document" />
36:             <input>
37:                 <soap:body use="literal" />
38:             </input>
39:             <output>
40:                 <soap:body use="literal" />
41:             </output>
42:         </operation>
43:     </binding>
44: </definitions>
```

Web Service Definition Including the service Element, viewable at http://local-host/Ch4WSDL/Service17.asmx?WSDL.

```
1:  <?xml version="1.0" encoding="utf-8" ?>
2:  <definitions
3:      xmlns:http="http://schemas.xmlsoap.org/wsdl/http/"
4:      xmlns:soap="http://schemas.xmlsoap.org/wsdl/soap/"
5:      xmlns:i1="http://scottseely.com/MyWS"
6:      xmlns:s="http://www.w3.org/2001/XMLSchema"
7:      xmlns:soapenc="http://schemas.xmlsoap.org/soap/encoding/"
8:      xmlns:tns="http://tempuri.org/"
9:      xmlns:tm="http://microsoft.com/wsdl/mime/textMatching/"
10:     xmlns:mime="http://schemas.xmlsoap.org/wsdl/mime/"
```

```
11:        targetNamespace="http://tempuri.org/"
12:        xmlns="http://schemas.xmlsoap.org/wsdl/">
13:        <import namespace="http://scottseely.com/MyWS"
14:            location=
15:              "http://localhost/Ch4WSDL/Service1.asmx?schema=schema1" />
16:        <import namespace="http://scottseely.com/MyWS"
17:            location=
18:              "http://localhost/Ch4WSDL/Service1.asmx?wsdl=wsdl1" />
19:        <types />
20:        <service name="Service1">
21:            <port name="MyWebServiceBinding"
22:                binding="i1:MyWebServiceBinding">
23:                <soap:address
24:                    location="http://localhost/Ch4WSDL/Service1.asmx" />
25:            </port>
26:        </service>
27:    </definitions>
```

The last WSDL document uses WSDL import statements to bring in the schema and other information into the last WSDL document. If you look at the `location` attribute in the second and third WSDL definitions, you will see that ASP.NET is automatically generating the extra documents as well through the query string. This query string only returns information when the separate namespace exists. Otherwise, ASP.NET will generate nothing for you.

If you are actually implementing a Web Service whose primary definition resides elsewhere, you can tell ASP.NET not to generate the first two documents shown in Listing 4.21. Of course, the Web Service definitions must exist somewhere. To tell ASP.NET where that is, the `WebServiceBindingAttribute` has one more property you can set—Location. This will cause ASP.NET to include an `import` element that points to the WSDL document at the specified URL. Listing 4.21 shows the code needed to make this change and the resulting WDSL document with the new location reflected on line 14 of the WSDL portion. If you are following along with the text, do not try to actually create a proxy with the resulting WSDL. It will fail because the location property points to a document that does not actually exist.

LISTING 4.21   Source Code to Set the Location of the WSDL (`service18.asmx.vb`)

```
1:  <WebServiceBinding(Name:="MyWebServiceBinding", _
2:      Namespace:="http://scottseely.com/MyWS", _
3:      Location:="http://scottseely.com/MyWS/Ch4BindingEx.WSDL"), _
4:      System.Web.Services.WebService()> _
5:  Public Class Service1
```

Effect on WSDL, viewable at `http://localhost/Ch4WSDL/Service18.asmx?WSDL`.

```
 1:  <?xml version="1.0" encoding="utf-8" ?>
 2:  <definitions
 3:      xmlns:http="http://schemas.xmlsoap.org/wsdl/http/"
 4:      xmlns:soap="http://schemas.xmlsoap.org/wsdl/soap/"
 5:      xmlns:s="http://www.w3.org/2001/XMLSchema"
 6:      xmlns:soapenc="http://schemas.xmlsoap.org/soap/encoding/"
 7:      xmlns:i0="http://scottseely.com/MyWS"
 8:      xmlns:tns="http://tempuri.org/"
 9:      xmlns:tm="http://microsoft.com/wsdl/mime/textMatching/"
10:      xmlns:mime="http://schemas.xmlsoap.org/wsdl/mime/"
11:      targetNamespace="http://tempuri.org/"
12:      xmlns="http://schemas.xmlsoap.org/wsdl/">
13:      <import namespace="http://scottseely.com/MyWS"
14:          location="http://scottseely.com/MyWS/Ch4BindingEx.WSDL" />
15:      <types />
16:      <service name="Service1">
17:          <port name="MyWebServiceBinding"
18:              binding="i0:MyWebServiceBinding">
19:              <soap:address
20:                  location="http://localhost/Ch4WSDL/Service1.asmx" />
21:          </port>
22:      </service>
23:  </definitions>
```

That's about it for shaping your WSDL. Using the information in this section, you should be able to do anything you need to do with respect to your WSDL document.

Creating a Custom SOAP Extension

In this section, we will take a look at how to create a custom SOAP extension for use with your source code. These custom extensions are useful for adding many things to your applications that do not make sense within the actual Web Method. For example, you may want some special processing to happen whenever a particular header comes through. If the header is used by many of your procedures and the processing for that header is always the same, a custom SOAP extension may be just the thing that you need. SOAP extensions have other uses as well. Some of those uses include the following:

- Encrypting pieces of the message

- Implementing extensions to SOAP, such as WS-Routing

- Adding auditing of the Web Service

- Anything else that you have to do to more than one message

The extensions can be used on clients and proxies. If you apply the extension to a client, you will want to create the proxy using the WSDL.EXE command-line tool instead of adding a Web Reference through Visual Studio .NET. Why? It is too easy to erase any changes to the Visual Studio .NET generated proxy, because all you have to do is right-click the Web Reference and select Update Web Reference. When you update the Web Reference, all of your changes are destroyed.

In this section, we will cover how custom SOAP extensions work. After this is described, we will create an actual extension. Let's start by covering the basics.

Custom SOAP Extension Basics

To implement a custom SOAP extension, you need to override two base classes from the System.Web.Services.Protocols namespace—SoapExtensionAttribute and SoapExtension. SoapExtensionAttribute provides the mechanism to attach the custom extension to a particular item. You can associate the attribute with anything that the System.AttributeTargets enumeration allows. Typically, these items will be attached to methods, classes, or structs. The class derived from SoapExtensionAttribute must override two properties—Priority and ExtensionType. The Priority property is used to indicate the relative priority of the extension with respect to other extensions. The priority influences the order in which the attributes will be applied. For example, you may want a cryptographic extension to decrypt data so that other custom SOAP extensions have access to the unencrypted data. An application that uses the attribute sets the priority through the web.config or app.config file. Listing 4.22 shows an entry that would modify the web.config file for the example project to set the Priority to 3.

LISTING 4.22   Setting the Priority of the Example Extension to 3

```
<configuration>
    <system.web>
        <webServices>
            <soapExtensionTypes>
                <add type=
            "Ch4CustomAttribute.ReverseExtension, Ch4CustomAttribute"
                    priority="3" group="0" />
            </soapExtensionTypes>
        </webServices>
    </system.web>
</configuration>
```

This entry tells the framework that whenever it uses the attribute class that refers to Ch4CustomAttribute.ReverseExtension from the assembly named Ch4CustomAttribute, the extension is at priority 3 within group 0. The extension itself can be in group 0 or group 1. Group 0 has higher priority than any extension in group 1. Priority is then sorted within the groups where the lower numbers reflect a higher priority. Typically, you can avoid using this feature within this first version of ASP.NET. The default behavior works just fine. Besides that, my experience shows that setting this item within the config file typically results in unexpected behavior that is hard to debug. Unless you are applying a large number of extensions to one part of your Web Service, you should not use this feature.

The other property every override of SoapExtensionAttribute must implement is ExtensionType. ExtensionType returns the type that implements the workhorse of the SOAP Extension, the class that overrides SoapExtension. This class requires five overrides:

- GetInitializer   Two versions of this function exist. Both must be overridden. These functions allow a Web Service extension to do some one-time initialization. The first version takes a Type as a parameter and returns a value of type Object. This version gets called when the attribute applies to anything other than a Web Method. The other version passes a LogicalMethodInfo struct and an instance of the associated SoapExtensionAttribute-derived class. It also returns a value of type Object. This value is then used for each individual initialization of the class.

- Initialize   This function receives the object returned by the first call to one of the GetInitializer functions. You have no guarantees that the same instance of the class will call both GetInitializer and Initialize. As a result, do not depend on this happening and treat GetInitializer as if it belongs to a separate instance.

- ChainStream   This function passes in a Stream and returns a new Stream. Typically, you will save the reference to the stream passed in and return a stream of your own. When a message comes in, the passed in Stream contains the serialized message. Outgoing messages appear in the Stream returned by this method. The custom extension is responsible for copying data between Streams at the correct stage. (What's a stage? Keep reading.)

- ProcessMessage   This part actually handles the various stages of processing. As input, it takes a value from the SoapMessageStage enumeration. A message may go through either two or four stages, two for each direction the message travels. The BeforeDeserialize and AfterDeserialize stages handle the message as it comes in. If performing encryption of a message, you would use the BeforeDeserialize stage to decrypt the message before it is sent to the appropriate objects. I set `AfterDeserialize` after the message has been deserialized and just before the method itself gets called. The other pair of stages is `BeforeSerialize` and `AfterSerialize`. `BeforeSerialize` gets called just after the method gets called but before and serialization occurs. `AfterSerialize` gets called after the message is in XML format but before the message gets returned to the client.

Now that you know what these two classes do, it is time to create an example showing the collaboration in action.

An Example SOAP Extension

I could do a lot of different things for a SOAP extension. The .NET Framework SDK documents and many articles cover an extension that writes all messages out to a file. While that is a great example, something more people will need to do is actually manipulate the XML contained in the messages. To give you a feel for how to get into the XML and change the message contents without delving too deeply into concepts like cryptography, this section presents an extension that reverses the text in the first element in the `Body` of the message response. The code for this example is contained in the `Ch4CustomAttribute` project. Because the attribute will be used to reverse text, the two classes will be named `ReverseExtensionAttribute` and `ReverseExtension`.

`ReverseExtensionAttribute` derives from `SoapExtensionAttribute` and overrides the `Priority` and `ExtensionType` properties. If the extension was used for something more sophisticated, the attribute class would have other properties specific to it. An encryption attribute would likely contain a location of a key or the key itself to be used for encryption. A SOAP extension attribute can have as many or as few attributes as makes sense. Because our extension does very little, it contains no extra attributes. Listing 4.23 shows the code for the attribute class.

LISTING 4.23 The `ReverseExtensionAttribute` Class

```
Imports System.Web.Services
Imports System.Web.Services.Protocols


<AttributeUsage(AttributeTargets.Method)> _
Public Class ReverseExtensionAttribute
    Inherits SoapExtensionAttribute

    ' Stores the priority for the class
    Private m_priority As Integer
```

LISTING 4.23 Continued

```
' Returns the type that inherits from
' SoapExtension
Public Overrides ReadOnly Property ExtensionType() As Type
    Get
         Return GetType(ReverseExtension)
    End Get
End Property

' Stores the Priority as set in the config file
' and returns that value on demand.
Public Overrides Property Priority() As Integer
    Get
         Return m_priority
    End Get
    Set(ByVal Value As Integer)
        m_priority = Value
    End Set
End Property

End Class
```

The attribute at the class declaration level declares that this class targets methods only. An attribute could target an entire Web Service or another item as well. This attribute associates itself with the SoapExtension derived class through the ExtensionType property. It tells ASP.NET that when a class uses this attribute, ASP.NET should use the ReverseExtension class to handle any SOAP requests that come through. Listing 4.24 shows the implementation of the ReverseExtension class.

LISTING 4.24 The ReverseExtension Class

```
1:  Imports System.Web.Services
2:  Imports System
3:  Imports System.Web.Services.Protocols
4:  Imports System.IO
5:  Imports System.Xml
6:
7:  Public Class ReverseExtension
8:      Inherits SoapExtension
9:
```

LISTING 4.24   Continued

```
10:        Private m_oldStream As Stream
11:        Private m_newStream As Stream
12:
13:        ' Save the Stream representing the SOAP request or SOAP response into
14:        ' a local memory buffer.
15:        Public Overrides Function ChainStream(ByVal stream As Stream) As Stream
16:            m_oldStream = stream
17:            m_newStream = New MemoryStream()
18:            Return m_newStream
19:        End Function
20:
21:        ' Both GetInitializer overrides are present but do nothing.
22:        Public Overloads Overrides Function GetInitializer( _
23:            ByVal methodInfo As LogicalMethodInfo, _
24:        ByVal attribute As SoapExtensionAttribute) As Object
25:            ' No initializer used. By default, this returns Nothing
26:        End Function
27:
28:        Public Overloads Overrides Function GetInitializer( _
29:            ByVal WebServiceType As Type) As Object
30:            ' No initializer used. By default, this returns Nothing
31:        End Function
32:
33:        ' Implemented because it has to be but does nothing.
34:        Public Overrides Sub Initialize(ByVal initializer As Object)
35:            ' No initializer is used. No point in writing any actual
36:            ' code.
37:        End Sub
38:
39:        ' Handle any chaining of the message between old and new.
40:        ' Besides that, manipulate the stream as needed
41:        Public Overrides Sub ProcessMessage(ByVal message As SoapMessage)
42:            Select Case message.Stage
43:                Case SoapMessageStage.BeforeSerialize
44:                Case SoapMessageStage.AfterSerialize
45:                    HandleOutput()
46:                Case SoapMessageStage.BeforeDeserialize
47:                    HandleInput()
48:                Case SoapMessageStage.AfterDeserialize
49:                Case Else
50:                    Throw New Exception("invalid stage")
```

LISTING 4.24   Continued

```
51:          End Select
52:      End Sub
53:
54:      ' Reverse the contents of the first child of
55:      ' the soap:Body element.
56:      Public Sub HandleOutput()
57:          Dim xmlDoc As New Xml.XmlDocument()
58:          Dim xmlRdr As New StreamReader(m_newStream)
59:
60:          ' Read the stream into the XML Document
61:          m_newStream.Position = 0
62:          xmlDoc.LoadXml(xmlRdr.ReadToEnd())
63:
64:          ' Create a namespace manager. This way, whatever
65:          ' the SOAP namespace is mapped to, we can refer
66:          ' to it using a namepsace nomenclature that we
67:          ' know will work.
68:          Dim nsManager As New XmlNamespaceManager(xmlDoc.NameTable)
69:
70:          ' Map the XMLNS name "soap" to the correct URI.
71:          nsManager.AddNamespace("soap", _
72:              "http://schemas.xmlsoap.org/soap/envelope/")
73:
74:          ' Pick out the Body node.
75:          Dim nodeBody As XmlNode = xmlDoc.SelectSingleNode( _
76:              "/soap:Envelope/soap:Body", nsManager)
77:          Dim value As String = _
78:              nodeBody.FirstChild.FirstChild.InnerText
79:
80:          ' Reverse the contents of the first child of the response
81:          ' element within the body.
82:          nodeBody.FirstChild.FirstChild.InnerText = StrReverse(value)
83:
84:          ' Reset the length of the stream to 0.
85:          m_newStream.SetLength(0)
86:          Dim xmlWriter As New XmlTextWriter(m_newStream, _
87:              New System.Text.UTF8Encoding())
88:          xmlDoc.WriteContentTo(xmlWriter)
89:          xmlWriter.Flush()
90:          m_newStream.Position = 0
91:
```

LISTING 4.24   Continued

```
92:              ' Chain this to the output: the old stream.
93:              Copy(m_newStream, m_oldStream)
94:          End Sub
95:
96:          ' Handle the physical chaining of the old stream and
97:          ' the new stream that we created.
98:          Public Sub HandleInput()
99:              Copy(m_oldStream, m_newStream)
100:             m_newStream.Position = 0
101:         End Sub
102:
103:         Sub Copy(ByVal fromStream As Stream, ByVal toStream As Stream)
104:             Dim reader As New StreamReader(fromStream)
105:             Dim writer As New StreamWriter(toStream)
106:             writer.WriteLine(reader.ReadToEnd())
107:             writer.Flush()
108:         End Sub
109:    End Class
```

You will often use the code like that in Copy to help finish the chaining of the message streams. The only method in here that really does anything is HandleOutput. HandleInput just does the chaining in between streams to make sure the message gets processed correctly. In HandleOutput, the message from the m_newStream member variable is loaded into an XML document. The code then goes into the XML and looks for the element containing what will be the text "Hello World" in the sample Web Service. That text gets reversed within the XML. Finally, the XML is streamed back out to the m_newStream variable and copied to the m_oldStream, which gets returned to the original caller. To use the attribute, just apply it to any method that also uses the WebMethodAttribute class. Listing 4.25 shows a simple Hello World method that uses the attribute.

LISTING 4.25   A Hello World Example That Uses the Custom SOAP Attribute

```
Imports System.Web.Services

<WebService(Namespace:="http://scottseely.com/")> _
Public Class Service1
    Inherits WebService

    <ReverseExtension(), _
    WebMethod()> Public Function HelloWorld() As String
```

LISTING 4.25   Continued

```
        HelloWorld = "Hello World"
    End Function


End Class
```

Figure 4.3 shows the output of a client that uses the Web Service in Listing 4.25.

FIGURE 4.3   A simple message box that calls the Web Service in Listing 4.25.

The example is not exactly a general purpose attribute, but custom SOAP attributes don't have to be. If the attribute fills the need on a small set of methods and you want to write it, go for it. When does writing the attribute make sense? Any time you need to manipulate the XML, write an attribute. You can encrypt sections of the message, handle other extensions to the SOAP protocol, and so on. Attributes can be applied to the client and the server. Keep that in mind when working with Web Services.

Creating a Server Based on a WSDL File

Many different businesses and industries are embracing SOAP, including investigating the possibility of creating standardized SOAP interfaces. The first large-scale instance of WSDL being used to define an industry-wide interface is UDDI itself. All operators must implement a common set of interfaces. If they did not, operator sites could not easily share data. The developers on the Visual Studio team have anticipated this and have included the capability to generate a server based on a WSDL file. So, what would you do and what would you get?

In an effort to standardize simple SOAP examples, let's create a standard AddService WSDL. This WSDL file exposes one method that adds two integers and returns the result. Listing 4.26 shows the WSDL file.

LISTING 4.26   AddService WSDL File

```
1:  <?xml version="1.0" encoding="utf-8"?>
2:  <definitions xmlns:soap="http://schemas.xmlsoap.org/wsdl/soap/"
3:      xmlns:tns="http://mathguys.org/MathService"
4:      xmlns:s="http://www.w3.org/2001/XMLSchema"
```

LISTING 4.26   Continued

```
 5:        xmlns:soapenc="http://schemas.xmlsoap.org/soap/encoding/"
 6:        targetNamespace="http://mathguys.org/MathService"
 7:        xmlns="http://schemas.xmlsoap.org/wsdl/">
 8:      <message name="AddSoapIn">
 9:        <part name="x" type="s:int" />
10:        <part name="y" type="s:int" />
11:      </message>
12:      <message name="AddSoapOut">
13:        <part name="AddResult" type="s:int" />
14:      </message>
15:      <portType name="AddServiceSoap">
16:        <operation name="Add">
17:          <input message="tns:AddSoapIn" />
18:          <output message="tns:AddSoapOut" />
19:        </operation>
20:      </portType>
21:      <binding name="AddServiceSoap" type="tns:AddServiceSoap">
22:        <soap:binding
23:            transport="http://schemas.xmlsoap.org/soap/http"
24:            style="rpc" />
25:        <operation name="Add">
26:          <soap:operation
27:            soapAction="http://mathguys.org/MathService/Add"
28:            style="rpc" />
29:          <input>
30:            <soap:body use="encoded"
31:                namespace="http://mathguys.org/MathService"
32:                encodingStyle=
33:                    "http://schemas.xmlsoap.org/soap/encoding/" />
34:          </input>
35:          <output>
36:            <soap:body use="encoded"
37:                namespace="http://mathguys.org/MathService"
38:                encodingStyle=
39:                    "http://schemas.xmlsoap.org/soap/encoding/" />
40:          </output>
41:        </operation>
42:      </binding>
43:    </definitions>
```

Notice that the WSDL file does not have a service element. The file should not include one because this WSDL defines the interface only. The WSDL has no knowledge of any existing endpoints. Using this WSDL file, we want to generate a server that implements the interface. That way, any clients that know how to use this predefined interface will know how to use our implementation. To do this, we need to use the WSDL.EXE command line tool.

Open up a Visual Studio .NET command prompt by choosing Start, Programs, Microsoft Visual Studio .NET, Visual Studio .NET Tools, Visual Studio .NET Command Prompt. This makes sure that all the tools are accessible via the command line. To create the skeleton for the service, type in the following command:

```
WSDL.EXE /server /language:VB /out:AddService.vb AddService.WSDL
```

This line tells WSDL.EXE to create a server skeleton in Visual Basic .NET. The skeleton must be based on AddService.WSDL and written to AddService.vb. Listing 4.27 shows the result of this command.

LISTING 4.27   Resulting Skeleton from WSDL Command

```
 1: Option Strict Off
 2: Option Explicit On
 3:
 4: Imports System
 5: Imports System.ComponentModel
 6: Imports System.Diagnostics
 7: Imports System.Web.Services
 8: Imports System.Web.Services.Protocols
 9: Imports System.Xml.Serialization
10:
11: '
12: 'This source code was auto-generated by wsdl, Version=1.0.3427.0.
13: '
14:
15: <System.Web.Services.WebServiceBindingAttribute( _
16:     Name:="AddServiceSoap", _
17:     [Namespace]:="http://mathguys.org/MathService")> _
18: Public MustInherit Class AddServiceSoap
19:     Inherits System.Web.Services.WebService
20:
21:     <System.Web.Services.WebMethodAttribute(), _
22:      System.Web.Services.Protocols.SoapRpcMethodAttribute( _
23:         "http://mathguys.org/MathService/Add", _
```

LISTING 4.27   Continued

```
24:              RequestNamespace:="http://mathguys.org/MathService", _
25:              ResponseNamespace:="http://mathguys.org/MathService")>  _
26:      Public MustOverride Function Add(ByVal x As Integer, _
27:          ByVal y As Integer) As Integer
28:  End Class
```

Using this interface, your implementation simply has to implement the Add function and you are done. The interface is included by adding the interface file to the Web Service implementing the interface. Listing 4.28 contains one sample implementation.

LISTING 4.28   An Actual Implementation Using the AddServiceSoap Abstract Base Class

```
1:   Imports System.Web.Services
2:
3:   <System.Web.Services.WebServiceBindingAttribute( _
4:       Name:="AddServiceSoap", _
5:       [Namespace]:="http://mathguys.org/MathService")> _
6:   Public Class MyAddService
7:       Inherits AddServiceSoap
8:
9:       <System.Web.Services.WebMethodAttribute(), _
10:          System.Web.Services.Protocols.SoapRpcMethodAttribute( _
11:          "http://mathguys.org/MathService/Add", _
12:          RequestNamespace:="http://mathguys.org/MathService", _
13:          ResponseNamespace:="http://mathguys.org/MathService")> _
14:      Public Overrides Function Add( _
15:          ByVal x As Integer, ByVal y As Integer) As Integer
16:          Add = x + y
17:      End Function
18:  End Class
```

Most of the attribution is handled by Visual Studio .NET when you override the functions in the base class. If special types had been included in this WSDL file, we would have had those appear in the generated code as well. This tool will become more useful as Web Service interfaces become standardized.

Using Visual Studio to Register Your SOAP Endpoint in UDDI

After you have finished writing your Web Service, documented the interfaces, and generally made sure that others should be able to use the code, you then need to make the Web Service itself discoverable. One of the best ways to do this is register the endpoint with a UDDI registry. Visual Studio includes a facility to register a Web Service. In this section, we will walk through the registration of the Web Service created in Chapter 1, "Creating Your First Web Service." You will see a series of screen shots and simple steps showing you how easy this whole process is. The built-in wizard registers the Web Service with the Microsoft UDDI Web Service. A similar registration may be possible with other UDDI services as they become available.

To access the wizard, open up Visual Studio .NET and go to the Start Page. From the Start Page, select the XML Web Services topic. This brings up a page with two tabs. Select the Register a Service tab. You can also use the tab, Find a Service, to search for Web Services registered with UDDI. You should see the screen in Figure 4.4.

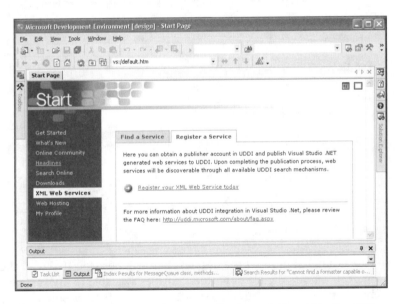

FIGURE 4.4   Preparing to register a Web Service through Visual Studio .NET.

When on the Register a Service page, click the Register Your XML Web Service Today link. Doing so brings up the screen shown in Figure 4.5. Here, you log in using a Microsoft Passport. If you have not completed development or if you are not quite ready to put the Web Service out for general consumption, you can publish to the test directory. Otherwise, publish to the production registry. Because this example will not be available except through this book, we will register this particular Web Service with the test directory. For this to work, you will have to go to the UDDI Test Directory and login at least once yourself. This directory is located at http://test.uddi.microsoft.com/register.aspx.

After you have logged in, create one business entity. The links there will help you along. Make sure to publish that business or you will not be able to follow along. While the site claims that the turnaround may take as long as 24 hours, I have rarely seen the publication take longer than a few seconds. The data will not get replicated to the other member servers for a day. As a result, you will not be able to browse to IBM's UDDI server until the next day.

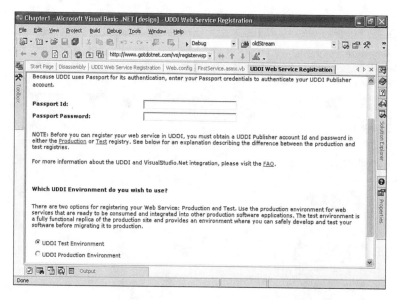

FIGURE 4.5   UDDI login screen.

Next, you are prompted to select the business that will be associated with the Web Service. Figure 4.6 shows the list of business entities available to my Passport ID. I select Seely Enterprises and continue. You will select whatever business you have created.

The next page allows you to publish the location of the Web Service and the associated WSDL file. Figure 4.7 shows one way to would publish the sample in Chapter 1.

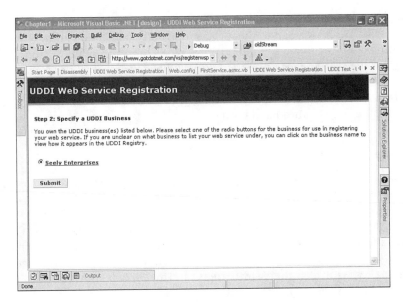

FIGURE 4.6   Select the business to associate with the Web Service.

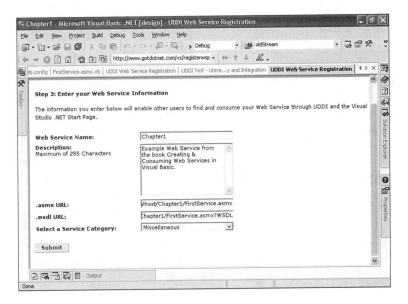

FIGURE 4.7   Describing the Web Service to UDDI.

From the screen in Figure 4.7, click the Submit button. If all goes well, you will see the message "Your Web Service has been successfully registered within UDDI." You can either continue to register more Web Services from this point or stop. If you later search for the Web Service using the Add Web Reference dialog, this Web Service will be discoverable using UDDI. Because it uses a localhost URL, any reader of this book who installs the Chapter 1 example should be able to add a Web Reference using the Test UDDI server. Go ahead and try it.

Summary

By now, you should be able to shape your WSDL to do anything you want. Not only can you change the name of almost all the pieces in the WSDL file, but you can split it up at will or cause other WSDL documents to be referenced by your Web Service. As for shaping the physical message, you can now apply many of the SOAP attributes to affect what the message looks like. The attributes covered in this chapter and the parts they affect are listed in Table 4.1 for your convenience. If you need extra functionality, write a custom SOAP extension. Finally, you know how easy it is to register a Web Service with Microsoft's UDDI registry.

TABLE 4.1   Attributes Covered in this Chapter and What They Affect

Classname (can appear in code without the final `Attribute` part of the name)	Affected parts of WSDL
SoapDocumentServiceAttribute	Specifies document/literal encoding. Influences type layouts.
SoapDocumentMethodAttribute	Sets method name, binding information, request, and response information for document/literal SOAP methods.
SoapElementAttribute	Specifies how to serialize an element within a SOAP message.
SoapEnumType	Specifies how to represent an enum value within a SOAP message.
SoapHeaderAttribute	Specifies a Header to use with a given message.
SoapIgnoreAttribute	Tells the XML serializer to not include a particular element when transforming an object to XML.
SoapRpcMethodAttribute	Sets method name, binding information, request, and response information for RPC/encoded SOAP methods.
SoapRpcServiceAttribute	Specifies RPC/encoded encoding. Influences type layouts.
SoapTypeAttribute	Allows the developer to specify namespace, type, and element name information when serializing data as a SOAP message.
WebMethodAttribute	Exposes a Public Sub or Function as a part of a Web Service. Also associates a method with a particular binding.
WebServiceAttribute	Allows code to set default namespace for the Web Service. Also sets documentation within the service element.

TABLE 4.1   Continued

Classname (can appear in code without the final `Attribute` **part of the name**)	Affected parts of WSDL
`WebServiceBindingAttribute`	Declares binding separation as well as the binding namespace. If the binding data exists in a separate file, this attribute also allows the code to declare the location of that file.
`XmlAttributeAttribute`	When serializing data as XML, this attribute declares that the element itself should appear as an XML attribute. Can also set the name and namespace of the attribute.
`XmlElementAttribute`	When serializing data as XML, this attribute declares that the element itself should appear as an XML element. Can also set the name and namespace of the element.
`XmlEnumAttribute`	When representing the value in an enumeration, this attribute allows the code to declare the namespace and representation of that value in the XML version of the enumeration.
XmlTypeAttribute	When representing a class or struct as XML, this attribute allows the code to declare the namespace and name of that class when represented as XML.

Knowing how to use this information should allow you to create Web Services that operate well with other SOAP toolkits. You should be able to mold your client code as well because these same attributes shape both the WSDL and the SOAP message. Occasionally, you will come across WSDL documents that contain errors or other sources of incompatibilities. With the information in this chapter and having a copy of a valid message exchange on hand, you should be able to write your own proxies if the need arises.

5

Troubleshooting Web Services/Consumers

Web Services are a bit different from other applications you have developed in the past. If you have spent a lot of time developing networked applications, you will find that it is a lot easier to look at and debug the messages going across the wire. On the other hand, if all you have ever written is desktop applications, you will have to get used to a few new skills. Don't worry; you still have the world of breakpoints and the ability to inspect the values of the variables available to you.

In this chapter, we will look at how to debug a Web Service. The following items will be covered:

- Viewing SOAP requests and the returned response

- Debugging a Web Service at the server

- Remote debugging of a Web Service

- Debugging Web Services under load

- Items to include in your test plan

That last item might be a bit of a shocker. When you deploy a Web Service, there is a set of common things that you will want to test for to make sure that your Web Service will be stable and accessible.

Viewing SOAP Message Exchanges

A good number of the bugs you tackle can be resolved by simply tracing the messages being exchanged between the client and server. One tool you will want is MSSOAPT.EXE, the trace utility provided with the Microsoft SOAP Toolkit v2. You can download the toolkit (SoapToolkit20.exe) from http://msdn.microsoft.com. To install just the trace utility, do the following:

1. Run the installation package. Step through the various dialogs until you see the dialog shown in Figure 5.1. Choose Custom installation.

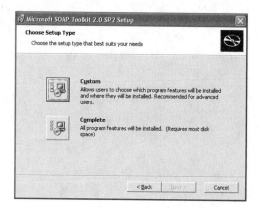

FIGURE 5.1   Choose Setup Type dialog.

2. On the Microsoft SOAP Toolkit 2.0 node, click the Drive icon and select Entire Feature Will Be Unavailable. This makes sure that most of the toolkit does not get installed.

3. On the Debugging Utilities node, click the icon next to the text and select Will Be Installed on Local Hard Drive. When you are done, the Custom Setup dialog should match Figure 5.2.

4. Click Next, Install.

5. When the install completes, click Finish. The trace utility will now be installed on your machine.

To start the trace utility, choose the Start button on the taskbar and select Programs, Microsoft SOAP Toolkit, Trace Utility (MSSOAPT.EXE).

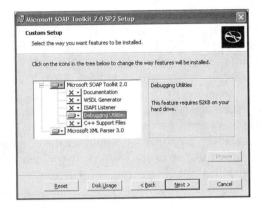

FIGURE 5.2   Custom Setup dialog.

The trace utility works by using a fairly simple store and forward mechanism. To make it easy to view SOAP messages, you should always set the URL Behavior property on Web references to Dynamic. Doing so allows you to change the Web Service endpoint without rebuilding your source code. Figure 5.3 shows where to do this in the Visual Studio .NET environment.

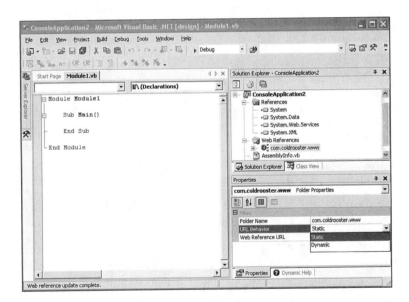

FIGURE 5.3   Changing the URL Behavior property.

Your first step in debugging should almost always be to open up this application and set it up to do a formatted trace. A formatted trace displays the requests and corresponding responses using the XML styles used by Internet Explorer. To access this functionality, open up the trace utility and select File, New, Formatted Trace. This will bring up the dialog shown in Figure 5.4. Typically, the default settings of listening on port 8080 and rerouting to `localhost` port 80 will work when debugging on the local machine. When debugging a client working with a remote server, just change the values appropriately. For example, a Web Service located on `http://www.scottseely.com` on port 9090 would set the destination host to `www.scottseely.com` and the destination port to 9090. When setting the Destination Host value, do not include things like the `http` prefix or the specific subdirectory. That information is carried in the SOAP message itself.

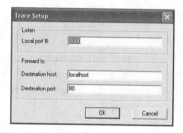

FIGURE 5.4   Trace Setup dialog.

After this is set up, you can now look at the SOAP messages and maybe figure out what is going wrong. You will want the WSDL definition of the operation being called available. Then, start with basic debugging and examine the SOAP request. Many of these items will not be wrong for a proxy created with Visual Studio .NET. Because your job may involve using toolkits created by companies other than Microsoft, I am including the full set of things to look at when debugging:

- Is the SOAP namespace correct? It must be `http://schemas.xmlsoap.org/soap/envelope/`.

- Is the enclosing element named `Envelope` and does the namespace match the one associated with `http://schemas.xmlsoap.org/soap/envelope/`?

- Is there a `Body` element, and does the namespace match the one associated with `http://schemas.xmlsoap.org/soap/envelope/`?

- Does the method being called use the namespace specified in the types element's `targetNamespace` attribute?

- Do the method names and element names match the operation information shown in the WSDL file? Depending on the Web Service type (RPC/encoded or document/literal), this may matter. This also matters on different SOAP implementations. Regardless, this is yet another thing to check and might be stopping you from connecting to the other Web Service.

A formatted trace (without problems) is shown in Figure 5.5.

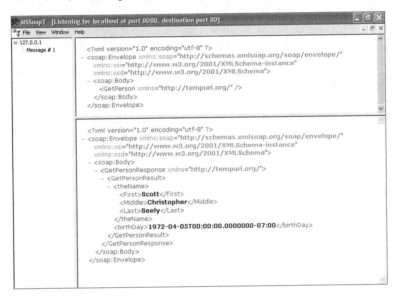

FIGURE 5.5   A formatted trace.

If everything looks correct, the other item you can check is the SOAPAction and the endpoint to which you are connecting. To see all of the information going between the two endpoints, select File, New, Unformatted Trace. The reading of data might be a bit cramped, but you can find out what the SOAPAction HTTP header is set to, as well as any other data being exchanged. Figure 5.6 shows an unformatted trace. See if you can spot the SOAPAction header.

When debugging client applications against a deployed Web Service, you can almost always be assured that if things are not working, it is your client code's fault. Because of this, you will spend a lot of time going over your SOAP messages making sure that all elements of the message are correct. Sometimes, the message might come back with no elements. Believe it or not, this can cause exceptions to be thrown on the client. During deserialization, the .NET runtime will try to take an empty element and deserialize that element into a value type (`int`, `string`, some class, and so on). If there is nothing to deserialize, this effort can sometimes cause an exception to be thrown. The only defense against this is to wrap the Web method call in a `try/catch` block.

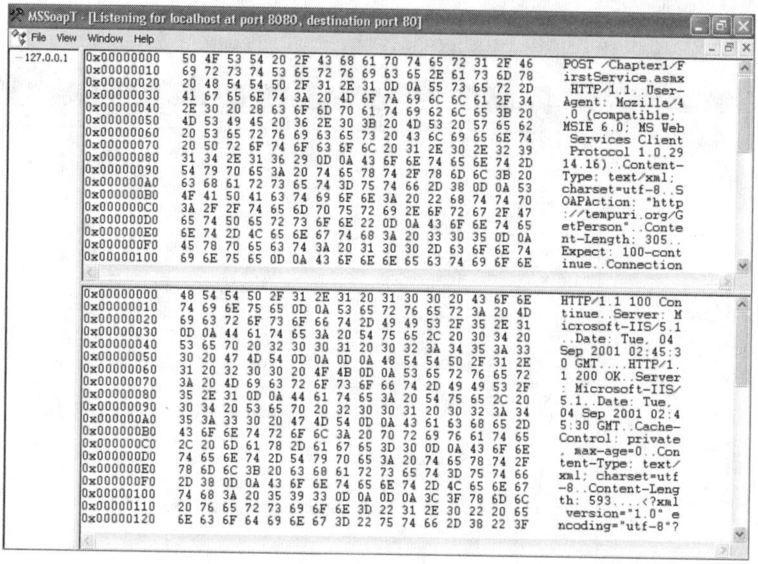

FIGURE 5.6   An unformatted trace.

NOTE

My experience indicates that most deployed, publicly available Web Services have already been tested with external clients. This means that issues revolving around permissions are typically worked out well before the Web Service itself is announced to the general public. Bad things can happen to the Web Service—the server goes down, domain name servers stop functioning, or the server is not able to handle the load. These things can happen but are not the most common reasons for clients failing to connect to the server.

Listing 5.1 shows an error handler that wraps the call and logs the error to a custom event log named `myNewLog`. The code itself calls to the Quote of the Day Web Service hosted by Microsoft at `http://www.gotdotnet.com`. To force the error to occur, the code contains a line that sets the URL to an endpoint that does not host the Web Service.

LISTING 5.1   A Simple Error Handler

```
Sub Main()

    Dim svc As New com.gotdotnet.www.Quote()
    svc.Url = "http://www.scottseely.com/"

    Try
        Console.WriteLine(svc.GetQuote())
    Catch soapEx As System.Web.Services.Protocols.SoapException
        Dim log As New System.Diagnostics.EventLog( _
            "myNewLog", ".", "SOAP")
        log.WriteEntry("SOAP Fault was caught at " & _
            DateTime.Now.ToString() & vbCrLf & _
            "Code: " & soapEx.Code.ToString() & vbCrLf & _
            "Actor: " & soapEx.Actor & vbCrLf & _
            "Detail: " & soapEx.Detail.InnerXml)
        log.Dispose()
    Catch ex As Exception
        Dim log As New System.Diagnostics.EventLog( _
            "myNewLog", ".", "Unknown")
        log.WriteEntry( _
            "An exception was caught at " & _
            DateTime.Now.ToString() & vbCrLf & _
            "URL to contact: " & svc.Url & vbCrLf & _
            "Exception details: " & ex.ToString())
        log.Dispose()
    End Try

    Console.ReadLine()

End Sub
```

This error log will be stored on the local machine. Assuming that Windows is installed in the c:\windows directory, the error log for the previous instance will be in the file named c:\windows\system32\config\myNewLog.evt. You will need to add this file in the event viewer to view any events.

We also have to consider that something may be wrong at the server and, if the server is ours, we are responsible for that too. How do you debug the server?

Debugging a Web Service at the Server

To debug a Web Service that resides on a machine that has Visual Studio .NET installed, you have two options—start the application or, if it has been started already, attach to the process executing the Web Service.

To start the Web Service from within Visual Studio .NET, you first have to make sure that the `aspnet_wp.exe` process has not been loaded. The surest way to do this is to open a command prompt and type **iisreset**. This stops and restarts IIS and any related applications. Then, in the Solution Explorer pane, right-click the `asmx` file you want to debug and select the Set as Start Page item from the pop-up menu. Then, go to the Debug menu and select Start. If the ASP .NET-generated Web pages allow you to interact with the Web method you need to debug, you should be set. If a client application is needed because the method takes a complex type or an array as an argument, you should be able to still hit the breakpoint.

One drawback to the previous method is that running `iisreset` all the time can be time consuming. Cycling IIS off and back on again can often take a minute or longer. Because of this, it might be more convenient to debug the already running process. ASP .NET Web Services run in the `aspnet_wp.exe` process. To debug a Web Service that has already been loaded into memory, you need to attach to `aspnet_wp.exe`. Do the following:

1. Open the project you want to debug.

2. Set your breakpoints.

3. Go to the Debug menu and select the Processes menu item.

4. In the Processes dialog (see Figure 5.7), make sure that the Show System Processes check box is checked. `aspnet_wp.exe` is a system process.

5. Select the `aspnet_wp.exe` process and click the Attach button.

6. In the Attach to Process dialog (see Figure 5.8), make sure that the Common Language Runtime item is checked.

7. Click OK.

8. On the Processes dialog, click the Close button.

9. Wait for the IDE to stop on your breakpoint. This last step assumes that you have a client application that you can invoke that will hit the Web Service. The client application does not need to be loaded within Visual Studio.

These techniques will help you find problems when the development tools and the Web Server are on the same machine. Now, what do you do when the Web Service is having problems and it is on a live server?

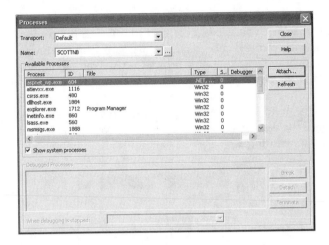

FIGURE 5.7   The Processes dialog.

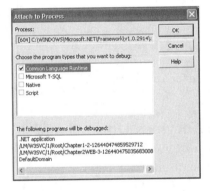

FIGURE 5.8   The Attach to Process dialog.

Debugging a Web Service Remotely

Leave it to your customers and co-workers to find a bug after you think you delivered a clean implementation. The good news is that the ASP .NET folks thought about this and have a solution—remote debugging. The first thing you will need to do is edit the web.config file on the Web server. Under the configuration\system.web element is an element named compilation. Set the debug attribute to true to enable debugging, set it to false to disable debugging. The only thing left to do is to connect your development machine to the Web server. No extra files need to be installed to do this.

Look again at Figure 5.7. At the top of the Processes dialog is a combo box named Name. If the machine you need to connect to is not in the combo box, click the ... button next to the Name combo box. This will bring up the Browse for Computer dialog box shown in Figure 5.9. Just browse to the Web server, select it, and click OK. Then, attach to the process the same way you would if you were debugging on your local machine. To do this, the user attaching to the process must be a member of the Debugger Users group on the remote machine. This works for cross domain relationships as well if the domain the server lives in can verify the identity of the debugger user from a different domain.

FIGURE 5.9   The Browse for Computer dialog.

Debugging Web Services Under Load

Sometimes, bugs only show up when the Web Service is serving a large number of requests. Setting breakpoints may not help if the behavior does not show up when things are slowed down (and nothing slows a service more than a breakpoint). To handle this, you enter the unhappy world of reviewing trace data. Because breakdown under load happens quite frequently, I recommend that you audit every entry point into the Web Service itself. By storing that information, the person analyzing the failure can recreate an accurate picture of what was happening at the time of the failure. This section will cover the things you should store at all times so that you can analyze where your code failed. As a developer, you will want to use this in conjunction with trace levels and such. The trace classes are typically covered quite well in introductory texts. If you do not have a basic reference, I would recommend that you purchase one very soon.

When auditing this information, do not place it in a file. As the file grows, and it will grow quickly under load, you will see file writes take longer and longer. Instead, consider logging your audit data to a database. Simple database inserts typically take very little time. As an added bonus, the database operations probably will not slow down as the amount of information grows. You may wind up making a large number of calls to figure out exactly what is going wrong. Decide what data you need to collect (each case will be different) and store it. A stored procedure may get you the best performance and impact the overall application the least.

For practical purposes, you might want to build this apparatus ahead of time, just to audit Web Service activity. When bugs start popping up, you can add extra lines of code to insert extra audit records. Some data items you may want to record are as follow:

- Method identifier. This can be a numeric value or a string.

- Date and time the audit record was created by the Web Service.

- Bit of data indicating whether the audit record represents success, failure due to server problems, failure due to client problems, or none of the above.

- User-defined string specific to the audit record. This can contain extra data useful in debugging or to give the audit record extra meaning.

Additionally, you will want to define a record key. A numeric index will work well. Because auditing should happen in the background, a form of delayed writes works very well. Either execute the recording of the audit record in a low priority asynchronous process or put the audit record in a queue to be stored in the database later. Writes to a message queue are often faster than a database insert.

Believe it or not, building an auditing mechanism is one of the best proactive things you can do. Discuss this with your database administrator (DBA) and figure out how often you want to archive the audit data. Your DBA may want to have the audit records exist in a separate database to make archiving easy. Regardless, you will see benefits from implementing auditing before problems happen.

Because auditing is so important, let's take a look at an example—a custom SOAP attribute that will log method calls in a synchronous manner. This attribute does not handle the asynchronous logging previously recommended. It does do the basic logging, though. To use the class, you need to have a SQL Server database installed. The SQL isn't too complex. This includes the Microsoft Data Engine (MSDE), a freely distributable database bundled with many applications. You can get MSDE at http://msdn.microsoft.com/vstudio/msde/msde.asp.

This code will work on any existing database that has a table named Audit and a stored procedure named AddAudit. The SQL to create the table and stored procedure is shown in Listing 5.2. The sql file, auditData.sql, contains some extra code that handles removing the table and procedure if they already exist.

LISTING 5.2   SQL to Create the Audit Table and AddAudit Stored Procedure

```
-- Create the Audit table
CREATE TABLE [dbo].[Audit] (
    [ID] [int] IDENTITY (1, 1) NOT NULL ,
    [startDate] [datetime] NOT NULL ,
    [endDate] [datetime] NOT NULL ,
    [result] [int] NOT NULL ,
    [methodName] [nvarchar] (100) NOT NULL ,
    [otherData] [nvarchar] (500) NULL
) ON [PRIMARY]
GO


ALTER TABLE [dbo].[Audit] WITH NOCHECK ADD
    CONSTRAINT [PK_Audit] PRIMARY KEY  CLUSTERED
    (
        [ID]
    )  ON [PRIMARY]
GO


-- Create the AddAudit stored procedure
CREATE PROCEDURE AddAudit
  @startDate as DATETIME,
  @endDate as DATETIME,
  @result as INT,
  @methodName as NVARCHAR(100),
  @otherData as NVARCHAR(500)
 AS
INSERT INTO Audit (startDate,
  endDate,
  result,
  methodName,
  otherData)
VALUES ( @startDate,
  @endDate,
  @result,
  @methodName,
  @otherData)
GO
```

After the database has been set up, you will need a way to tell any code how to open a connection to the database. The web.config file for any Web Service using the custom attribute about to be shown must contain the database connection string in the appSettings section of the configuration file. The name of the value must be AuditDB. Listing 5.3 shows a sample version of this section. The connection string points to the Northwind database that is installed by default with SQL Server.

LISTING 5.3   Setting the AuditDB Value in the web.config File

```
<appSettings>
    <add key="AuditDB" value=
        "user id=sa;password=dbpassword;initial catalog=northwind;
        ➥data source=localhost;Connect_Timeout=30"/>
</appSettings>
```

How is this used? To answer that, we need to look at the first of three classes used to audit the Web Service. The AuditEntry class is used to store our audit data and then save it to a database when the complete round trip (request and response) is all but done. The class contains some simple properties as well as a Save method that writes the properties to the database. This class assumes that users have already executed the SQL in Listing 5.2 and added the value to the web.config file as shown in Listing 5.3. Listing 5.4 shows the complete listing for this class.

LISTING 5.4   The AuditEntry Class

```
Imports System.Reflection
Imports System

Namespace com.scottseely

    Public Enum CallResult
        ServerFailure = 1
        ClientFailure = 2
        Success = 10
    End Enum

    Public Class AuditEntry
        Private m_methodName As String
        Private m_startTime As DateTime
        Private m_endTime As DateTime
        Private m_callResult As callResult
        Private m_otherData As String = ""

        ' Stores the name of the method being audited
        Public Property methodName() As String
```

LISTING 5.4   Continued

```
            Get
                Return m_methodName
            End Get
            Set(ByVal Value As String)
                m_methodName = Value
            End Set
        End Property

        ' Stores the time that the audit began
        Public Property startTime() As DateTime
            Get
Return m_startTime
            End Get
            Set(ByVal Value As DateTime)
                m_startTime = Value
            End Set
        End Property

        ' Stores the time that the audit finished
        Public Property endTime() As DateTime
            Get
                Return m_endTime
            End Get
            Set(ByVal Value As DateTime)
                m_endTime = Value
            End Set
        End Property

        ' Stores the result of the SOAP method
        Public Property callResult() As callResult
            Get
                Return m_callResult
            End Get
            Set(ByVal Value As callResult)
                m_callResult = Value
            End Set
        End Property

        ' Stores any other data related to the method call
        Public Property otherData() As String
            Get
```

LISTING 5.4   Continued

```
            Return m_otherData
        End Get
        Set(ByVal Value As String)
            m_otherData = Value
        End Set
    End Property

    ' Saves the audit information to a database
    Public Sub Save()
        Try
            ' Get the connection string from the
            ' application using this library
            Dim connStr As String = _
                System.Configuration.ConfigurationSettings. _
                AppSettings.Item("AuditDB")
            Dim conn As New SqlClient.SqlConnection(connStr)
            conn.Open()

            Dim comm As New SqlClient.SqlCommand()

            'Setup the command object
            comm.Connection = conn
            comm.CommandType = CommandType.StoredProcedure
            comm.CommandText = "AddAudit"
            Dim startDateParam As New SqlClient.SqlParameter( _
                "@startDate", SqlDbType.DateTime)
            Dim endDateParam As New SqlClient.SqlParameter( _
                "@endDate", SqlDbType.DateTime)
            Dim resultParam As New SqlClient.SqlParameter( _
                "@result", SqlDbType.Int)
            Dim methodNameParam As New SqlClient.SqlParameter( _
                "@methodName", SqlDbType.NVarChar, 100)
            Dim otherDataParam As New SqlClient.SqlParameter( _
                "@otherData", SqlDbType.NVarChar, 500)

            startDateParam.Value = m_startTime
            endDateParam.Value = m_endTime
            resultParam.Value = m_callResult
            methodNameParam.Value = m_methodName
            otherDataParam.Value = m_otherData
```

LISTING 5.4   Continued

```
            ' Add the parameters to the command object.
            comm.Parameters.Add(startDateParam)
            comm.Parameters.Add(endDateParam)
            comm.Parameters.Add(resultParam)
            comm.Parameters.Add(methodNameParam)
            comm.Parameters.Add(otherDataParam)

            ' Execute the query. No results come back.
            comm.ExecuteNonQuery()

            ' Clean up
            conn.Close()
        Catch ex As Exception
            Trace.WriteLine(ex.ToString())

            ' This code will throw an exception of its own
            ' if the default Web user does not have permission
            ' to write to a log file.
            Dim log As New System.Diagnostics.EventLog( _
                "AuditLog", ".", "AuditLogError")
            log.WriteEntry( _
                "An exception was caught at " & _
                DateTime.Now.ToString() & vbCrLf & _
                "Exception details: " & ex.ToString())
            log.Dispose()
        End Try
    End Sub
End Class

End Namespace
```

You will notice that the class is in its own namespace. I did this to help prevent name collisions with other classes. This code might get modified and reused quite a bit. If you modify this code, make sure to update the namespace to something appropriate for your Web site.

With a way to store the data, we now need to write the custom SOAP attribute. (Chapter 4, "Using Attributes to Shape the WSDL and XML," covered the particulars of custom SOAP attributes.) This particular attribute will allow a user to audit any individual Web Method. The first class we need to implement inherits from

SoapExtensionAttribute and is named `AuditAttribute`. This class, shown in Listing 5.5, allows the user of the class to set custom data through the `otherData` property.

LISTING 5.5   The `AuditAttribute` Class

```
Imports System.Web.Services
Imports System.Web.Services.Protocols
Namespace com.scottseely

    <AttributeUsage(AttributeTargets.Method)> _
    Public Class AuditAttribute
        Inherits SoapExtensionAttribute

        ' Stores the priority for the class
        Private m_priority As Integer

        Private m_otherData As String = ""

        ' Returns the type that inherits from
        ' SoapExtension
        Public Overrides ReadOnly Property ExtensionType() As Type
            Get
                Return GetType(AuditExtension)
            End Get
        End Property

        ' Stores the Priority as set in the config file
        ' and returns that value on demand.
        Public Overrides Property Priority() As Integer
            Get
                Return m_priority
            End Get
            Set(ByVal Value As Integer)
                m_priority = Value
            End Set
        End Property

        ' Store the random data as requested by the
        ' user of the attribute.
        Public Property otherData() As String
            Get
```

LISTING 5.5   Continued

```
                    Return m_otherData
            End Get
            Set(ByVal Value As String)
                m_otherData = Value
            End Set
        End Property


    End Class


End Namespace
```

Now comes the part that does the work of auditing the Web Method—
AuditExtension. It derives from SoapExtension and does most of the work in the
ProcessMessage override. This class uses the AuditEntry class to mark various events
in the call of the Web Method as well as store information discovered about the
method being called. The start time of the call is noted in the BeforeDeserialize
stage before the Web Method itself gets interpreted. After interpreting the message
but before calling the method (the AfterDeserialize stage), the attribute pulls out
the method name and stores that. Then, after the method has executed and the
response has been created, the AfterSerialize stage checks for any faults. If a fault
did occur, the cause of the fault is noted in the otherData member of the AuditEntry
instance and the method checks to see if the client or server is responsible for the
fault. Regardless of success or failure, the processing for the stage finishes by noting
the end time. The AuditEntry instance then saves itself to the database and auditing
for the method is complete. Listing 5.6 shows the code for the AuditExtension class.

LISTING 5.6   The AuditExtension Class

```
Imports System.Web.Services
Imports System
Imports System.Web.Services.Protocols
Imports System.IO
Imports System.Xml


Namespace com.scottseely

    Public Class AuditExtension
        Inherits SoapExtension

        Private m_auditEntry As AuditEntry
```

LISTING 5.6   Continued

```vb
' We don't manipulate the stream.
' Just throw it back at the caller.
Public Overrides Function ChainStream( _
    ByVal stream As Stream) As Stream
    Return stream
End Function

' Both GetInitializer overrides are present but do nothing.
Public Overloads Overrides Function GetInitializer( _
    ByVal methodInfo As LogicalMethodInfo, _
    ByVal attribute As SoapExtensionAttribute) As Object

    Dim theAttr As AuditAttribute = attribute
    Return theAttr.otherData
End Function

Public Overloads Overrides Function GetInitializer( _
    ByVal WebServiceType As Type) As Object
    ' No initializer used. By default, this returns Nothing
    m_auditEntry.otherData = "What the heck2" 'theAttr.otherData
    Return "No special data set"
End Function

' Implemented because it has to be but does nothing.
Public Overrides Sub Initialize(ByVal initializer As Object)
    m_auditEntry.otherData = CStr(initializer)
End Sub

' Handle any chaining of the message between old and new.
' Besides that, manipulate the stream as needed
Public Overrides Sub ProcessMessage(ByVal message As SoapMessage)
    Select Case message.Stage
        Case SoapMessageStage.BeforeSerialize
        Case SoapMessageStage.AfterSerialize
            m_auditEntry.endTime = DateTime.Now
            If (message.Exception Is Nothing) Then
                m_auditEntry.callResult = CallResult.Success
            Else
                m_auditEntry.otherData = _
                    message.Exception.ToString()
                If (message.Exception.Code Is _
                    SoapException.ClientFaultCode) Then
```

LISTING 5.6   Continued

```
                    m_auditEntry.callResult = _
                        CallResult.ClientFailure
              Else
                    m_auditEntry.callResult = _
                        CallResult.ServerFailure
              End If
          End If
          m_auditEntry.Save()
        Case SoapMessageStage.BeforeDeserialize
          m_auditEntry.startTime = DateTime.Now
        Case SoapMessageStage.AfterDeserialize
          m_auditEntry.methodName = _
            message.MethodInfo.Name
        Case Else
                    Throw New Exception("invalid stage")
        End Select
      End Sub


      Public Sub New()
          m_auditEntry = New AuditEntry()
      End Sub
    End Class


End Namespace
```

To use the attribute, just apply to a Web Method and you are ready to go. Listing 5.7 shows a couple of Web Methods that use the attribute to implement logging with just one line of code.

LISTING 5.7   Example of Using the Custom Attribute

```
<WebMethod(), _
 Audit.com.scottseely.Audit(otherData:="This is a test")> _
Public Function HelloWorld() As String
    Return "Hello World!"
End Function


<WebMethod(), _
 Audit.com.scottseely.Audit(otherData:="Another method")> _
Public Function AnotherMethod() As String
    Return "Yet another method"
End Function
```

The Web Service and a test application are included in the sample files on the companion Web site for you to see how everything works. The Web Service is named `AuditTestService` and the console application is named `AuditTestConsole`. Auditing is an often overlooked part of developing a Web Service. I hope the sample code here will help you add this basic functionality to your own Web Services.

Items to Include in Your Test Plan

Finally, you want to make sure that you think ahead and figure out what type of activity you expect your Web Service to see. For example, you should look at your Web methods and determine what you expect the distribution of calls to be. Something like, "We expect method A to be called 25% of the time, method B to be called 30% of the time, and the other 10 methods to be called with the same frequency over the remaining 45% of the time." Then, determine how many calls per second you want to be able to handle. If anything, make your estimates a little on the high side. An estimate of three calls per second equals 259,200 calls per day. The load you need to test for depends on whether people or computers will be your primary consumers. At this point in time, no historical data exists to tell just what an average load will look like.

After you determine the load you want to test for, you need to acquire some client machines and write an application that will hit the Web Service at the level you have determined. Plan some time for this and expect bugs to be discovered. At this point in time, no stress testing tools exist for Web Services. Any tools I have used were built for the specific Web Service. Some of the bugs you can expect to see under stress are connection timeouts and refused connections. If you access files or a database, you will probably uncover some race conditions as well that leave the Web Service locked up. Finally, you may see memory usage climb to points that your hardware cannot handle. These are all reasons that you need to see if your Web Service can handle loads at whatever you estimated to be the maximum load.

You will also want to test sending bad data. Send values that the Web Service should not allow. Send messages with the wrong contents. Have clients that send the message but do not wait for the response. This may all sound a little crazy, but it will work and show where you made mistakes in assuming that data would have a particular representation. Make sure that all this bad code can handle the inevitable SOAP Faults. By the time the server is made bulletproof, you will have a large number of SOAP Faults being returned.

In addition to all of this, you will want to include tests that look for things like:

- Time to respond to a message
- Verification that valid data works

- See how much stress the Web Service can take

- Test the Web Service when deployed on a Web Farm

Additionally, you will need to test things specific to your situation.

A Simple Example

Let's load up the example from Chapter 1, "Creating Your First Web Service," and set a breakpoint within the GetRandomNumbers function. As you may recall, that function returns a variable number of random numbers that all lie within a range as requested by the user. If we want to debug this method, we just open up the Chapter1 project and set a breakpoint within the GetRandomNumbers function, as shown in Figure 5.10.

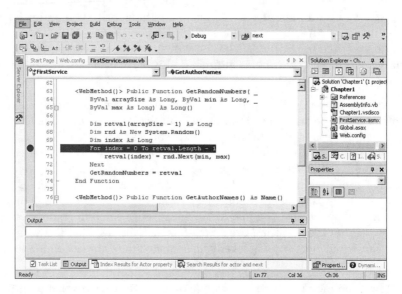

FIGURE 5.10   Setting a breakpoint in *GetRandomNumbers*.

With a breakpoint set, we next need to attach to the aspnet_wp.exe process, as shown in Figure 5.8. Doing so attaches the debugger and allows us to be notified when the breakpoint is hit. To generate a call, we can either fire up one of the applications from Chapter 2, "Consuming Your Web Service," or invoke the method from the ASP .NET-generated Web page. How we do it does not matter—from the debugger the call will look the same. So, I navigate to `http://localhost/Chapter1/FirstService.asmx?op=GetRandomNumbers` and load up the parameters with the values set as

- `arraySize: 5`

- `min: 1`

- `max: 20`

This means that I want the method to return 5 random values between 1 and 20. With this data entered, I click Invoke and see the debugger stop on the breakpoint. From here, I can inspect variables, step into any functions I have source code for, and perform any other debugging functions. Before leaving the chapter, try setting breakpoints in the other methods to make sure that you are familiar with how to set a breakpoint, attach to `aspwnet_wp.exe`, and step through a method.

When you are finished debugging, either stop debugging or exit the development environment. You will find that debugging is easiest on Windows XP, because XP allows you to attach and detach from a process. When detaching from a process under Windows 2000, .NET has to perform some extra tricks. This is because Windows 2000 (and earlier Windows versions) do not provide a mechanism to detach from a process without killing that process.

Summary

When developing a Web Service, you will inevitably run into bugs and other issues. After those bugs are eliminated, you will deploy the application and see more bugs pop up. As the bugs change, your debugging techniques will change as well.

One of the best things you can do for your own sanity is to include an auditing mechanism in your application. This auditing mechanism can be used to track Web Service use, as well as track down aberrant behavior. If mysterious bugs appear, the auditing mechanism can save the day.

Finally, design a test plan that looks for holes in your logic and in how your Web Service handles large numbers of clients. It is always better to find these holes before announcing that the Web Service is live and someone finds the bugs for you.

PART II

Going Deeper

This section deals with additional pieces of the Web Services puzzle, including security, availability, and state. Developers will be able to use this information to create more robust and secure applications that are based on a Web Service-based architecture and the .NET framework.

IN THIS PART

6

Security Issues with Web Services

When deploying a Web Service, you have to think about how you will secure that service. Yes, even if you decide to open up access to the service to everyone and anyone, you still have to think about security—for example, protecting yourself against people seeking to deny access to your service. Security encompasses the following:

- Equipment deployment
- Authenticating users
- Guarding data so that users only see what they should see
- Tracking user activity

Any and all of these items may be a part of your overall security plan. In this chapter, we will take a look at all of these items and show how you can use them to make your Web Service more secure.

Equipment Deployment

One of the easiest things to do to secure your corporate data is to use hardware in an intelligent way. When deploying a publicly accessible Web Service, you will want to expose as little of your internal infrastructure as necessary. There are a number of things you will want to do:

- Put your database machines behind a firewall.
- Use hardware to protect your equipment. For example, rely on routers instead of software firewalls.

Hardware is typically faster at routing and is easier to lockdown. The software firewall may have unknown interactions with which to deal.

- Make use of a demilitarized zone (DMZ). In other words, only put the machine serving the Web Service on the public Internet.

The basic theme in equipment deployment, as you have just seen, is that you should strive to keep the majority of your machines behind some sort of protective firewall. The recommended configuration looks something like what is shown in Figure 6.1.

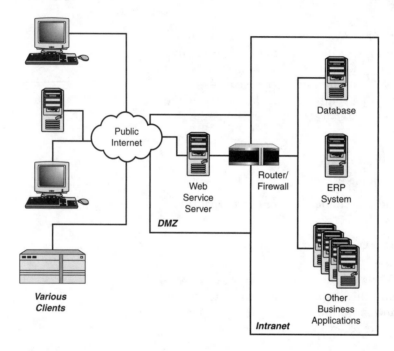

FIGURE 6.1   Web Service deployment behind a firewall.

By using a router, you can set up your equipment so that only one computer from your internal network is exposed in the DMZ. Alternatively, you can place a machine on the public Internet and set up the network such that only requests from the external machine can come through the firewall. Any requests that do not come from that IP address will not be allowed through. You may also be able to do more advanced items as well. Make sure to discuss this with your networking team or your vendor. They should be able to help you get things deployed correctly.

Authenticating Users

You authenticate a user to learn his or her identity. The identity information might be used to make sure a person should have access to the Web Service. You may also use the identity to track the user's activities. When it comes to authenticating your users, you have several options:

- *Application level authentication*—Users identify themselves via credentials supplied in the SOAP message.

- *HTTP Basic authentication*—The username and password are sent as clear text. This is not useful for secure applications, but it can be useful in combination with other identification techniques.

- *HTTP Digest authentication*—This tool sends a hashed version of the basic authentication credentials so that only the server can decode them.

- *Client certificates*—Using a certificate provided by a certificate authority, the client can prove its identity during SSL authentication.

- *Windows authentication*—Through HTTP Basic/Digest authentication or client certificates, IIS can map a user identity to a real Windows user.

All of these options have different uses. We will look at each of them in turn. For all except application level authorization, ASP.NET will assist us. Each section will discuss when to set the options, but here is a quick overview. The web.config file has a section describing the authentication mode to use. Listing 6.1 shows an excerpt of the authentication section from that file.

LISTING 6.1   Setting the Authentication Options Inside web.config.

```
<configuration>

  <system.web>

    <!-- AUTHENTICATION
         This section sets the authentication policies of the
         application. Possible modes are "Windows", "Forms",
         "Passport" and "None"
    -->
    <authentication mode="Windows" />

  </system.web>

</configuration>
```

The authentication mode can be any of the following values:

- none   No authentication is performed.

- Windows   Use Windows integrated authentication. This can be in the form of HTTP Basic or Digest authentication or NTLM.

- Passport   Uses Microsoft Passport to authenticate users. This is not a valid method of authentication for XML Web Services. A client with a user interface can use this data to identify the user via some custom methods.

- Forms   This form of authentication embeds the username and password in a cookie. If the cookie is not present, the user is redirected to a page where he or she can log in. Like Passport, this method will not work with XML Web Services. It can be used to identify the user and then use some other method to authenticate the user with the identity information.

Now, let's see how all these different methods can be used.

Application Level Authorization

At times, it may make sense to provide your own authentication mechanisms. Some of the reasons to do so include the following:

- Your Web Service is running on a corporate intranet and you want to grant access to departments, not individuals. You also can assume that all users are legitimate.

- Clients already are using credentials you manage for other items (for example, customer ID and password).

- Integration with other authentication systems does not make sense for your application.

Whatever the reason, creating your own authentication mechanism is possible. All I present here is a recommended way to accomplish this task.

Credentials are useful for establishing ownership of data, rights to view or manipulate data, and for tracking Web Service usage. Regardless of how they are used, the credentials are out-of-band data. By "out-of-band," I mean that the information on the entity calling a particular Web Method is extra. In a typical programmatic API, you would get user identity by calling some operating system-specific functions and would never make this data part of the function signature. With a Web Service, you cannot always do this. However, you can keep the credentials out of the actual function signature. To do this, require that the client send the credentials in the SOAP Header.

The most common form of application level authentication involves the use of a username and password. Typically, this initial exchange should happen over a secure connection, such as SSL. This operation should return a token of some sort for the caller to use in subsequent calls. This token is the out-of-band data used to identify the caller. You should give the tokens as short a lifespan as what makes sense. For highly secure data, the token may live only a few seconds. For less secure data, the token may live for an hour or more.

As the provider of a Web Service, you should tell clients what to expect for an error when their tokens become invalid. When the token's lifespan comes to an end, the user will have to log in again to get a new, valid token so that he or she can continue to use the Web Service.

Listing 6.2 shows how you might accomplish this task. The sample uses a plain HTTP URL and does not go over SSL. If this were a production system, you would perform the extra steps to turn off anonymous access and enable SSL for IIS. To use SSL, you would need a certificate from a certificate authority that you and your users could trust. For internal applications, this could be a machine running Microsoft Certificate Server. Microsoft Certificate Server is available through the NT 4 Option Pack and ships as part of later versions of Windows Server as an optional Windows component. For external applications, you would have to acquire a certificate from a publicly trusted certificate authority, such as VeriSign.

The usage scenario for the example is simple:

1. Login and acquire a token.

2. Using the token, call `HelloWorld`.

The login method uses a hard-coded username and password.

LISTING 6.2   Custom Authentication Login Method

```
<WebMethod()> Public Function Login(ByVal userName As String, _
   ByVal password As String) As String

   If (userName = "Admin") And _
      (password = "simplePW") Then
       Login = theToken
   Else
       Throw New System.Web.Services.Protocols.SoapException( _
           "Invalid username/password combination", _
           System.Web.Services.Protocols.SoapException. _
               ClientFaultCode)
   End If
End Function
```

The token is a constant string. Using that token, the user would call `HelloWorld` passing the token in the SOAP Header. Listing 6.3 shows how the service itself could check the token and make sure that the header matched the required credentials.

LISTING 6.3   The Token Class and the `HelloWorld` Declaration Using That Token

```
Public Class TokenHeader
    Inherits System.Web.Services.Protocols.SoapHeader

    Public theToken As String

End Class

Public m_tokenHeader As TokenHeader

Private Const theToken As String = "this_is_the_token"

<WebMethod(), _
    System.Web.Services.Protocols.SoapHeader("m_tokenHeader", _
    Direction:=System.Web.Services.Protocols.SoapHeaderDirection.In, _
    Required:=True)> Public Function HelloWorld() As String

    If (m_tokenHeader.theToken = theToken) Then
        HelloWorld = "Hello World!"
    Else
        Throw New System.Web.Services.Protocols.SoapException( _
            "You must login first", _
            System.Web.Services.Protocols.SoapException.ClientFaultCode)
    End If
End Function
```

To see this in action, we can use a simple console application, as shown in Listing 6.4. This application will just log in and, with the returned token, call `HelloWorld`. It uses the special URI `http://schemas.xmlsoap.org/soap/actor/next` to indicate that the `mustUnderstand` refers to the recipient of the message.

LISTING 6.4   A Simple Client Using Application Authentication

```
Sub Main()
    Dim svc As New localhost.Authenticate()

    Dim theToken As String
    Try
```

5

LISTING 6.4 Continued

```
        Dim userName As String
        Dim password As String

        ' For this sample, we already know
        ' the username and password.
        userName = "Admin"
        password = "simplePW"

        theToken = svc.Login(username, password)
        If (theToken.Length > 0) Then
            ' We were authenticated. Call HelloWorld

            ' First, setup the token header
            Dim theHeader As New localhost.TokenHeader()
            theHeader.theToken = theToken
            theHeader.MustUnderstand = True

            ' Set the actor to say who must understand.
            ' Yes, it's the one who receives the message.
                theHeader.Actor = _
                    "http://schemas.xmlsoap.org/soap/actor/next"
            svc.TokenHeaderValue = theHeader
            System.Console.WriteLine(svc.HelloWorld())


        End If
    Catch ex As System.Web.Services.Protocols.SoapException
        System.Console.WriteLine(ex.Detail)
    End Try
    System.Console.WriteLine("Press return to exit")
    System.Console.ReadLine()
End Sub
```

If everything works correctly, the console should have the text "Hello World!" on it. To write a longer lived version of the client in Listing 6.4, you would store the token and only change it when a Web Service method indicated that the token was no longer valid. The downside to this approach is that someone with a packet sniffer and the ability to watch a piece of the network could capture the token and start using it. If this is a worry, you could run the entire communication over SSL so that the token would be encrypted. This all depends on how secure the data needs to be.

HTTP Basic and Digest Authentication

HTTP Basic and Digest Authentication are used to secure HTTP traffic. They are both defined in RFC 2617 and are variations on the same theme. With both forms of authentication, the user credentials are passed in the HTTP Authorization header field. User credentials always include a username and password and may include information regarding the domain to which the user belongs. When these credentials are passed using Basic authentication, the username and password travel as clear text. Well, not exactly. The text is base64 encoded. For a user named TestUser who has a password of password, the username and password will be represented in the HTTP headers as follows:

```
Authorization: Basic VGVzdFVzZXI6cGFzc3dvcmQ=
```

The header states that Basic authentication is being used and that the base64 encoded copy of the username and password is VGVzdFVzZXI6cGFzc3dvcmQ=. Decode this information, and you will discover that this says TestUser:password.

> **NOTE**
>
> How does one go about decoding base64 encoded data? The XML classes support base64 encoding and decoding natively. One easy way to transform a value between base64 and its regular text representation is to make use of those XML classes. In particular, use the XmlTextReader to do the transformation. To see how to do this, take a look at how I decoded a string that was in the HTTP Authorization header. (You will see this username/password combination in use in the example for this section.)
>
> The first thing I had to do was capture the HTTP conversation. This can be done by using the SOAP Toolkit and capturing an "Unformatted Trace." While a "Formatted Trace" displays only the XML exchanged between client and server, the "Unformatted Trace" shows every byte that goes back and forth. A base64 encoded string ends with a =. With the ability to locate the string easily, the following lines will decode and print the string to the console:
>
> ```
> Dim str As String = "<ROOT>VGVzdFVzZXI6cGFzc3dvcmQ=</ROOT>"
> Dim reader As New _
>     System.Xml.XmlTextReader(New System.IO.StringReader(str))
>
> reader.Read()
> Dim buffer(1) As Byte
> Dim AE As New Text.ASCIIEncoding()
>
> ' When done, will write out TestUser:password
> While reader.ReadBase64(buffer, 0, 1) <> 0
>     Console.Write(AE.GetChars(buffer)(0))
> End While
> ```

Because the base64 representation comes back as a byte, you have to convert that byte into the correct representation. Because base64 encoding can be used on many different types of data (images, executables, spreadsheets, and so on), the reader of the data is expected to know what to do with the bytes. In our case, we know that the string contains encoded ASCII characters, so we use the ASCIIEncoding class to transform those bytes into characters.

Basic authentication works well over an SSL channel because the entire HTTP message exchange will be encrypted.

How do you set up the Web Service to use Basic Authentication? To demonstrate how, we will develop a simple Web Service. A variant on Hello World, this one uses Basic (and later, Digest) authentication to say Hello to the user calling the Web Service.

The first thing we need to do is create an XML Web Service. So, fire up Visual Studio and create a new Visual Basic Web Service named **Ch6BasicAuth**. Open up `Service1.asmx.vb` and look for the spot where the sample `HelloWorld` method is commented out. Uncomment that method and change the second line so that the whole method reads as shown in the following code:

```
<WebMethod()> Public Function HelloWorld() As String
    HelloWorld = "Hello " & Me.User.Identity.Name
End Function
```

This function uses some of the built-in functionality of ASP.NET to figure out who the caller is. It takes the name tied to the calling identity and says `"Hello"` to it. The bulk of the work for making this work lies primarily in the land of Web Service deployment. You have to make sure that both the `web.config` file and the Web Application configuration in IIS are set up correctly. Here, make sure that the authentication type is set to Windows.

```
<authentication mode="Windows" />
```

To complete the necessary steps, you will need to go to the Internet Information Management Services console. You can get there by right-clicking My Computer and selecting Manage. After expanding a series of nodes, you should see things looking much like Figure 6.2.

After you locate this node, perform the following steps to turn on Basic HTTP authentication. While the steps shown are only for the Ch6BasicAuth application, they will work for any Web application.

1. Within the Internet Information Services node, open up Web Sites, Default Web Site, and locate the `Ch6BasicAuth` node (shown in Figure 6.3).

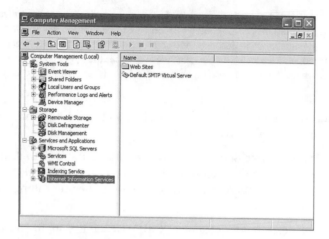

FIGURE 6.2 Main IIS node.

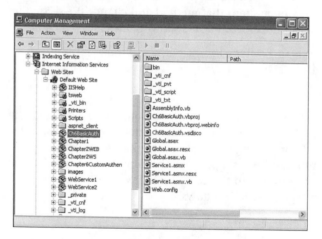

FIGURE 6.3 Locating the Ch6BasicAuth application in IIS.

2. Right-click the Ch6BasicAuth node and select Properties.

3. Click the Directory Security tab and click the Edit button.

4. Uncheck the Anonymous Access checkbox and check the Basic Authentication checkbox. If you want to only allow valid Windows Users, select the Integrated Windows Authentication checkbox too. This is shown in Figure 6.4.

NOTE

Important: If you don't turn off Anonymous Access, many of the authentication samples in this chapter will not work.

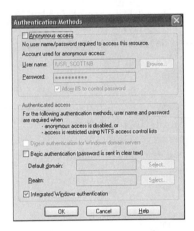

FIGURE 6.4 Security setup for Ch6BasicAuth virtual directory.

5. Click OK twice and you should be returned to the management console. The application will now only accept authenticated users who have Windows accounts.

6. In the `web.config` file for the Web Service, make sure that the authentication mode is set to Windows. This section of the `web.config` file was described in this chapter in the "Authenticating Users" section.

Now that the Web Service is locked down and will only access authenticated users, how do you access it? To do this, you need to get on speaking terms with two classes—`CredentialCache` and `NetworkCredential`. Both of these classes live in the `System.Net` namespace and they work together. For our purposes, `CredentialCache` is used to make associations between the servers we want to access and the username/password that we use to authenticate ourselves to the servers. You then tell the proxy to use the `CredentialCache` when it needs a username/password combination. Listing 6.5 shows a very simple client that uses HTTP Basic authentication to validate itself to use the Web Service.

LISTING 6.5   A Simple Basic HTTP Authentication Client

```
Sub Main()
    Dim svc As New localhost.Service1()

    ' Tell the proxy to use the current user's credentials
    ' whenever it needs to authenticate this client.
    svc.Credentials = System.Net.CredentialCache.DefaultCredentials
    svc.AllowAutoRedirect = True
    svc.PreAuthenticate = True

    ' Show the results and exit
    ' The expected output is "Hello [user name]"
    System.Console.WriteLine(svc.HelloWorld())
    System.Console.WriteLine("Press return to exit")
    System.Console.ReadLine()
End Sub
```

To change this over to HTTP Digest Authentication, the client remains the same. Just go back through the steps outlined in this section and select Digest Authentication for Windows Domain Servers instead of Basic Authentication. The rest will just work. Digest authentication works by encrypting the HTTP Authentication header. The user identification information travels inside a MD5 hash. On a Windows network, this information can only be authenticated by a domain controller. Digest authentication is only available on Windows 2000 and later.

X509 Client Certificates

X509 client certificates present yet another way to authenticate users. Typically, a certificate is issued by an entity called a Certificate Authority (CA). An example of a public CA is Verisign. Many companies use Microsoft Certificate Server (part of Windows Server products) as an internal CA. Certificates make use of public key infrastructure (PKI) to encrypt data. They use private/public key pairs to secure the data. The sender of the data encrypts the data using a private key that only the sender knows. The data can be decrypted using his or her public key. This arrangement allows the receiver of the data to verify that the data was sent by a known party. If the private key is compromised, the owner of the certificate needs to invalidate the certificate and get a new one. How does this work with Web Services?

As you know, ASP.NET transmits SOAP requests using HTTP. SSL, a widely adopted HTTP technology, typically uses server certificates to guarantee that a client is talking to who he or she claims to be. Clients verify this by requesting the server certificate and making sure that data encrypted by the server can be decrypted with the public key. If needed, the server can request a client certificate that verifies the client's identity using the same techniques. A full discussion on SSL and certificates is beyond the scope of this book. For more information, Netscape has an excellent explanation at http://developer.netscape.com/tech/security/basics/index.html.

How do you set this up on your own server? Well, the first thing you will want to do is enable SSL on the server. Without SSL, the certificate exchange will not happen.

Setting up a Certificate Authority

This section contains supplemental information about setting up a certificate authority and has very little to do with Web Services. If you do not need to do this, feel free to skip ahead to the next section.

To run SSL on the server, you will need to have a certificate to prove the identity of the server. If you want to experiment with SSL without paying a certificate authority, such as Verisign for a certificate, you can set up your own certificate authority. Windows 2000 Server and later ships with a component called Certificate Server. You install this component through the Add/Remove Programs dialog by selecting "Add/Remove Windows Components." A certificate authority is an organization that provides public key infrastructure facilities. A certificate identifies the user and issuer of the certificate and provides keys that can be used in encrypting and decrypting data. A full discussion of certificates with respect to PKI, public key infrastructure, is beyond the scope of this book.

The following instructions explain how to set up SSL on a server using a local certificate authority.

1. Open up IIS administration console (inetmgr) and select the Web site on which you want to use SSL. On most machines, this will be the Web site named Default Web Site.

2. Right-click the Web site and select Properties.

3. Select the Directory Security tab and click the Server Certificate... button. This button will be enabled only if a certificate has not been applied to the Web site. Pressing the button brings up the Web Server Certificate wizard.

4. Click Next.

5. Select the Create a New Certificate radio button and click Next.

6. Select the Send the Request Immediately to an Online Certification Authority radio button and click Next again.

7. On the Name and Security Settings dialog, leave the defaults as is. This is shown in Figure 6.5. Click Next.

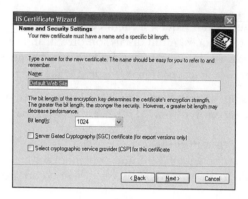

FIGURE 6.5   Name and Security Settings dialog.

8. On the Organization Information dialog, fill in some values for Organization and Organizational Unit. An example is shown in Figure 6.6.

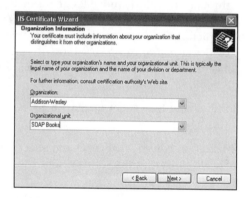

FIGURE 6.6   Organization Settings Wizard dialog.

9. On the Your Site's Common Name dialog, leave the common name alone for testing. When accessing the site over SSL, make sure to use the computer name and not localhost. For a production site, you would want the common name to be the name of the Web site. For example, www.scottseely.com would use www.scottseely.com as the common name. Click Next.

10. On the Geographical Information dialog, fill in the information for the country, state/province, and city/locality that applies to your machine. Figure 6.7 shows what I filled in for my development machine. Click Next.

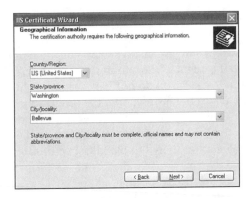

FIGURE 6.7   Geographical Information dialog.

11. Click a certification authority on the Choose a Certification Authority dialog. If you set up an in-house certification authority, choose that one. Click Next.

12. The request is now ready. Click Next to submit the request and install the certificate on the machine. When this is done, click Finish to exit the wizard.

    After the certificate is installed, you can view the certificate by pressing the View Certificate button on the Directory Security tab of the Web site property sheet. Figure 6.8 shows the first tab of the certificate installed for my development computer.

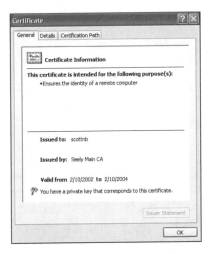

FIGURE 6.8   General information about the installed certificate.

Client-Side Certificates

After SSL is set up, you are done with the server side of things. Things become a bit more difficult on the client side. Normally, when you are in a client, such as Internet Explorer, you will install a client certificate so that IE can send it at will. When developing a client application, you do not have access to the certificates IE knows. Instead, the certificate needs to be stored in a file (preferably a file secured to the owner only using the NT File System, NTFS). After this is done, you load the file at runtime and add it to the list of certificates being used by the proxy. The client presented in Listing 6.5 can be altered to use client certificates. The altered client is presented in Listing 6.6.

LISTING 6.6   When Configured for SSL, Using the Ch6BasicAuth Service Using Client Certificates for Authentication

```
Sub Main()
    Dim svc As New localhost.Service1()
    ' Load the certificate from a file.
    Dim x509 As X509Certificate = _
        X509Certificate.CreateFromCertFile("c:\example.cer")

    ' Add the certificate to the service cache
    svc.ClientCertificates.Add(x509)

    ' Show the results and exit
    Try
        System.Console.WriteLine(svc.HelloWorld())
    Catch ex As Exception
        System.Console.WriteLine(ex.ToString())
    End Try
    System.Console.WriteLine("Press return to exit")
    System.Console.ReadLine()
End Sub
```

The requirements for this to work are simple—a certificate authority that the server trusts must issue the client's certificate. This is the same requirement that the client places on the server when deciding to trust the server. Because the server side of the authentication is all handled by IIS, the Web Service itself does not change. The things that change are the client and the way it is deployed.

Setting up IIS for Client Certificates

Most developers have never set up IIS to accept a client certificate or requested a certificate for client authentication. This section assumes that you have a copy of

Windows Server set up somewhere (a 120-day evaluation version will work) and that Certificate Server is installed on that computer. To make X509 certificates work, you have to set up the client and the IIS server correctly. Doing this consists of two larger steps—getting a client certificate and mapping that certificate to a Windows account.

To get a client certificate, do the following:

1. Navigate to `http://[cert server]/certsrv`. Figure 6.9 shows the page on my network at home. Select Request a Certificate.

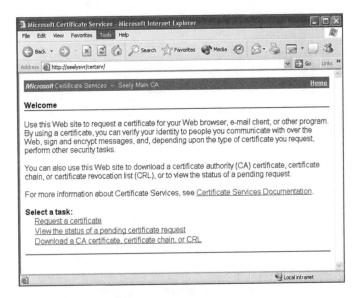

FIGURE 6.9   Web interface for requesting a client certificate.

2. Figure 6.10 shows the next screen. From here, select User Certificate because this is the certificate type we want to use.

FIGURE 6.10   Select certificate type.

3. On the next page, click Submit to get the certificate. Figure 6.11 shows the result of this submission. From here, select the Install This Certificate link. This will add the certificate to the client certificates available through Internet Explorer.

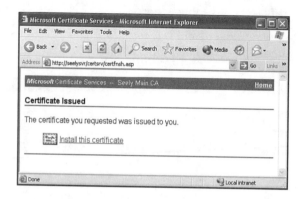

FIGURE 6.11   Result of requesting a client certificate.

4. With the certificate installed, from within Internet Explorer select the Tools, Internet Options menu option.

5. Select the Content tab. On that tab, select the Certificates button.

6. Select the just installed certificate on the Personal tab and click the Export... button. This tab is shown in Figure 6.12.

FIGURE 6.12   Personal certificates installed within Internet Explorer.

7. From within the Certificate Export Wizard, click the Next button. On the Export Private Key page, select No, Do Not Export the Private Key. As a rule you should not give someone your private key because that certificate can be used to impersonate you. The person would thus know the key you use to encrypt your data. Click Next.

8. On the Export File Format dialog, select DER Encoded Binary X.509 (.CER). The Base64-encoded option would work equally well, although it would result in a larger file to transmit during authentication. Base64 encoding typically introduces a 30 percent increase in size. Click Next.

9. For the filename, type in **c:\example.cer** as shown in Figure 6.13. This will allow you to duplicate the results in Listing 6.6. Click Next, and then click Finish. You now have exported the certificate.

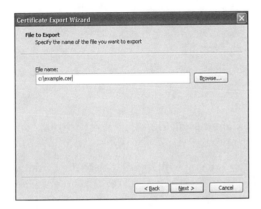

FIGURE 6.13 Exporting the certificate to a file.

Now that the client certificate has been exported, you need to map that certificate to an individual or group of individuals in IIS. Let's look at how to map the certificate to an individual from within IIS.

1. Open up the IIS management console—inetmgr.

2. Select the Web site you want to protect. In our case, select Local computer, Web Sites, Default Web Site, Ch6BasicAuth. Right-click the Ch6BasicAuth node and select Properties.

3. Select the Directory Security tab. In the Secure Communications group box, click the Edit... button.

4. On the Secure Communications dialog, select the Require Secure Channel (SSL) check box. Select the Require Client License radio button. Finally, select the Enable Client Certificate Mapping check box. The dialog should look as shown in Figure 6.14.

FIGURE 6.14   Configuring the virtual directory to use SSL and client certificates.

5. Click the Edit... button.

6. In the Account Mappings dialog, select the 1-to-1 tab. Click the Add... button to add a new mapping.

7. The Open common dialog will appear. Select the certificate you just saved from the first set of steps in this sidebar, `c:\example.cer`. Click Open.

8. The Map to Account dialog will be open. Make sure that the Enable This Mapping check box is selected. Pick an account from your machine for the Account text box. Then, enter that user's password. Figure 6.15 shows the dialog as filled out on my home machine. After the data is filled in correctly for your environment, click OK and then confirm the password.

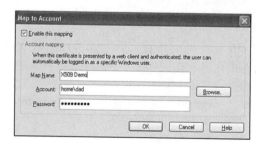

FIGURE 6.15   Configuring the user mapped to a given certificate.

9. Click OK, until all property pages are closed and you are back at the IIS management console.

If you follow these directions, you should be able to use X509 certificates to authenticate clients.

Guarding Data

When you make your data, you can use the user authentication mechanisms discussed to guard the data. You can use Access Control Lists to guard files and SQL-based security to guard data in your database. As part of your security for the Web Service, consider using a combination of user identity and other security mechanisms as a way to protect your data. For example, SQL server allows you to limit who can and cannot access various databases, tables, and stored procedures. NTFS limits what files a particular user can access. Active Directory can be used to limit what network resources to which the user has access. An effective security plan uses a combination of methods to keep things safe. By authenticating the user using Windows Integrated Authentication and denying anonymous access to the Web Service, the Web method will impersonate the caller when it executes. Any rights given to that caller will be enforced. This includes access to files, network resources, and database objects.

Tracking User Activity

Many applications require that you give users access to sensitive resources. When the users are using those resources, you will want to be able to see what was done. What did they look at? What actions did they fire? What data did they change? Most of the time, the users will not abuse their privileges. However, when the users are new and when they are trying to do something wrong, you want to see what they did. It will help you back out the changes the newbie made. As a forensic tool, tracking the changes will help you identify who did what and when.

All of this involves creating some sort of an auditing strategy. In the best of all worlds, you will know exactly who is calling you. Auditing was discussed as a debugging tool in Chapter 5, "Troubleshooting Web Services/Consumers." For security, you can use auditing to determine what the user did and when he or she did it. What information do you track when auditing user activity? This set of data is specific to security:

- *User identity (if available)*—This lets you know who executed the action.

- *IP Address of caller*—This allows you to track the call back to a specific machine. This comes in handy, even if the user is coming through some sort of proxy server.

- *Free text field*—You will want some sort of generic field that allows you to put all audit data into one table. Within this field, you can enter information particular to the action the user was performing. Think of putting in information that would be helpful when capturing details about what happened.

- *Time of action*—By knowing when things happened, you will be able to figure out the order of the actions and string together what the user did.

Keep in mind that a lot of this information will be used only when something odd happens. Depending on what the Web Service allows users to do, you may want to write programs that analyze the audit data, looking for use patterns that look suspicious. So, what would this logging mechanism look like? Ideally, the auditing mechanism would use some sort of delayed write mechanism, such as inserting the item in to a queue and having a listener actually log the item to a database. I will highlight the one function you would want to adapt to actually use Microsoft Message Queue (MSMQ) instead of writing to a file, as is done in the example.

The code presents a class named `Audit` that handles extracting the audit data from the Web Service and storing the audit to a file. This class is used by a `HelloWorld` Web Method. The code, shown in Listing 6.7, is written using what I consider to be the recommended setup for making sure that the audit record always gets recorded for every Web Method that you audit.

LISTING 6.7   Auditing `HelloWorld` and Making Sure That the Audit Data Is Always Written

```
<WebMethod()> Public Function HelloWorld() As String
    Dim theAudit As New Audit(Me, "Service1.HelloWorld", AuditLog)

    Try
        HelloWorld = "Hello World"
        theAudit.FreeText = "This is some free text."
    Catch ex As Exception
        theAudit.FreeText = ex.ToString()
    Finally
        theAudit.Store()
    End Try
End Function
```

The Web Service should be set up to use HTTP Basic Authentication. This will allow us to easily track who is using the Web Service. The `Audit` class takes a reference to a `WebService` class, the name of the method being audited, and the name of the log file. In the constructor, shown in Listing 6.8, `Audit` captures everything but the free text and stores it to be written a little bit later.

LISTING 6.8   Constructor for the Audit Class

```
Public Sub New( _
    ByRef theContext As System.Web.Services.WebService, _
    ByVal methodName As String, _
    ByVal logFileName As String)

    ' Extract and store the important data.
    m_methodName = methodName
    m_logFileName = logFileName
    m_actionTime = DateTime.Now
    m_userID = theContext.User.Identity.Name
    m_callerIP = theContext.Context.Request.UserHostAddress
End Sub
```

When the method being audited is ready to return, the code should store the log information. This gives the Web Method a chance to set the free text to anything that may happen while it is executing. Listing 6.9 shows how the data is then stored to the log file. This is the method you would want to update to write to an MSMQ because even file access can get to be time consuming as the file grows in size.

LISTING 6.9   Storing the Audit Data to the Log

```
Public Sub Store()
    Dim fs As New System.IO.StreamWriter(m_logFileName, True)
    fs.Write(m_actionTime.ToString() & vbTab)
    fs.Write(m_methodName & vbTab)
    fs.Write(m_callerIP & vbTab)
    fs.Write(m_userID & vbTab)
    fs.WriteLine(m_freeText)
    fs.Close()
End Sub
```

Table 6.1 shows the data that was stored in the log file when I logged in using two different accounts on my computer.

TABLE 6.1   Data Stored by Simple Audit Class

Time	Method	Client IP	User ID	Free Text
12/4/2001 9:34:55 PM	Service1.HelloWorld	127.0.0.1	SCOTTNB\TestUser	This is some free text.
12/4/2001 9:35:13 PM	Service1.HelloWorld	127.0.0.1	SCOTTNB\Dad	This is some free text.

The method presented here depends on knowing the User ID. For a free Web Service, you could omit this data and still store the client IP address. Knowing this information will come in handy when particular addresses seem to be abusing your Web Service. Abuse includes looking for ways to bring your Web Service down, denial of service attempts, or anything else that you don't want to see happening on your server.

Summary

You will need to use more than one technique to secure your Web Service. The combination of techniques depends on what your security requirements are. Pay attention to where you deploy the Web Service, and make sure that your critical data is protected from the public Internet. Web Services, by providing a well-defined interface, can offer quite a bit of data protection by putting the Web Service on the public Internet and allowing only the Web Service server to get at the data.

By locking down the boxes and allowing only authenticated users to access the data, you lock out a number of malicious users. Of the users you do allow through, you will want to monitor what they are doing and store that data in a log. Even if you allow everyone through, you should include logging mechanisms and design these early in the development process. Adding logging after the fact is error prone and time consuming.

If you follow the recommendations in this chapter, you will have a more secure Web Service. By monitoring who is calling the Web Service, you will be able to figure out how it is being used. If you notice abuse, you will be able to figure out what group of machines is misusing the service and block them from any more transgressions.

7

Looking at the "Abilities"

When you deploy a Web Service, there are a number of things you can do to make it successful. A lot of those items have to do with designing for a set of specific targets referred to as the "abilities."

- *Availability*—The goal of availability design is avoiding a single point of failure. We will look at how to build your Web Service so that another box could easily take over if another one failed.

- *Scalability*—You want your Web Service to handle more concurrent users as it gains popularity. One of the worst things that can happen to a Web Service is for it to fail because it became too popular and could not handle all the users.

- *Manageability*—When deploying a Web Service, you want to make sure that your systems operations people can easily monitor what is happening inside the system. We will discuss things you can do to make system monitoring easier.

- *Performance*—Of the four "abilities," this one does not follow the naming pattern. Nevertheless, you need to design things around performance. You need to define minimum response times under given user loads so that you know how fast things ought to perform. Because every application is different, we will discuss deployment options that will make your Web Services more responsive.

Much like Chapter 6, "Security Issues with Web Services," this chapter should help you think about what you need to do as a developer to make your Web Service perform well on the Internet. One thing that can cause a Web Service (or any Internet-based application) to fail is unanticipated success. By thinking about success early in the design and coding process, you can make sure that the Web Service is ready to handle success without adding much cost. With any luck, you will save time rewriting the Web Service too. The things you will do for Web Services are not much different from things you would do to make a Web ready to handle the "abilities."

Availability

One of the reasons that you provide a Web Service is so that other applications can use it. If the Web Service has problems maintaining availability due to server failure, application crashes, network outages, or anything else, the usefulness of the Web Service will be greatly reduced. Your users want to be able to depend on the service being available when they need it. So, what are some of the things you can do to make the Web Service more available?

- *Clustered servers*—Protect against power outages and server failure.

- *Multiple deployment locations*—Allows the same Web Service to be accessed from multiple locations. This approach will also be discussed within the context of increasing performance.

- *Reporting*—By providing reporting mechanisms through system counters, Web Service-specific reports, and other mechanisms, you can gauge how the Web Service is used. Knowing what is happening with the Web Service will let you know when you are approaching known limits.

- *Administrator communication*—Make sure that you have installed software that will notify the system administrator of situations such as power failures, routing errors, and suspected attacks. Administrative software has become increasingly useful and should be used to keep tabs on your servers and other network equipment.

Let's dig a little deeper into each of these approaches.

Clustered Servers

Clustering on Windows involves taking at least two to four machines and setting them up so that one can take over the duties of another in case one machine fails for some reason. Most clusters contain two machines that are configured either as active-passive or active-active. An active-passive configuration contains one server that handles requests and another that does nothing. The passive server just monitors the active server, waiting for it to become unreachable. It might be unreachable for any number of reasons—power failure, a component stops working, or some other reason. When that happens, the passive server takes over. Networked users of the machine will not be able to tell what happened.

The other option is an active-active cluster. This allows you to use the two machines in the cluster for different purposes. If one machine fails, the working machine assumes the workload of the failed machine. This can result in performance degradation on the machine doing the work of the pair. The upside is that client applications will continue to function, albeit with a slower response time. This configuration has the advantage over an active-passive cluster that both machines are actually being used.

The clustering technology in Windows NT 4.0, and later, provides for the ability to keep both machines in the cluster in sync. For example, they can be set up to have the same specific files, applications, and database transactions on both the main machine and the backup. For information on how a specific product supports clustering, refer to its documentation. (Microsoft SQL Server is one product you will rely on that does support clustered servers.)

For a Web Service, you would most likely use clustering for any machines that the Web Service uses. You would not use clustering for the machines on which the Web Service lives. For example, if the Web Service uses a database, consider locating the database server on a clustered pair of servers. The Web Service itself could be placed in a Web farm where any request would be routed to one of many servers in the farm. You could use something like Windows Application Center Server to maintain all the machines in the Web farm. (Application Center has facilities that allow you to write a file to one server. Depending on how the server is configured, that change is replicated to other servers.)

Multiple Deployment Locations

If the Web Service is used by geographically dispersed locations and requirements for accessibility and redundancy are high, consider deploying the Web Service and related databases to more than one physical location. To keep the databases synchronized, you can use SQL Server's built-in replication and merge technologies. How would you write client applications to take advantage of this redundancy?

First off, you have to assume that the exact same setup will exist at each endpoint. The same Web Service is deployed at each location. Because of this, the same client code will be able to access any one of the endpoints. If the redundant endpoints were registered using either a private UDDI registry (such as what will be available with Windows .NET Server) or using one of the public registries, a client can locate an endpoint based on location. Private UDDI registries are typically hosted internally and are not accessible to external entities. Public registries, such as `uddi.microsoft.com`, allow you to make your endpoints known to the world.

UDDI allows you to categorize Web Services based on ISO 3166 Geographic Taxonomy and GeoWeb Geographic classification. Both methods let you specify the location using different granularity. To make use of this information, each client could be preloaded with a set of endpoints on a location-by-location basis. Individual clients could also be built to look for endpoints on a certain scale out basis. For example, a client could be told that it is in Spokane, Washington, United States, North America. To locate a preferred server, possibly at startup time, the client would look for Web Services located in Spokane. It would continue to increase the size of the geographical search until it located a working server.

In a best-case situation, the client would find the Web Service implementation closest to it. This provides for good response times. When the closest endpoint fails for whatever reasons, the client could contact UDDI and query for all tModels implementing the Web Service in Washington. The client would continue scaling out this way until it either found a functioning endpoint somewhere on the globe or all endpoints failed.

Multiple deployment locations facilitate availability by giving clients an alternative endpoint if a server or network link fails. If the link from the computer to the Internet is blocked, you are in trouble. However, if that link is functioning, the client should be able to find at least one endpoint that works. Multiple deployment locations also benefit performance by helping the client locate the closest endpoint. The less distance the message has to travel, the faster it will get from one end of the conversation to the other.

Reporting

Yes, reporting is a theme that you should be getting used to by now. Auditing has been discussed in Chapter 5, "Troubleshooting Web Services/Consumers" as a way to make your Web Service easier to debug and secure. Using that audit data, you can also collect information on how available the Web Service has been. This can help you decide how to make the Web Service more responsive.

For example, your test plan may have made sure that you can handle an average of five requests per second (that's 432,000 requests per day!). What do you do when you discover that that you are getting 200,000 requests per day but that 70 percent of the requests come through during a four hour period? That would translate into a rate of 9.7 requests per second—almost double what you tested for. Reporting would tell you one of two things: you did a really good job or that it is time to scale the system up. Reporting can also tell you what parts of the Web Service are the most popular. Optimizing those methods might allow you to service more users with less hardware, decreasing the chances that a user will have problems accessing the Web Service.

Administrator Communication

Again, you want to make sure that your administrators have ways of being notified when the Web Service and its hardware need attention. If the server hardware is monitored by software that can alert a person when something bad happens, you can respond to problems before your customers alert you. Servers can and do fail. By making it possible for administrators to respond in a timely manner, you reduce your downtime. Less downtime translates into better availability.

Scalability

Scalability can mean a lot of things to many people. For the purposes of this discussion, we will define scalability as the ability to adapt to increases in client requests. Ideally, we will set things up such that on a certain hardware configuration we can handle X requests per second. If we need more capacity, adding a second box will be all we need to do to handle somewhere between 1.8 * X requests/second and 2 * X requests/second. What can you do to be able to handle this kind of scalability? You do a lot of the same things that you would do to make a Web site more scalable:

- Make the Web Service stateless.
- Use a Web Farm to deploy the Web Service.
- Use components that can scale with you.
- Use your head.

That last item, use your head, is the most important item to follow. Every decision you make can potentially help or hinder scalability. Just ask yourself, "Will this decision make it difficult to have two machines running the same application?" If the answer is Yes, figure out how to accomplish the task another way. For example, always use stored procedures when accessing the database. A stored procedure executes faster and returns the data quickly. Use disconnected datasets. By programming SQL Server (or some other database) to return the data to you as a disconnected dataset, you spend less time in the database and allow other users to do their work. Use this same kind of thinking whenever you have to access a shared resource. Now, let's look at the first three items.

Stateless Web Service and Using a Web Farm

A Web Farm is a collection of servers to which a load balancing mechanism, such as a router, can send requests. To take advantage of this load balancing, your Web

Service should not maintain any internal state between Web Service calls. When you maintain state, you hamper the ability of the client to use machines deployed in a Web Farm. When the server maintains state, this adds the requirement that the Web Service calls themselves are sticky. A *sticky* relationship means that the load balancing mechanism routes the client to some server and then routes all future requests from that client to the same server. If one server bunches up on requests, the benefits of the Web Farm decrease. What do you do if a need for state management exists on a per-client basis?

If state information is required between invocations, the state data should be maintained on the server and stored within SQL Server. ASP.NET allows for the storage of state data across a Web Farm. Using this feature is covered in Chapter 9, "Stateful Services."

Scalable Components

If you use other, pre-existing components, make sure that they can also scale. If they can, you are in luck, and you do not have to do any extra work. However, if those components do not scale, what can you do? This question is important. In an effort to reuse existing code, many developers do not think about the scalability of that code. If you must use an existing, poorly-scaling component, there are ways to use it and not hurt your Web Service. It may make sense to place the objects into a COM+ application or library to take advantage of the COM+ object pooling and other capabilities. Do this if startup costs for the object are expensive. If the object can handle only a small number of concurrent connections, consider wrapping the access to that code via Microsoft Message Queue (MSMQ). The MSMQ approach allows you to be responsive to the client while queuing up completion of the requests. A request in a queue will not slow down the Web Service. The worst thing that happens when you use MSMQ is that the client may not be able to get the response immediately.

Manageability

In the section on availability, we discussed the need for applications that communicate with the system administrators when bad things happen. Reporting was yet another item that helps with availability. Not too surprisingly, availability and manageability items are closely related. To make your Web Service more manageable, you will have to design how reporting will work and specify what tools will be purchased or created so that administrators can find out about server health. In this section, we will look at a number of items that will make your Web Service easier to manage. In particular we will look at the following items:

- *Using performance monitor*—Performance monitor can track counters and send alerts when the counters start reaching "warning" levels.

- *Deployment packages*—If the Web Service has to be installed, you can save yourself a lot of time by making installations easy for the installer.

- *Reporting*—If you are auditing the Web Service, reports will help you extract the information into a more meaningful dataset.

This section does not cover all the management items that you will need to do a good job. For example, you need to make sure that the right people are in charge of your servers. Get the operations people the training they need to understand what you are trying to do with a Web Service. A Web Service is like running an RPC server and a Web site. My experience indicates that the best candidates will have experience running larger Web sites. You can teach the administrator the transactional, Web Service stuff pretty easily. Now, let's look at the items that you can control as a developer.

Performance Monitor

The performance monitor and related counters can be a big help in monitoring the Web Service and the hardware on which it runs. Using these counters can give you a good picture of the health of the system. Decide what "acceptable" looks like for your system. For example, you may decide that a sustained CPU load of 80 percent indicates that you need to add servers. By monitoring the page file use, you will know when it is time to add more physical memory to a machine. To give you a start in identifying counters to watch, the following is a list of some that ought to be applicable most of the time, including a brief explanation of why the counter is useful. The list is enumerated as *[Object Name].[Counter Name]*.

- `Processor.% ProcessorTime`   This counter reports back how busy the processor has been. If the processor use stays too high for too long, odds are pretty good that the server is getting overloaded. For example, if the CPU sits at a sustained 80 percent and above use, you may need a faster machine or more machines to handle the request load.

- `Memory.Available Mbytes`   The memory object actually exposes three counters of interest—Available MBytes, Available KBytes, and Available Bytes. Each counter is just a change in how tight you need to be. This counter shows how much physical memory is available on the computer. If this number starts getting close to 0, say only 10MB left of physical memory, you should look at increasing the amount of RAM in the machine. If the Web Service is memory bound, you may need more machines to handle the request load.

- `ASP.NET.Requests Queued`   This states how many requests are waiting to be processed. If the queue grows too long, more machines need to be added to the Web Farm.

- `ASP.NET.Request Wait Time`   States how long the most recent request was waiting in the queue. If this number gets to be too long (you should decide what is acceptable), take a look at the application and see what functions might need further optimization work.

- `ASP.NET.Requests Rejected`   If the queue grows to a point that requests are being turned away, you should look at either speeding the Web Service up or at adding more machines.

- `ASP.NET Applications.Requests/sec`   This counter indicates how many requests are executed per second. Monitoring this value will tell you how accurate your test plan was. When this value drifts above the threshold you tested for, you will want to pay attention to how well the Web Service is handling the additional, unplanned load. Make sure that the Web Service can handle the added stress. Note: there are counters for each application running on the server. Make sure you monitor the correct instance of the ASP.NET Applications object. You can monitor the `_Total` object when that makes the most sense.

Besides these items, you may find that other counters make sense. For example, if you have a large number of objects that are not being picked up by the garbage collector, you will want to look at the counters exposed by the .NET CLR Memory object. When using this one, look at the `aspnet_wp` instance; it contains data pertaining to your ASP.NET Web Service. Take some time to familiarize yourself with the other objects added by Visual Studio .NET and see if they give you any extra information. If you cannot find what you need, you may even want to consider providing your own objects and counters. To view these counters, follow these simple steps:

1. From the taskbar, select Start, Run. In the edit box, type in **perfmon**.

2. To add a counter, either press Ctrl+I or press the plus button on the toolbar.

3. Select an object to monitor. The ones starting with `ASP.NET` or `.NET CLR` will be useful. Figure 7.1 shows a number of the objects available to you.

4. Select some individual counters and the instance you want to watch. For example, if you are watching counters for ASP.NET Applications, you can pick from actual, running applications or from the aggregate. Figure 7.2 shows the `Ch6BasicAuth` application being selected.

5. Pick as many or as few counters as you want from an assortment of objects.

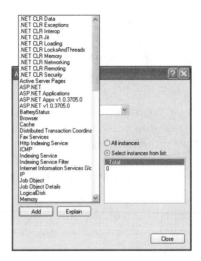

FIGURE 7.1   .NET Objects available for monitoring.

FIGURE 7.2   Selecting a counter from an instance of an object.

After you select the objects that you want to watch, you can save that selection for later use. Just choose File, Save, and then save the selection. When you want to use that profile later, find the file in Windows Explorer and double-click it. Everything will come up just as you saved it.

Deployment Packages

Whenever possible, script the installation procedures for the administrator. By scripting, I do not mean writing out a long list of instructions that must be followed.

Instead, go to the trouble of writing a Microsoft Installer package (MSI). These packages can run other batch files, executables, or Windows Scripting Host compatible scripts (VBScript or JScript). Through script, you can create virtual directories, install or modify databases, or any number of things. By providing an MSI, you make the administrator's job a lot easier and improve his or her chances of success.

How long does it take to put together an installation script? That all depends on how much you need to set up and how complicated the installation is. After you create this package, you will have something that you can give to your testers as well as your server administrators. This also guarantees that everyone installs the Web Service the same way, and that no crucial steps get skipped.

For manageability, the MSI makes it easy for the administrator to set up new boxes as the need arises. Need an installation on the other side of town or around the world? No problem. Just make sure the administrator of the Web Service box has access to the MSI and you are set.

Reporting

The operations staff will need a way to regularly check on the health on the Web Service. For one Web Service deployment, the operations staff I worked with used a combination of reports generated by some Web site monitoring software and our own custom reports to monitor the health and usage of the Web Service. The packaged software reported on which endpoints were getting called and how frequently that was happening. The software also generated an analysis of when the site had the highest traffic. A lot of packages exist that can do basic Web Site monitoring. These packages do not come cheap, but they are worth the money because they help prevent a large number of expensive problems.

You will not be able to escape writing custom reports. Find out what information the systems operations staff needs to know, as well as the information you need to know as a developer. If you plan ahead, you can easily instrument your Web Service to report how much time it takes to service a request, as well as the status of the request. Knowing who your heaviest users are will allow you to talk to them and find out what features the Web Service is lacking. Finally, custom reports can deliver extra information regarding the health of the system.

Performance

One of the most important of the "abilities" is performance. The Web Service needs to be able to return results back to the user as fast as possible. Most of the time, there will be simple things you can do to improve speed. Occasionally, you will have situations where the Web Service call will take several minutes or even hours to complete. In this section, we will look at the simple cases and then the hard case of long-lived calls.

First, let's take a look at some simple gains you can get through improvements to your own hardware. The first thing you should do is identify which Web Methods tied to the Web Service get called the most. Identify the Web Methods that make up 80 percent of the calls to the Web Service. Then, look at them for the following characteristics:

- *Input/Output (I/O) Bound*—Determine if the Web Method mostly accesses the disk. Examples include a simple lookup in a database or reading a file off the hard drive.

- *Computation Intensive*—Determine how much the Web Method taxes the CPU. If the Web Method does a lot of math, image manipulation, general analysis, or fires a complex SQL query, you have a computation intensive Web Method.

- *Memory Hog*—Okay, this is not a great name, but you get the idea. If the Web Method uses lots of memory to perform its job, you have a memory hog.

Hardware solutions to these three items come pretty easily. For each, I will discuss what you can do with hardware and software to improve speed. These tactics are not secrets, by any means. Rather, this discussion is a reminder about some of the best practices. A particular Web Method may have all three items as issues, although that is unlikely for the majority of cases. After you identify which combination of these three exist, you can apply some hardware remedies.

I/O Bound

An I/O bound Web Method will benefit the most from faster hard drives. Look at how fast the drive spins as well as seek times. Also, keeping the hard drive defragmented will make it easier for the disk to deliver all the information in one burst.

In addition to buying faster hard drives, you can also look at how you gather the information from the disk. For example, it may be faster to do all of your data reads and writes in one spot in the code—that is, do all your reads at one time. When writes happen, save them for one burst as well. Most programs do not read and write to more than one or two files. By doing the reads and writes in a batch, you increase the likelihood that the drive's heads are near where your data lives. If the drive does not have to seek a location on the disk, your reads will happen faster.

Why would the head move? If the routine is doing sporadic reads, other processes may get a slice of processor time and need to go to another location on disk. If your reads happen sporadically, the head may have moved by the time you get control back. You also can take advantage of any buffering the operating system may be doing for you. Even if you only read one byte at a time, the operating system is reading data back in larger chunks.

Computation Intensive

A computation-intensive task will benefit from a combination of a faster CPU and memory bus. The faster the data can get to and from the processor, the faster the computation will complete. Of course, if the operation is not manipulating data but is simply crunching numbers, a faster memory bus will have no benefits.

To speed things up as a programmer, look at using some simple best practices. For example, you can allocate all of your memory in one batch and avoid creating objects in any loops. Allocating the objects all at once increases the likelihood that they are near each other in memory. When they get transferred from memory over to the CPU, you increase the likelihood that those objects live on the same page of memory. You can also unravel loops, use methods that are faster, and so on.

Find some way to profile your code and identify the bottlenecks. If you are profiling the method, you can either time the method yourself or use profiling tools. To time the method yourself, just note the time down to the millisecond, execute the method, and check the time again. Then, write the difference out using either the Trace or Debug objects. When you identify the slower methods, you can use the same technique to profile blocks of code within the method. After some checks, you will know what parts of the code you need to examine and make faster.

Memory Hog

As far as hardware goes, all you can do for an application that needs a lot of memory is give it more memory. Memory prices have fallen sharply in recent years, making it easier to throw memory at the problem.

Sometimes, more memory is not the solution. In that case, look at how you are allocating memory. If you think you are doing a good job, you can always tell the garbage collector to clean up. You may need to do this when the Web Service gets to be so popular that the service is grabbing memory faster than the garbage collector can manage. When you are running a .NET-based application, CPU utilization becomes something that you really want to watch. If that CPU does not have some spare cycles, the garbage collector may only run in crisis situations. This can severely affect performance. What can you do?

First, look and see if the code calls new too much. You may be able to reuse objects occasionally. Some of the code may overdo things as well.

Second, conduct a code review (this is a good idea for I/O-bound and computation-intensive services as well). By having others look at your code, you should be able to avoid some problems. Those extra eyes will identify potential problems, such as memory bloat. Also, if the Web Method is doing its job correctly, you will be able to update the specifications on the hardware so that it will be able to perform well with the Web Service.

Long-Lived Web Method Calls

Some Web Method calls can take a long time to complete. When a given call takes a minute or longer to return, what should you do? Forcing synchronous execution means that you would have to keep the communication channel open for the duration of the processing. This is not the best approach. Instead, you want to provide some method of asynchronous processing. The method that you use will depend on what types of demands you can place on clients. The following are just a few of the options available to you:

- Return the results to a Web Service provided on the client.

- Return a unique ID that the client can use to poll for results.

- Have the client provide a place for the results to be delivered, such as an e-mail address or MSMQ location.

When are these different options good ideas?

If you can require clients to provide their own Web Service that complies with a WSDL that you define, you can return the results to the client asynchronously when the call completes. The advantage of this approach is that the client can act on the information as soon as it arrives, and they do not have to poll to get the results. This may also be an option when you provide the client and the main Web Service.

If the client cannot run a Web Service, you will want to look at polling or delivery to a non-Web Service endpoint. The client may not be able to run a Web Service for any number of reasons—device constraints, deployment difficulties, or security concerns. If any of these items occur, you will want to look at alternatives. One alternative is to return a GUID to the user. Then, when the Web Service completes, it can store the result and associate it with the GUID. The client will periodically poll the server asking if the request is done. The server will return a status value of either "ready" or "keep waiting." As soon as the server has completed, the client will then request the actual data and the server can remove the result from its stores.

You could also provide a drop point for the data when it is ready. Because the result will come back as XML, this XML can be delivered to a predetermined location as well. The client simply needs to tell the server where to put the data, and to make sure that the server has access to it. Good things to use are e-mail, secured FTP directories, and file shares if the Web Service and client are on the same, secure network. When depositing the file to a filename, the client should decide what the file will be named. Alternatively, the Web Service could send back as a return value the name it will be giving the file. [GUID].xml will always be a safe thing to name the file because GUIDs are globally unique. ("Globally unique" is in the name, right?) If it makes sense, the returned file does not even need to contain XML. Inside the WSDL, you could indicate the MIME type of the returned item instead.

Polling and sending the XML results are the approaches that place the lowest demands on the client in terms of services it needs to run. The flip side is that the client program may be the hardest to write. Conversely, requiring a Web Server to listen for responses places extra demands on the client in terms of capability and security. The client's Web Server does open the client up for possible attacks, especially if it is on the public Internet. You can limit the potential for attack by limiting access to the client to the server machine only.

Summary

In this chapter, you looked at how to make a Web Service more available, scalable, manageable, and able to perform well. These best practices should be understood by everyone on your team from management to the system designers, developers, and testers. By understanding these items, you will get better Web Services that can be used by greater numbers of people and applications.

8

Asynchronous Web Services

This chapter will focus on the issues of consuming Web Services asynchronously and the benefits of doing so. Because this book's title references both creating and consuming Web Services, you might be wondering why the focus here will be only on consuming Web Services. That is because there is nothing special that needs to be done to create an asynchronous Web Service. Web services can be consumed either synchronously or asynchronously.

We will examine examples of multiple types of consuming applications, as well as the various techniques for calling Web Services asynchronously.

Synchronous Versus Asynchronous Calls

As applications evolve, some components' method calls can take a long time to complete. This can occur when a method has to perform a complicated operation or search for a record or set of records from a database that has a large volume of records.

An example is a flight reservation system, where a search could be looking for a flight on day X from location A to location B and returning on a day Y from location B to location A. There are over 6000 flights per day in the United States alone. In addition, the search may have to access legacy systems to retrieve the possible flights that match the given criteria, and this can take some time.

When a synchronous call is made to a method, the client application is blocked until the method call has completed. In the case of the flight reservation system, once the user clicks the Search button, the client application would freeze and be released only when the method call is completed.

When an asynchronous call is made to a method, the client is not blocked and can, therefore, continue to perform additional processing tasks while the method is being executed. This fact allows the client application to present some kind of notice to the user that the request is being processed (a progress bar for example). When the method call has been completed, the information generated can then be used.

Asynchronous calls are made possible by decoupling the thread used to issue the method call from the thread that is used to perform the operation. This means that the client-side thread issues the call asynchronously and regains control immediately. On the server-side, the object acts as an asynchronous server and dispatches the method call to another thread, permitting the calling thread to be returned immediately.

Making calls to Web services is very similar to calls made to other components' methods. When a client makes a call to a Web Service method, the client will be "blocked" while waiting for the method execution to complete. As mentioned previously, this gives the end user the feeling that the application has frozen. To solve this problem, the Web Service method can be called asynchronously.

Fortunately for developers, the .NET Framework already does most of the plumbing, so this task is quite painless. As you will see in the following section, to perform an asynchronous call to a Web Service method, the developer of that Web Service does not have to write any additional code to handle asynchronous calls. Instead, the developer of the client application makes the decision to call a method synchronously or asynchronously.

Design Pattern for Asynchronous Method Calls

The .NET Framework defines a design pattern for calling methods asynchronously. It is important to use a common design pattern to avoid confusion among developers. This pattern dictates that there are two asynchronous methods for every synchronous method. Specifically, for every synchronous method there is a `Begin` and an `End` asynchronous method. The `Begin` method is called by a client to initiate the execution of the method. With this call, the client tells the method to begin processing the method and control is returned immediately to the client. There are a few options for determining if the call has been completed. These include specifying a *callback method* that will be called when the execution has been completed or performing periodic checking to see if the execution has completed. After it has been stipulated that the execution has completed, the End method is called by the client. The End method performs the retrieval of the results of the Web Service method call.

> **NOTE**
>
> Some functions need to send information back to an application, and callback methods can be used to accomplish this. A callback method provides a way for client applications to complete an asynchronous operation by supplying a callback delegate when the operation is initiated. The callback delegate referenced by a call could then receive any notification from the execution methods. With asynchronous calls, the callback method is notified that the execution has completed.

The Begin and End methods are exposed by the proxy object and are created for each public Web Service method exposed by the Web Service. (Generation of the proxy is discussed in Chapter 2, "Consuming Your First Web Service.") This is also true, even if there is only a synchronous implementation of the Web Service method.

Table 8.1 describes the synchronous and asynchronous methods.

TABLE 8.1   Description of Methods Exposed in the Proxy Class

Method Name in Proxy Class	Description
<WebServiceMethodName>	Invokes a Web Service method named <WebServiceMethodName>
Begin<WebServiceMethodName>	Begins an asynchronous call to a Web Service method named <WebServiceMethodName>
End<WebServiceMethodName>	Ends an asynchronous call to a Web Service method named <WebServiceMethodName>, retrieving return values from the Web Service method

There are two built-in mechanisms available in the .NET Framework for the client to find out whether the method has completed processing the call and is ready to produce the results:

- The client passes a callback function into the Begin method. The callback function is called when the method has completed processing.

- The client waits for the method to complete. The WaitHandle class exposes some methods that can be used to allow the client to wait for the method to complete its execution. In this case, the call made by the client will return an object implementing the IAsyncResult interface.

The `IAsyncResult` object can be used to receive information about the status of the asynchronous call. It also contains an `AsyncWaitHandle` property of type `WaitHandle`. The `WaitHandle` object implements methods that support waiting for the synchronization object to be signaled. The possible signals are `WaitOne`, `WaitAny`, and `WaitAll`. These are discussed in more detail in the section "Using the `WaitHandle` Methods," later in this chapter.

Calling a Web Service Asynchronously

To demonstrate calling a Web Service asynchronously, we will begin by creating a Web Service that will be consumed in all of the examples that follow.

Listing 8.1 demonstrates a Web Service with a WebMethod that will take some time to execute. Create a new Web Service Project called `VirtualFlights`. Add Listing 8.1 to the service.

LISTING 8.1   `Flights.asmx.vb` Shows the Source Code for a Slow Web Service

```
Imports System.Web.Services
Imports System.Threading

Public Class Flights
    Inherits System.Web.Services.WebService

    <WebMethod()> Public Function FlightSearch( _
                            ByVal Departure As String, _
                            ByVal Destination As String, _
                            ByVal DepartureDate As Date, _
                            ByVal ReturnDate As Date, _
                            ByRef Flight As String, _
                            ByRef Time As String) As String
        'Simulate lengthy search...
        Thread.Sleep(5000)
        'Return a Flight Number
        Flight = "VF" & CInt(Rnd() * 100).ToString
        Time = "9:00 AM"
        FlightSearch = "VF" & CInt(Rnd() * 100).ToString
    End Function

End Class
```

Listing 8.1 includes a typical WebMethod that would receive 6 parameters. Four parameters are passed into the WebMethod by value and will be used to perform some lengthy search. Two additional parameters are passed by reference. These parameters will be modified by the WebMethod to return the results of the execution. To simulate the lengthy operation, the Thread will pause for 5 seconds and then set the parameters, passed in by reference to the result values, which in this case are dummy results.

Using the Callback Function

Now that we have a Web Service, let's create a client that will make use of a callback method to retrieve the results from the Web Service. The client will include implementations of both synchronous and asynchronous calls.

1. Add a new Visual Basic Windows Application Project to the solution. Rename the project **FlightTest**.

2. Because this project needs to consume the Web Service, add a Web Reference to the VirtualFlights Web Service you previously created.

3. Now it's time to prepare the Windows Form. Add the controls listed in Table 8.2 to the form and set their properties as listed. The resulting form should look similar to Figure 8.1.

TABLE 8.2   Control Properties for the Consumer Form

Control	Property	Value
Label	Name	lblResult
Button	Name	cmdSearchAsync
	Text	Search (Async)
Button	Name	cmdSearchSync
	Text	Search (Sync)
Timer	Name	Timer1
	Interval	1000
StatusBar	Name	StatusBar1
StatusBarPanel1	Name	StatusBarPanel1
	Text	
	ShowPanels	False

4. Add Listing 8.2 to the form.

5. Change all references to localhost1 to the name of the Web Reference created in step 2.

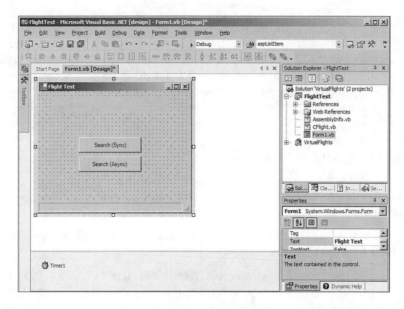

FIGURE 8.1   The consumer form for the sample client.

LISTING 8.2   `Form1.vb` Shows the Code That Will Be Used to Consume the Web Service Asynchronously

```
Private Sub cmdSearchSync_Click(ByVal sender As System.Object, _
                                ByVal e As System.EventArgs) _
                                Handles cmdSearchSync.Click
  Dim FlightNumber As String
  Dim Time As String
  Dim svcFlightSearch As New localhost1.Flights()
  StatusBar1.Text = "Initializing execution..."
  svcFlightSearch.FlightSearch("Point A", "Point B", _
                        "10/12/2001", "12/12/2001", _
                        FlightNumber, Time)
  lblResult.Text = FlightNumber & " at " & Time
  StatusBar1.Text = "Synchronous Execution Completed"
End Sub

 Private Sub cmdSearchAsync_Click(ByVal sender As System.Object, _
                        ByVal e As System.EventArgs) _
                        Handles cmdSearchAsync.Click
  Dim FlightsSvc As New localhost1.Flights()
```

LISTING 8.2   Continued

```
   Dim cb As AsyncCallback
   Dim ar As IAsyncResult

   StatusBar1.Text = "Initializing execution..."
   cb = New AsyncCallback(AddressOf SearchCallback)
   ar = FlightsSvc.BeginFlightSearch("Point A", "Point B", _
                                     "10/12/2001", "12/12/2001", _
                                     Nothing, Nothing, _
                                     cb, FlightsSvc)
   seconds = 0
   Timer1.Enabled = True
 End Sub

Public Sub SearchCallback(ByVal ar As IAsyncResult)
  Dim FlightNumber As String
  Dim Time As String
  Dim FlightSvc As localhost1.Flights
  FlightSvc = ar.AsyncState
  FlightSvc.EndFlightSearch(ar, FlightNumber, Time)
  Timer1.Enabled = False
  StatusBar1.Text = "Async. Execution Completed (" _
                          & seconds.ToString & " second/s)"
  lblResult.Text = FlightNumber & " at " & Time
End Sub

  Private Sub Timer1_Tick(ByVal sender As System.Object, _
                          ByVal e As System.EventArgs) _
                          Handles Timer1.Tick
      seconds = seconds + 1
      StatusBar1.Text = "Executing (" & _
                              seconds.ToString & " second/s)"
  End Sub
```

Before we analyze the code, take a moment to execute the application and click each of the Search buttons. You will notice that each of the Search buttons has a different user experience. As mentioned earlier in this chapter, the synchronous button leaves the user waiting, not knowing what to expect. On the other hand, the asynchronous call allows the application to notify the user of the progress of the process being executed.

cmdSearchSync_Click() is the subroutine used for the synchronous execution of the WebMethod (Lines 7—14). You should be familiar with the code in this method because this call is like many of the other calls seen in earlier chapters of this book.

cmdSearchAsync_Click() is the subroutine used for the synchronous execution of the WebMethod (Lines 15—30).

On line 19, you can see that we declared an AsyncCallback object. This object allows us to declare a Callback function (Line 23) that will receive the results from the Web Service method. Next, an IAsyncResult object is declared. This object is used as the return value for the BeginFlightSearch WebMethod and allows the WebMethod to be executed asynchronously.

Within the call to BeginFlightSearch (Lines 24–27), there are a few important aspects to take note of with respect to the method call. You will notice that the first four parameters correspond with the first four parameters of the FlightSearch WebMethod that appears in Listing 8.1. Next, you will notice that the fifth and sixth parameters were passed in as Nothing. In the Web Service declaration, these parameters (Flight and Time) are declared by reference (ByRef). They are used to return results from the WebMethod.   Since the thread that is executing the BeginFlightSearch will not be continuous, the results can not be returned to the variables directly. The next thing that you will notice is that the last two parameters were not included in the FlightSearch WebMethod listing in Listing 8.1. These parameters are added to the asynchronous methods automatically. The first parameter is a reference to the Callback method, while the second is a reference to the Web Service itself. After the WebMethod has been called, the timer control is enabled and displays an ongoing counter while the method is being executed by the Web Server.

SearchCallBack (Lines 32–42) is the subroutine passed into the BeginFlightSearch call (Lines 24–27). This subroutine will be invoked by the Web Service as soon as the execution has been completed. The AsyncState returned from the IAsyncResult object (Line 36) returns the object that was provided as the last parameter of the BeginFlightSearch call. A final call is then made to the EndFlightSearch method (line 37) to retrieve the results from the asynchronous execution. In addition to the IAsyncResult variable, two additional parameters are passed into the EndFlightSearch method to receive the results of the method's execution. You will notice that apart from the IAsyncResult parameter that is added by the proxy generator, only parameters declared ByRef are returned in the EndFlightSearch method.

To summarize, following are the steps for creating an application that calls a Web Service method asynchronously using the callback mechanism:

1. Create an application from which you want to access a WebMethod asynchronously.

2. Add a Web reference to the Web Service.

3. Implement a callback method.

4. Within the callback method, make a call to the End<*WebServiceMethodName*> method exposed by the proxy. This method will return the results of WebMethod's execution.

5. Within the method that calls the WebMethod, create an AsynCallback object that will act as a wrapper to the callback method.

6. Call the Begin<*WebServiceMethodName*> method exposed by the proxy, passing in the callback method as a parameter.

7. Continue to perform additional operations while waiting for the execution of the WebMethod to complete.

8. After the WebMethod finishes processing and returns the result to the proxy, the proxy will call the callback method.

Using the WaitHandle Methods

An alternative to using a callback function when calling Web Services asynchronously is to use the WaitHandle methods of the IAsyncResult.AsyncWaitHandle class. The WaitHandle methods make it possible to make asynchronous calls and then wait for these calls to complete. When using the WaitHandle class, the client can also specify a timeout. When the timeout is met, the WaitHandle will expire and the application flow will be returned to the thread. The WaitHandle class exposes three different variations, which are listed in Table 8.3.

TABLE 8.3   Possible WaitHandle Methods

Method	Description
WaitHandle.WaitOne	Blocks the current thread until the current WaitHandle receives a signal
WaitHandle.WaitAny	Waits for any of the elements in the specified array to receive a signal
WaitHandle.WaitAll	Waits for all of the elements in the specified array to receive a signal

To make multiple asynchronous calls simultaneously, use either WaitHandle.WaitAny or WaitHandle.WaitAll. If the process should not continue until all of the asynchronous calls have been made, use WaitHandle.WaitAll. This will allow the thread to be blocked while multiple calls are being executed.

If it is enough for only one of the simultaneous calls to be completed or if each returning call should be processed as it returns, use the WaitHandle.WaitAny. The WaitHandle.WaitAny will indicate that a call has completed and will allow the client to identify the call.

To demonstrate this mechanism, we will begin by adding another button and another label to the form.

Add the controls listed in Table 8.4 to the form and set their properties as listed. The resulting form should look similar to Figure 8.2.

TABLE 8.4   Additional Controls and Their Properties for the Consumer Form

Control	Property	Value
Label	Name	lblResult2
Button	Name	cmdSearchAsyncWait
	Text	Async w Wait

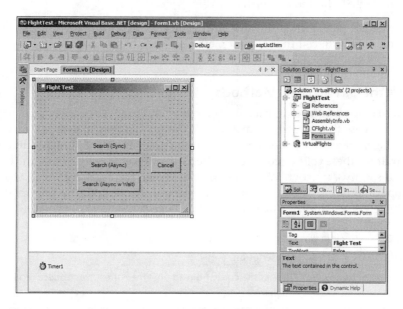

FIGURE 8.2   The consumer form with additional properties.

Double-click the cmdSearchAsyncWait button and add Listing 8.3 to the event's subroutine.

LISTING 8.3   Code that Handles the Click Event of the Command Button cmdSearchAsyncWait

```
Private Sub cmdSearchAsyncWait_Click(ByVal sender As System.Object, _
                                     ByVal e As System.EventArgs) _
                                     Handles cmdSearchAsyncWait.Click
    Dim FlightNumber As String
    Dim Time As String
```

LISTING 8.3 Continued

```
Dim FlightsSvc As New localhost1.Flights()
Dim ar As IAsyncResult
ar = FlightsSvc.BeginFlightSearch("Point A", "Point B", _
                        "10/12/2001", "12/12/2001", _
                        FlightNumber, Time, _
                        Nothing, Nothing)
'Simulate additional work that can be performed concurrently (4 secs)
Dim StartTime As DateTime = DateTime.Now
Dim curTime As DateTime = StartTime
Do While (DateDiff(DateInterval.Second, StartTime, curTime) < 4)
  If curTime < DateTime.Now Then
    curTime = DateTime.Now
    StatusBar1.Text = "Executing Asynchronously (" _
                        & (DateDiff(DateInterval.Second, _
                          StartTime, curTime) _
                          + 1).ToString() _
                        & " second/s)"
  End If
Loop
StatusBar1.Text = "Waiting..."
ar.AsyncWaitHandle.WaitOne()
FlightsSvc.EndFlightSearch(ar, FlightNumber, Time)
lblResult.Text = FlightNumber & " at " & Time
StatusBar1.Text = "Async. Execution Completed"
End Sub
```

You may notice that Listing 8.3 starts very much like the cmdSearchSync method in Listing 8.2. The first difference that can be noticed is within the call to BeginFlightSearch; the last two parameters are passed in as Nothing (Lines 8–11). This is due to the fact that we are not interested in using a callback method in this case. Lines 12–24 demonstrate the ability to perform additional processing while the WebMethod is executing. After the additional processing is completed, the WaitOne method is used to wait for the WebMethod to complete its execution (Line 26). The WaitOne method will block indefinitely until the current instance receives a signal, and will freeze until the execution is completed.

After the WebMethod has completed the execution, the results may be retrieved by using the EndFlightSearch method, much like the SearchCallback method in Listing 8.2.

Run the application to see how this asynchronous mechanism executes.

Evaluating the Length of the Wait

How long should you wait for a WebMethod to return? This is a common question and it has a common answer—it depends. This might sound like an evasive answer, but the truth is that some methods take longer to execute than others. The person that will know best about how long to wait while a WebMethod executes is normally the developer (even though the end user usually is the one with the stopwatch). A common practice would be to execute the WebMethod multiple times with different amounts of data and different loads on the Web Server to see how long the method normally takes to execute. After a decision has been made on the maximum time that the method should be allowed to execute, you can make use of the WaitOne method of the AsyncWaitHandle object to specify how long the wait should be.

An overloaded version of the WaitOne method receives two parameters—timeout and exitContext. The timeout parameter is the number of milliseconds the method should wait for the thread to receive a signal. The exitContext parameter is set to true to ensure that the execution will exit the synchronization domain for the context before the wait (if in a synchronized context) and reacquire it.

To see how we can make use of this technique, we will add the following code to the cmdSearchAsyncWait_Click method that was added in the previous example. Replace the last four lines (excluding the End Sub command) with the code in Listing 8.4.

LISTING 8.4   Code That Handles a Predetermined Wait

```
If ar.AsyncWaitHandle.WaitOne(3000, True) Then
  FlightsSvc.EndFlightSearch(ar, FlightNumber, Time)
  lblResult.Text = FlightNumber & " at " & Time
  StatusBar1.Text = "Async. Execution Completed"
Else
  lblResult.Text = "Please try again at a later time..."
  FlightsSvc.Abort()
  StatusBar1.Text = "Async. Execution Not Completed"
End If
```

In Listing 8.3, Lines 12–24 simulate additional processing with a duration of 4 seconds. In Line 1 of Listing 8.4, a wait of 3 seconds is specified with the WaitOne(3000, True) method call.

You will notice that the duration of the simulation of additional work (4 seconds) and the wait (3 seconds) will exceed the execution time of the WebMethod (5 seconds). However, if you time the execution, you will notice that the execution takes exactly 5 seconds. When the AsyncWaitHandle object receives the execution completed signal, it will no longer wait for the entire timeout period but will continue with the execution of the method.

The `WaitOne` method will return a value of `true` if the current instance receives a signal that the execution has completed. (This is also known as waiting for an object to be *signaled*.) If, by the time the `timeout` expires the method has not received a signal, it will return a value of `false`.

If the method does not complete on time, it is good practice to `Abort` the asynchronous call. By calling the `Abort` method, exposed by the Web Service, the asynchronous call is stopped immediately.

To see what happens when the WebMethod takes longer to execute than the wait, change the `timeout` parameter to 500 milliseconds (equivalent to half a second).

Another variation to Listing 8.4 would be to replace the first line with the following two lines:

```
ar.AsyncWaitHandle.WaitOne(3000, True)
If ar.IsCompleted Then
```

In this code, the `IsCompleted` method is used to verify whether the asynchronous call has been completed. `true` will be returned if the call has been completed; otherwise, `false` will be returned.

To summarize, the following steps create an application that calls a Web Service method asynchronously using the `WaitHandle` mechanism:

1. Create an application from which you want to access a WebMethod asynchronously.

2. Add a Web reference to the Web Service.

3. Create an instance of the proxy object.

4. Create an interface to an `AsyncResult` and call the `Begin<WebServiceMethodName>` method exposed by the proxy, passing in the callback method as a parameter.

5. Continue to perform additional operations while waiting for the execution of the WebMethod to complete.

6. At a point where the results of the WebMethod are required, wait for the execution of the WebMethod to complete by using the `WaitHandle` to halt the processing.

7. After the WebMethod finishes processing and returns the results, make a call to the `End<WebServiceMethodName>` method exposed by the proxy.

Permitting Users to Cancel a Call

Many applications give the end user the power to decide if he or she would like to wait for a process to complete or cancel it. This power is given to the end user by means of a dialog that includes a Cancel button. There are many types of users—some that will use this power wisely and some that are just impatient and get fed up waiting for a process that takes more that a couple of seconds. For both of these types of users, it is very important to supply a clean way to cancel an asynchronous call.

In Listing 8.4, you saw that the FlightsSvc.Abort() command was used to abort a call to a WebMethod after it did not complete in time. The cancellation of a WebMethod by the user is very similar to the way that this is handled. (The timer in this case is in the user's hands.) There is one small difference. To abort an asynchronous WebMethod call, the scope of the variable used to reference the Web Service proxy needs to be changed. The Cancel subroutine needs to share the scope of the variable with the subroutine making the initial asynchronous call. This is so that the Abort call is being made to the same instance of the Web Service as the initial asynchronous call.

To demonstrate this, we will remove the Web Service proxy declaration from the cmdSearch_Click method (Listing 8.2, Line 28), and place it in the declarations section of the form. (It can be placed after line 4.)

Now, add an additional command button to the forms and rename it **cmdCancel**. Change the Text property of the button to **Cancel**. Double-click this new button and add the following to the event's code:

```
Private Sub cmdCancel_Click(ByVal sender As System.Object, _
                          ByVal e As System.EventArgs) _
                          Handles cmdCancel.Click
    FlightsSvc.Abort()
    Timer1.Enabled = False
    StatusBar1.Text = "Execution aborted."
End Sub
```

Run the application and click the Search (Async) button. After a second or two, click the Cancel button. The asynchronous call will be cancelled and the user interface will display the Execution Aborted message.

Another issue that should be dealt with is the end user's ability to close the application at will. This too can cause unpredictable results and should be handled appropriately. In the case of a Windows Application, code that aborts an existing asynchronous call should be added to the form's Closing event handler.

Handling Web Pages That Make Asynchronous Calls to WebMethods

In this section, we will take a look at how a Web Service can be consumed asynchronously by an ASP.NET WebForm.

This scenario is a little different from using Windows Forms, because there is no form resident in memory to catch the callback method when the method executed has completed. To get around this obstacle, we will use a technique that will cause the page to refresh itself and then check to see if any results have been returned. Listing 8.5 contains the HTML that will be used to display the ASP.NET WebForm.

LISTING 8.5   `FlightSearchForm.aspx` Is a Demo Flight Search Page That Calls the Web Service Asynchronously

```
<%@ Page Language="vb" AutoEventWireup="false"
    Codebehind="FlightSearchForm.aspx.vb"
    Inherits="VirtualFlightsWeb.FlightSearchForm"%>
<!DOCTYPE HTML PUBLIC "-//W3C//DTD HTML 4.0 Transitional//EN">
<HTML>
    <HEAD>
        <title>Flight Search Form</title>
        <meta name="GENERATOR" content="Microsoft Visual Studio.NET 7.0"/>
        <meta name="CODE_LANGUAGE" content="Visual Basic 7.0"/>
        <meta name="vs_defaultClientScript" content="JavaScript"/>
        <meta name="vs_targetSchema"
            content=http://schemas.microsoft.com/intellisense/ie5/>
        <meta http-equiv='refresh' content='2'
            visible="false" id="metaTag" runat="server"/>
    </HEAD>
    <body>
        <form runat="server">
            <P align="center">
              <b><asp:Label ID="lblMessage" runat="server" /></b>
              <br><br>
              <asp:Label id="lblMessage2" runat="server" align="center">
                  To perform a search - hit the search button.
              </asp:Label>
              <br><br>
              <asp:Button ID="cmdsearch" Text="Search" Runat="server"/>
            </p>
        </form>
    </body>
</HTML>
```

Most of Listing 8.5 should be quite familiar to you. On lines 13–14, a <meta> tag is
defined to instruct the browser to refresh the page contents at a predefined interval.
In this case, the refresh rate has been set to 2 seconds. The <meta> tag has been
defined as a server control so that the tag's visible status can be changed programmatically. By default, the tag's visible status will be set to `false` because, until a
search has been executed, there is no reason to refresh the browser.

LISTING 8.6   FlightSearchForm.aspx.vb Shows the Code Behind Listing 8.5
(FlightSearchForm.aspx)

```
01: Imports System.Web.UI
02:
03: Public Class FlightSearchForm
04:     Inherits System.Web.UI.Page
05:
06:     Protected WithEvents lblMessage As WebControls.Label
07:     Protected WithEvents lblMessage2 As WebControls.Label
08:     Protected WithEvents cmdsearch As System.Web.UI.WebControls.Button
09:     Protected WithEvents metaTag As HtmlControls.HtmlGenericControl
10:
11:     Private Sub Page_Load(ByVal sender As System.Object, _
12:                         ByVal e As System.EventArgs) Handles MyBase.Load
13:     ' Checking is a search is currently in progress for this session
14:     If Not Session("SearchInProgress") Is Nothing Then
15:       'Checking if a result has yet to be returned
16:       If Session("Result") Is Nothing Then
17:         lblMessage.Text = "Still waiting...(" & _
18:                         DateDiff(DateInterval.Second, _
19:                                 Session("SearchInProgress"), _
20:                                 DateTime.Now) & _
21:                         " second/s)"
22:         lblMessage2.Visible = False
23:         'Enabling the refresh meta tag
24:         metaTag.Visible = True
25:       Else 'A result has been returned
26:         'No more need for browser refresh
27:         metaTag.Visible = False
28:         Try
29:           Dim FlightNumber As String
30:           Dim Time As String
31:           Dim FlightsSvc As New localhost.Flights()
32:           Dim ar As IAsyncResult
33:           'Retrieving the Asynchronous Result object
```

LISTING 8.6 Continued

```
34:          ar = Session("Result")
35:          FlightsSvc.EndFlightSearch(ar, FlightNumber, Time)
36:          lblMessage.Text = FlightNumber & " at " & Time
37:          Session("SearchInProgress") = Nothing
38:          Session("Result") = Nothing
39:        Catch ex As Exception
40:          lblMessage.Text = "Still searching..."
41:        End Try
42:      End If
43:    End If
44:  End Sub
45:
46:  Protected Sub SearchCallback(ByVal ar As IAsyncResult)
47:    Session("Result") = ar
48:  End Sub
49:
50:  Private Sub cmdSearch_Click(ByVal sender As Object, _
51:                        ByVal e As System.EventArgs) Handles cmdsearch.Click
52:    metaTag.Visible = True
53:    If Session("SearchInProgress") Is Nothing Then
54:      lblMessage.Text = "Searching..."
55:      Dim FlightsSvc As New localhost.Flights()
56:      Dim cb As AsyncCallback
57:      Dim ar As IAsyncResult
58:      cb = New AsyncCallback(AddressOf SearchCallback)
59:      ar = FlightsSvc.BeginFlightSearch("Point A", "Point B", _
60:                                "10/12/2001", "12/12/2001", _
61:                                Nothing, Nothing, _
62:                                cb, FlightsSvc)
63:      Session("SearchInProgress") = DateTime.Now
64:      lblMessage2.Visible = False
65:    End If
66:  End Sub
67: End Class
```

Lines 11–44 contain the Page_Load event subroutine. Depending on the current status, different blocks of code will be executed. The first check (Line 14) is made is to see if a search is in progress. If a search is not in progress, the page will load without performing any actions. If a search is in progress, a second check will be made (Line 16) to see if there is a result in the `Session` object. If no result is available, a message will be displayed to the user explaining that the system is still waiting for a response; the time lapsed since the execution of the search will also be displayed (Lines 17–22). The `<meta>` tag that deals with the browser refresh rate is set to visible, thus making sure that the browser will refresh itself at the appropriate moment (Line 24).

If a result is received, the block dealing with the result will be executed (Lines 25–42). The first action that is performed is that the `<meta>` tag that deals with the browser refresh rate is set to invisible (Line 27) and the results are retrieved from the `EndFlightSearch` method (Lines 34–25). The results are then displayed to the user and the various `Session` objects are cleared (Lines 37–28).

Lines 46–48 contain `SearchCallback`, which is the customary callback method for the WebForm.

Lines 50–66 contain the `cmdSearch_Click` event subroutine. This event is triggered when the user clicks the Search button on the form. The first action that takes place is that the `<meta>` tag that deals with the browser refresh rate is set to visible. A check is performed to see if a search is already in progress (Line 53). If no search is in progress, a search is executed, and the `SearchCallback` method is specified as the `Callback` method. The `SearchInProgress` key in the `Session` object is set to the current time (Line 63).

Server to Server Asynchronous Communications

Sometimes the time between request and response will be really long. The processing may take a long time, a person may need to do some work before returning a result, or it just might not make sense to wait until the call completes. For example, when placing a purchase order, the client may only care that the order was received. Later, the server can notify the client of the following events:

- Payment processed

- Order being processed

- Order shipped

- Changes in order location up through delivery

These changes may happen over several days, making it difficult to keep any connections alive. Instead of keeping a connection alive, why not send the request and response over independent connections? To do this, both ends of the SOAP message exchange need to be able to listen for another computer initiating a connection. The other requirement is that the server needs to know what the response message should look like.

In general, you will need to have a SOAP server on each end. Each server implements a different Web Service. When a request goes out, the client sends a one-way message to the server. The message should have at least two pieces of information associated through method arguments or SOAP Header information—the URL to send the response to and an identifier that the client can use to match the response with the original request. The identifier is very important to have, because the client may send several messages before the server gets around to responding. The client needs to implement a Web Service interface with which the server knows how to work. The way of doing this that makes the most sense to me is to have the server define that interface and require clients to implement the interface.

Because the time between request and response may be great, it may make sense for the actual Web Service to store the essential data from the requests for processing by a client-side or server-side application. Why would you do this? On the server side, if the transaction is long lived, you do not want to tie up the Web endpoint while it processes the request. Instead of launching thread in IIS, you may be better off processing the request in another process.

For the client side, the client that issued the request may not be active when the response comes back. Here again, the Web Service handling the response should store the results in a place where the client will know to look.

Because we have given a brief overview of when you would want to implement a Web Service capable of returning results later and viewed a few of the requirements for what the server and client would need to do, let's look at an example—the "Hello World" of disconnected asynchronous processing.

This application consists of two Web Services—a console application and a WinForm application. You can obtain the source for these applications from the companion Web site. The applications live in the following projects:

- Client Web Service: `Server1`
- Server Web Service: `Server2`
- Client Application: `ServiceClient`
- Server Application: `ServiceProcessor`

To run the example, you will need to have Microsoft Message Queue installed. We will start with the server Web Service.

Server Web Service

The Server Web Service is implemented by the `RequestService` class. This class has one `Sub`, `HelloWorld`. `HelloWorld` takes a unique identifier and a URL to which to send the response. It stores this information in a queue for the console application to process at a later time. Listing 8.7 shows this class in detail.

LISTING 8.7   The RequestService Class (Server2\RequestService.asmx.vb)

```
1:  Imports System.Web.Services
2:  Imports System.Web.Services.Protocols
3:  Imports System.Messaging
4:
5:  <WebService(Namespace:= _
6:      "http://scottseely.com/Request/RequestService.asmx"), _
7:   SoapDocumentService()> _
8:  Public Class RequestService
9:      Inherits System.Web.Services.WebService
10:
11:     ' The name of the queue that this Web Service reads.
12:     Private Const QUEUE_NAME As String = _
13:         ".\Private$\Ch8HelloWorldRequest"
14:
15:     <WebMethod(), _
16:         SoapDocumentMethod(OneWay:=True)> _
17:     Public Sub HelloWorld(ByVal theGUID As Guid, _
18:         ByVal theURL As String)
19:         Dim theQueue As MessageQueue
20:
21:         ' Open up the request queue and place the
22:         ' notification there. The client application knows
23:         ' to listen on that endpoint.
24:         If Not (MessageQueue.Exists(QUEUE_NAME)) Then
25:             theQueue = MessageQueue.Create(QUEUE_NAME)
26:         Else
27:             theQueue = New MessageQueue(QUEUE_NAME)
28:         End If
29:
30:         theQueue.Send(theURL, theGUID.ToString())
31:         theQueue.Close()
32:
33:     End Sub
34:
35: End Class
```

The HelloWorld Web Method is designed to not return a response. Line 16 instructs .NET that any callers should not to wait for a response. When WSDL is generated, the operation element will only contain an input member. This also tells the underlying framework to close the connection after the request is received and not to return anything back to the client. When the request has been received, all information pertaining to the request is saved in a private queue. The actual work will occur in the console application. If you are following this model, you will want to do something similar and store the data for the method call for another application to process.

Lines 17 and 18 of listing 8.7 show the Web Service taking two string values as arguments. The first value, theGUID, is stored for later use in mapping the result to the original request. The second value, theURL, tells the server where to send any response. For a simple example or intranet application, this is good enough. The sender can be trusted and worries about abuse are fairly low.

If this same approach is used to give external clients access to the Web Service, the Web Method should do some extra work before having any work done for the message. To do this, you could make sure that the caller and the host name in the response URL mapped to the same computer. If mapping to one computer does not make sense, because the client could be behind a firewall and have its address obscured or because of deployment issues, such as many clients using one Web Server to store responses, the preceding verification would not be a good option. Instead, the server could maintain a list of clients that it will respond to in a database, configuration file, or other location. When a request comes in, the response URL would be validated against that table. This solution could be expanded to map client address ranges to specific response URLs. It would also mean that the server could throw away any requests not coming from a valid IP address. To work, this type of validation would have to be set up before the client accessed the Web Service.

Client Web Service

Before covering the console application that processes a request, I would like to show the Web Service that handles any responses. The Web Service "client" implements a class named ResponseService. ResponseService is almost an exact copy of the RequestService class. The main differences are that the second parameter contains a result instead of a URL, and the response is stored to a different queue.

LISTING 8.8   The ResponseService Class (Server1\ResponseService.asmx.vb)

```vb
 1: Imports System.Web.Services
 2: Imports System.Web.Services.Protocols
 3: Imports System.Messaging
 4:
 5: <WebService(Namespace:= _
 6:     "http://scottseely.com/Response/ResponseService.asmx"), _
 7:   SoapDocumentService()> _
 8: Public Class ResponseService
 9:     Inherits System.Web.Services.WebService
10:
11:     ' The name of the queue that this Web Service reads.
12:     Private Const QUEUE_NAME As String = _
13:         ".\Private$\Ch8HelloWorldResponse"
14:
15:     <WebMethod(), _
16:         SoapDocumentMethod(OneWay:=True)> _
17:     Public Sub ReturnHelloWorld(ByVal theGUID As Guid, _
18:         ByVal theResponse As String)
19:
20:         ' Open up the response queue and place the
21:         ' notification there. The client application knows
22:         ' to listen on that endpoint.
23:         Dim theQueue As MessageQueue
24:         If Not (MessageQueue.Exists(QUEUE_NAME)) Then
25:             theQueue = MessageQueue.Create(QUEUE_NAME)
26:         Else
27:             theQueue = New MessageQueue(QUEUE_NAME)
28:         End If
29:
30:         theQueue.Send(theResponse, theGUID.ToString())
31:         theQueue.Close()
32:
33:     End Sub
34:
35: End Class
```

Like the server-side Web Service, this Web Method supports one-way messaging. It uses the GUID in the return message as a way to map the original request to the response. Because the response sits in a queue, the client can process the message when it is ready.

Console Application

The console application reads the messages from the request queue and responds to each request. In a production environment, this application probably would be written as a Windows Service. In this example, I use a console application so that I can easily show what is happening to the user. Listing 8.9 shows the complete listing for the server-side message handler. In lines 18–27, the application handles initialization. After that little bit of works is complete, the application sits and waits for messages to arrive. Message processing happens between lines 30 and 61. The console blocks on line 38 wait for messages to arrive. When a message does arrive, the application simulates work by waiting five seconds on line 44 before sending the response to the client Web Service. The wait is important if you are running the client and the server at the same time. When the wait is absent, the response comes back immediately and more or less ruins the effect of the sample. If you want to see the quick turnaround, just comment out line 44 and re-run the example on your machine.

LISTING 8.9   The Module1 Class (ServiceProcessor\Module1.vb)

```
 1: Imports System.Messaging
 2:
 3: Module Module1
 4:
 5:     ' The name of the queue the app reads from
 6:     Private Const QUEUE_NAME As String = _
 7:         ".\Private$\Ch8HelloWorldRequest"
 8:
 9:     Sub Main()
10:         Dim theQueue As MessageQueue
11:         Dim theMsg As Message
12:         Dim svc As New localhost.ResponseService()
13:         Dim theResponse As String
14:         Dim theBody As Object
15:
16:         ' If the queue exists, create it. Otherwise,
17:         ' simply open it.
18:         If Not (MessageQueue.Exists(QUEUE_NAME)) Then
19:             theQueue = MessageQueue.Create(QUEUE_NAME)
20:         Else
21:             theQueue = New MessageQueue(QUEUE_NAME)
22:         End If
23:
24:         ' Tell the queue object how to read data
25:         ' out and what it should place the type into.
```

LISTING 8.9   Continued

```
26:            theQueue.Formatter = New XmlMessageFormatter(New Type() _
27:                    {GetType([String])})
28:
29:        ' Run forever.
30:        While True
31:
32:            Try
33:                ' Tell the user how to quit
34:                Console.WriteLine("Press CTRL-C to stop listening")
35:
36:                ' Wait synchronously for the next message in the
37:                ' queue.
38:                theMsg = theQueue.Receive()
39:
40:                ' Read the body in as a string.
41:                theBody = CType(theMsg.Body, [String])
42:
43:                ' Simulate work
44:                System.Threading.Thread.Sleep(5000)
45:
46:                ' Create the response and send it to the
47:                ' client's Web Service.
48:                svc.Url = theBody.ToString()
49:                theResponse = "Message returned at " & _
50:                    DateTime.Now.ToString()
51:                svc.ReturnHelloWorld(New Guid(theMsg.Label), _
52:                    _theResponse)
53:            Catch ex As Exception
54:                ' The Url probably did not work.
55:                Console.WriteLine(ex.ToString())
56:            End Try
57:            ' Show the user that something happened on
58:            ' this end.
59:            Console.WriteLine("Just processed " & theMsg.Label & _
60:                vbCrLf & theBody.ToString())
61:        End While
62:        theQueue.Close()
63:    End Sub
64:
65: End Module
```

Lines 59 and 60 send some output to the console. In particular, they print the GUID that was just processed and the destination URL. The output for one message exchange is shown in Figure 8.3

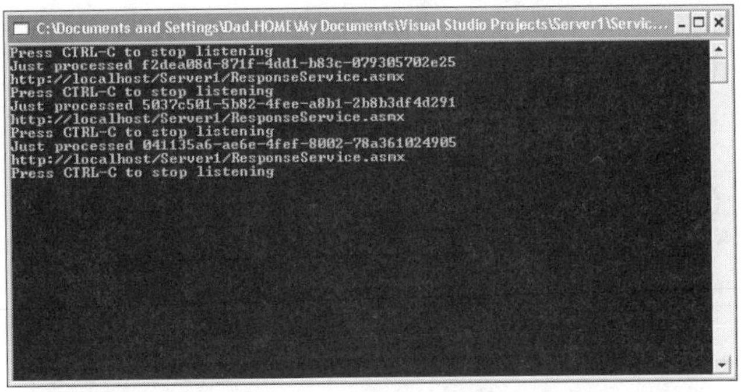

FIGURE 8.3   Figure 8.3 console application processing three messages from the client.

While testing this console application, I tried filling the queue up with hundreds of messages before running the console. After seeing how slow the processing was going, I decided to try running several instances of the console application. Of course, the request queue started shrinking faster and faster. Due to the highly disconnected nature of this architecture, its use gives a developer great scalability options. If the machines processing messages read from a common queue or other data source, it should be pretty easy to scale out by adding extra hardware as needed whenever request levels exceed the capabilities of the current hardware. Yes, this is something that queues allow for, and I thought it was pretty neat that even this simple example can show the benefit.

WinForm Application

The WinForm application sends all requests and processes all responses. Listing 8.10 shows the code that does all the work for the WinForm. The form sends requests whenever its button is clicked. The request itself is pretty simple. On lines 10 and 11, HelloWorld is called and a new Guid is created. In a real world implementation, the Guid would be saved somewhere to map the request message to the response message.

Every second, a timer event occurs. When that happens, the response queue is opened and the code checks to see if any responses are in the queue. Lines 43–47 peek into the queue and check if any messages are waiting. When a message is found, the code pulls the response out and displays the Guid and response message in a list box.

LISTING 8.10   The WinForm Client (ServiceClient\Form1.vb)

```vb
1:  ' The name of the queue we check for messages.
2:  Private Const QUEUE_NAME As String = _
3:      ".\Private$\Ch8HelloWorldResponse"
4:
5:  Private Sub Button1_Click(ByVal sender As System.Object, _
6:      ByVal e As System.EventArgs) Handles btnSendRequest.Click
7:
8:      ' Execute the "HelloWorld" of inter-endpoint async
9:      Dim svc As New WindowsApplication1.localhost.RequestService()
10:     svc.HelloWorld(Guid.NewGuid(), _
11:         "http://localhost/Server1/ResponseService.asmx")
12:
13:     ' Let the user that the message went out already.
14:     MsgBox("Test Succeeded", 0, Nothing)
15:
16: End Sub
17:
18: Private Sub tmrCheckQueue_Tick(ByVal sender As System.Object, _
19:     ByVal e As System.EventArgs) Handles tmrCheckQueue.Tick
20:
21:     ' Stop the timer while handling this event
22:     tmrCheckQueue.Enabled = False
23:     Dim theQueue As MessageQueue
24:     Dim theMsg As Message
25:     Dim waitTime As New TimeSpan(100)
26:
27:     ' Check the queue. If it doesn't exist,
28:     ' create it.
29:     If Not (MessageQueue.Exists(QUEUE_NAME)) Then
30:         theQueue = MessageQueue.Create(QUEUE_NAME)
31:     Else
32:         theQueue = New MessageQueue(QUEUE_NAME)
33:     End If
34:
35:     ' Tell the queue how to read values
36:     theQueue.Formatter = New XmlMessageFormatter(New Type() _
37:         {GetType([String])})
38:
39:     Try
40:         ' If any messages are in the queue, read them
41:         ' and place the body text in the Response
```

LISTING 8.10   Continued

```
42:              ' listbox.
43:              While Not (theQueue.Peek(waitTime) Is Nothing)
44:                  theMsg = theQueue.Receive()
45:                  Me.lbResponses.Items.Add("GUID: " & theMsg.Label & _
46:                      " " & CType(theMsg.Body, [String]))
47:              End While
48:          Catch ex As MessageQueueException
49:              ' This is expected whenever no messages are
50:              ' sitting in the queue.
51:          End Try
52:
53:          ' Close the queue.
54:          theQueue.Close()
55:          tmrCheckQueue.Enabled = True
56:  End Sub
```

Figure 8.4 shows the client application after reading the responses generated when Figure 8.3 was captured. Visually, you can match the request and response messages.

In situations where the client and the server can both host a Web Service and when a near term response is not needed, you can achieve asynchronous messaging by using pairs of one-way messages. When using this model, it seems to work best when the Web Service stores the request for another application to process. Likewise, the client needs to have a Web Service that can listen for responses. Then, the client can periodically check to see results have returned. The server needs to cooperate by persisting the unique identifier and by being able to use the client-side Web Service. The client-side identifier only needs to be unique enough. A monotonically increasing number would work just as well as a GUID. The example used a GUID only because it is globally unique, limiting the probability of a mismatched request/response pair.

Summary

Asynchronous calls should be used when a synchronous call would leave an application waiting for an extended amount of time. The .NET Framework allows Web Services to be called asynchronously without any additional work on the part of the Web Service developers. Web Services can be called asynchronously while specifying a callback method to be executed when the asynchronous call completes, or the application can "wait" for the execution to complete. The consumer of the Web

Service can decide how long to wait for an asynchronous Web Service method to complete execution and whether to cancel the execution. If the response may take a long time to return, the request and response can be completely disconnected. In this situation, both the client and the server need to implement a Web Service and provide a mechanism to map requests and responses.

9

Stateful Services

A stateful service is a Web Service that maintains data
between WebMethod calls. Application state may include
any piece of information that is required by the application to be stored and possibly recovered at a later stage.
This information could be any of the following: user
options, hit counts, shopping carts, catalogs, and any
other of data that the application might need for the
successful execution of its workflow.

State management for ASP.NET Web Services have the
exact same options as those available for other ASP.NET
applications. As long as the implementation of the Web
Service derives from the WebService class, the application
will have access to some of the common objects that any
ASP.NET application has. These objects include the Session
and Application objects.

This chapter will focus on the issue of maintaining state
and the benefits of doing so. In particular, two important
benefits of maintaining state are preventing unnecessary
roundtrips to the server and keeping turn-around time to a
minimum. We will examine three techniques for maintaining state—The Session object, the Application object, and
the Cache object.

Benefits of Maintaining State: Performance and Scalability

As a Web Application's user community grows, there is an ever-growing amount of stress placed on the Web Server as it attempts to accommodate this larger volume of calls. As more stress is placed on a Web server, the performance will take a hit. A slow Web Service, like a slow Web site, will not only waste expensive company resources, but it can potentially drive customers away, causing even greater losses. When you design and implement a high-performance Web Service, it is extremely important to carry out performance tuning. There is no set recipe for improving the scalability or the performance of a Web Service. Some tweaking may need to be performed in various places within the Web Service. The balance between scalability and performance can be delicate, which is why the term *performance tuning* is so appropriate.

The following are some of the important goals that should be taken into account:

- *Conserving CPU cycles*—Keep the volume of operations performed by the Web server hosting the Web Service to a minimum.

- *Conserving time*—Keep turn-around time on the Web server to a minimum by reducing the number of calls to the database. Also, make sure that the code is optimized and performs well.

- *Conserving resources*—Keep the amount of reserved memory on the Web server to a minimum.

As you may have noticed from the previous list, performance tuning is almost like nature preservation (conserve, conserve, conserve...)—the more we save, the better it is for humankind! Unlike nature preservation (where the more you do for the environment, the better it is), when dealing with improving the scalability and the performance of a Web Service, we need to find an optimal point and stop there. This is due to the fact that scalability and performance go hand-in-hand for most of the time, but there are times when this is not the case. Improving performance will almost always improve scalability, but the reverse is not always true—sometimes, improving scalability can have a negative effect on performance.

Improving Performance

A typical application receives data from a back-end system, manipulates that data, and then presents it to the user. Regardless of the speed of a database server, retrieving data from memory will always be much faster than retrieving from a database. Performance can be improved by caching frequently used data on the Web server. This can either be in memory or on disk. You can think of caching as a space-versus-time tradeoff. If the correct data is cached, there will definitely be a performance gain. If too much data is cached, a performance gain is not guaranteed; sometimes the exact opposite could occur because too many resources have been allocated for caching.

Enhancing Scalability

Scalability can be enhanced by making sure that the application can handle an ever-growing user community. So how can state management help to enhance scalability? Instead of making calls to a database every time, you should develop your applications such that frequently used information is retrieved from cache. This would improve the performance by reducing the time needed to retrieve the data. If a method call's performance is improved, the Web Service can serve more users in less time and, as a result, scalability has been improved too. Figure 9.1 contrasts the data retrieval time for uncached and cached data.

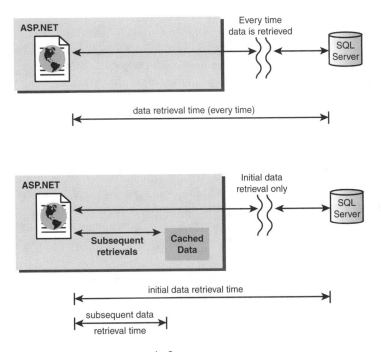

FIGURE 9.1   To cache or not to cache?

Of course, we should not oversimplify the relationship between scalability and performance. Take for example an application that caches 50KB of data per user. If the application has 10 users, almost half a megabyte of memory is reserved for this cache. Now consider 1000 concurrent users using that same application; the cost will be almost 50MB of reserved memory! Of course, with the price of memory today, more and more memory can be "thrown" at a single server. This example is intended to demonstrate the effect that an increasing number of users and their maintained state have on the server's available memory.

The outcome of this would be reduced performance and eventual crash of the Web server.

Although each one of the conservation measures mentioned previously should be weighed according to the nature of the Web Service, we will not discuss them all here. This chapter will focus on two of the important issues—preventing unnecessary roundtrips to the server and keeping turn-around time to a minimum. One of the ways of preventing roundtrips to a server, for example an application server or a database server, is to maintain state on the Web Server.

Facilitating Web Farms

To accommodate a growing number of users and give each one a satisfactory level of responsiveness, the Web application needs to be scalable. One method of scaling a Web application is to throw additional hardware at the problem.

For example, one solution is to upgrade the Web Server to a computer with a faster CPU or multiple CPUs. This solution, known as *scaling-up*, will provide a new computer that will have the ability to handle a larger number of requests. At some point, this solution will become extremely expensive.

Another hardware solution is to add new processors spread across multiple machines, thereby dividing the workload among multiple machines. This solution is known as *scaling-out* and, at a certain point, becomes much more cost-effective. In actual fact, what this solution creates is a *Web Farm*. A Web Farm consists of a number of Web Servers that are situated on a number of machines with the same Web Application residing on each Web Server.

One of the issues that was a big problem with state management and scalability when the Web Server needed to be scaled out was if state is managed on the same Web Server as the Web Service (or page) being requested, a problem might occur the next time a Web Service is requested. There is a good chance that the next request to a Web Service or even the same Web Service may not be hosted by the same machine as the previous request. This would mean that the state that was maintained in the previous request would not necessarily be available for the current request. Later in this chapter, in the "Using the ASP.NET State Service" section, we will see what functionality has been added to ASP.NET to allow us to successfully manage state in a Web farm.

Maintaining State with the Session Object

The Session object provides a mechanism that allows data to be stored on a per-client basis. Before delving into how to use the Session object, you need to understand the concept of a session state.

ASP.NET Session State

What is a session? A session is a period of time during which a unique user interacts with a Web Server. Session state is the ability to retain data for this unique user during the session.

The Session object is very similar to a hash table, in that it stores data in key-value pairs. Data stored in the Session object can be retrieved for a predetermined amount of time.

The following is the syntax used to store data in the Session object:

```
Session("Key") = Value
```

The following is the syntax used to retrieve data from the application object:

```
Value = Session("Key")
```

Session state is managed individually for each active ASP.NET session. The session state can be maintained either in memory, in the memory of a remote server, or in an SQL Server database.

The session state is identified and tracked by means of a 120-bit SessionID. This SessionID is generated using an algorithm that guarantees uniqueness so that there cannot be more than one ASP.NET session with the same SessionID, thus preventing collisions. The same algorithm is responsible for guaranteeing that the SessionID is created randomly, making it more difficult for malicious users to attempt to calculate an existing session's SessionID.

The SessionID is transmitted as part of the Web requests. Depending on the type of application, the SessionID is transmitted either by using an HTTP cookie or by modifying a URL.

Choosing which session state provider to use is a serious decision. The four distinct ways to store session state for an application are in-process session state, out-of-process session state with ASP.NET State Service, out-of-process session state in an SQL database, and out-of-process session state as a Web Service. Each of these has advantages and disadvantages. In-process session state is the fastest solution, but cannot be used for Web farms. Out-of-process session state solutions are better suited for scaling an application across multiple processors or multiple computers. Out-of-process session state should be used when the data being processed cannot be lost in the case of a server or a process being restarted.

Before considering these methods in more detail and getting our hands dirty with some implementations of session state, let's take a look at how session state is configured.

Like most other Web application configuration settings, ASP.NET Session State settings are configured through the ASP.NET XML configuration file web.config.

The following is the default sessionState element used to configure the session state setting from within the web.config file:

```
<sessionState
  mode="InProc"
  cookieless="false"
  timeout="20"
  stateConnectionString="tcpip=127.0.0.1:42424"
  sqlConnectionString="data source=127.0.0.1;user id=sa;password="
/>
```

Let's take a look at each of the attributes that appear in the sessionState element.

The mode attribute specifies where to store the session state data; mode is the only mandatory attribute.

There are four possible settings for the mode attribute:

- Off   Indicates that session state is not enabled

- InProc   Indicates that session state is stored locally

- StateServer   Indicates that session state is stored on a remote server

- SQLServer   Indicates that session state is stored on the SQL Server

The mode options will be discussed in more detail throughout this chapter.

The cookieless attribute is a Boolean value that specifies whether sessions without cookies should be used to identify client sessions. A value of true indicates that sessions without cookies should be used. The default value, false, indicates that sessions without cookies should not be used.

The timeout attribute specifies the number of minutes a session can be idle before it is abandoned. The default value is 20.

The `stateConnectionString` attribute specifies the server name and port where the session state is stored remotely. The default setting is `tcpip=127.0.0.1:42424`. This attribute is required only when the `mode` attribute is set to `StateServer`.

Finally, the `sqlConnectionString` attribute specifies the connection string for a SQL Server database. The default setting is `data source=127.0.0.1;user id=sa; password=`. This attribute is required only when the `mode` attribute is set to `SQLServer`.

In-Process Session State

The in-process mode is the default setting for ASP.NET (see Figure 9.2). In-process session state is, as the name suggests, managed within the ASP.NET process. This means that if the ASP.NET process is recycled, any data stored in session state is lost.

FIGURE 9.2   When you use in-process session state management, the State Manager runs as part of the ASP.NET process.

Why use in-process, if there are other settings that are available and will give better reliability? The most important reason for using in-process is performance. Because in-process session state is managed locally, it will be much faster to read from and write to than the other available options. The other options will normally entail cross-process calls that take significantly longer to process. In-process state maintenance cannot be used with Web Farms because the state will be managed on a specific instance of Microsoft Internet Information Service (IIS). Each additional request made to the Web Service will not necessarily be made to the same instance of IIS, therefore the state may not exist there.

To see how the `Session` object is used within a Web Service, we will create a simple Web Service that uses the `Session` object to store the number of searches that users have performed on specific criteria. To simplify this example, the return value of the `WebMethod` will be the search count.

Create a new ASP.NET Web Service project. In the Solution Explorer, select `Service1.asmx` and rename it **`StatefulService.asmx`**. Expand the `StatefulService.asmx` node and open the `StatefulService.asmx.vb` file for editing. Add the following code to the `StatefulService.asmx.vb` file:

```
<WebMethod(EnableSession:=True)> _
Public Function UserSearch(ByVal Criteria As String) As Integer
    If Session(Criteria) Is Nothing Then
```

```
            Session(Criteria) = 1
        Else
            Session(Criteria) = CInt(Session(Criteria)) + 1
        End If
        UserSearch = CInt(Session(Criteria))
    End Function
```

This `WebMethod` is very similar to the other implementations that you have seen up
to now. The only difference that you may have noticed is that a new property,
`EnableSession`, has been added to the `WebMethod` attribute. Setting this property to
true is necessary to enable storage and retrieval of data stored in the session state.

The method starts off by checking whether a variable, with a key identical to criteria
that was passed into the `WebMethod`, has already been stored in the `Session` object
(Line 3). Based on the outcome, the method either initializes the variable with the
value of 1 or increments that variable by 1.

Let's take a look at how state is maintained by executing this sample Web Service. To
do this, open a Web browser and set the URL to point to the `StatefulService.asmx`
file. Select the `UserSearch` WebMethod by clicking the UserSearch link at the top of
the page. The Test interface should now appear. Enter a value for the Criteria and
click the Invoke button.

A new browser should open up to produce the results of the `WebMethod` call.

Now click the Refresh button to execute the `WebMethod` again. You will notice that
the result has been incremented by one.

To get a picture of how the call would be made from other environments, such as a
Win32 application or another Web Service, we will make a small modification to the
`Web.config` file. In the `sessionState` element, change the `cookieless` attributes
value to true. The following code shows the settings:

```
<sessionState
  mode="InProc"
  cookieless="true"
  timeout="20"
  stateConnectionString="tcpip=127.0.0.1:42424"
  sqlConnectionString="data source=127.0.0.1;user id=sa;password="
/>
```

Close the browser with the `WebMethod` results. Now click the Invoke button within
the browser that shows the `WebMethod`'s test interface. The window should look
similar to Figure 9.3. Notice that the `SessionID` is displayed within the URL.

FIGURE 9.3   The results returned from the *UserSearch WebMethod*.

As an introduction to the next section, open up a command prompt and type the following line:

```
iireset
```

After the Internet Information Services have been restarted, go back to the browser displaying the results from the *UserSearch WebMethod*'s execution. Click the Refresh button again.

It would seem that we are back to "square one." What you have just done is simulate the recycling of the ASP.NET process. As you have noticed, all session state has been erased.

Out-of-Process Session State

The new out-of-process state management option in ASP.NET exists in two variations:

- Out-of-process state management with the ASP.NET State Service

- Out-of-process state management with SQL Server

We will begin by introducing the new ASP.NET State Service and continue later to the SQL Server implementation.

Using the ASP.NET State Service

The ASP.NET State Server is implemented by the new ASPState Service, included in the .NET Framework. Because this is a Windows NT service, this option will only be available on the Windows NT-based operating systems (Windows NT 4.0, Windows 2000 and Windows XP). Figure 9.4 shows how the State Manager exists in a separate process when using the ASP.NET State Server.

To use the ASP.NET State Service for out-of-process state management, the service must be running. If the service is not running, it can be started by opening up the Settings Microsoft Management Console, right-click the ASP.NET State Service, and select Start from the pop-up menu. Figure 9.5 demonstrates how the ASP.NET State Service can be started.

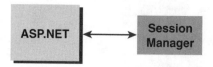

FIGURE 9.4   When used with ASP.NET State Server, State Manager runs as a separate process.

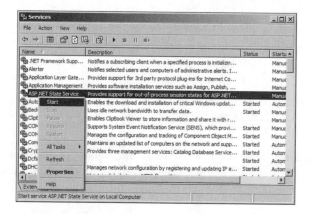

FIGURE 9.5   Starting the ASP.NET State Service.

Another way to start the service is to open a command prompt and type the following:

```
net start aspnet_state
```

NOTE

If you use the ASP.NET State Service for state management, it is advisable to set the startup parameter for the service to automatic.

After the ASP.NET State Server has been activated, the Web application needs to be configured to take advantage of this option. Again, configuring the Web application to use this option will be performed by editing the web.config file. The following code shows the settings:

```
<sessionState
  mode="StateServer"
  cookieless="true"
```

```
    timeout="20"
    stateConnectionString="tcpip=127.0.0.1:42424"
    sqlConnectionString="data source=127.0.0.1;user id=sa;password="
/>
```

Only two changes need to be made from the default settings, thus moving from in-process to out-of-process state management. The mode attribute needs to be changed to StateServer and the stateConnectionString needs to be configured. Note that the stateConnectionString attribute is made up of three parts. The syntax is in the following format:

stateConnectionString="<protocol>=<server>:<port>"

At the time of this book's publication, the only known value for *protocol* is tcpip. *Server* indicates the name or IP address of the server that will act as the state management server, and the value of *port* is the port number to be used.

The value of the stateConnectionString specifies the local server.

Again, we will take a look at how state is maintained by executing the sample Web Service just as we did in the previous section. Open a Web browser and test the UserSearch WebMethod again.

As you did before, click the Refresh button a few times and you will notice that after each click, the result is incremented by one. Now, restart the Internet Information Services. Once again, click the Refresh button in the Web browser. Notice that the state is maintained, even though the ASP.NET process has been recycled.

There is, of course, a downfall to this mechanism. If the machine hosting the Session Manager becomes unavailable, or worse, is restarted, all session state is lost. This brings us to the next option, out-of-process state management with SQL Server.

Using SQL Server
Out-of-process state management with SQL Server is very similar to out-of-process state management with the ASP.NET State Server, except that it is even more robust. When using the previous mechanism (ASP.NET State Service in StateServer mode), the session state is stored in memory on the designated machine. When using the ASP.NET State Service in SQLServer mode, the state is maintained in a database. If the server with ASP.NET State Service mode set to StateServer is restarted, all state is lost. On the other hand, when using the SQLServer mode, even if the server hosting the SQL Server in which the state is being maintained is restarted, the state will be retained. When the server becomes available again, the state will be available again. Figure 9.6 displays the process boundaries that exist when using the SQLServer mode.

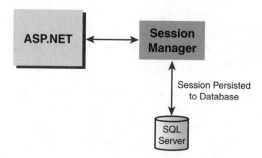

FIGURE 9.6   When used with SQL Server, ASP.NET state management not only runs as a separate process but is persisted to the database.

Configuring ASP.NET to manage state with SQL Server requires two steps. The first step is a setup procedure that needs to be performed only once. The second step entails making two minor changes to the web.config file.

To manage session state by using SQL Server, the necessary tables and stored procedures need to be created. ASP.NET will use the stored procedures to persist state into the tables. The .NET Framework SDK includes an SQL script that will create all of the SQL Server objects needed to perform this task.

The SQL script file is named InstallSqlState.sql and is found in the [system drive]\winnt\Microsoft.NET\Framework\[version]\ directory.

To execute this SQL script, you can use the command line tool osql.exe that is provided by SQL Server. (When installing the .NET Framework, a lightweight version of SQL Server is installed.) You can also use the Query Analyzer utility if you have a full version of SQL Server installed. Administrator rights equivalent to that of sa are needed to execute the script because modifications will be made to the SQL Servers master database.

To use the command-line tool (osql.exe), the following syntax is used:

```
osql /S [server name] /U [user] /P [password] /i InstallSqlState.sql
```

You need to replace [server name] with the name of the server that you are going to use as the State Server. Also replace [user] and [password] with the corresponding machine's administrator's credentials.

After executing the script, you should receive a result similar to that shown in Figure 9.7.

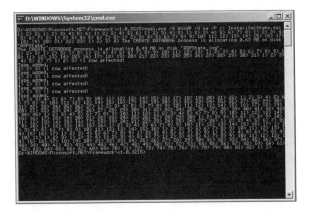

FIGURE 9.7   Execution of the *InstallSqlState* script.

Next, as mentioned earlier, the web.config file needs to be configured to specify the mode and the database.

```
<sessionState
      mode="SQLServer"
      stateConnectionString="tcpip=127.0.0.1:42424"
      sqlConnectionString="data source=127.0.0.1;
                            user id=sa;password=password"
      cookieless="true"
      timeout="20"
  />
```

The mode attribute is changed to SQLServer and the sqlConnectionString points to a database that has been set up on either the local machine or a remote machine.

Maintaining State with the Application Object

In contrast to the Session object, which provides a mechanism for storing data on a per-client basis, the Application object can be used to store and access any data that is specific to the Web application to which the Web Service belongs.

The Application object is very similar to the Session object with the exception that is does not manage Session IDs. Like the Session object, the Application object stores data in key-value pairs. Data stored in the Application object can be retrieved throughout the life of the Web application. This benefit is also a potential downfall of using the Application object—any data stored there will be kept in memory for the entire life of the application, therefore not allowing other processes to use the memory allocated.

The following is the syntax used to store data in the application object:

```
Application("Key") = Value
```

The following is the syntax used to retrieve data from the application object:

```
Value = Application("Key")
```

To see how the `Application` object is used within a Web Service, we will create a simple Web to store the number of searches that users have performed on specific criteria.

Add the following method to the `StatefulService` Web service created earlier:

```
<WebMethod()> _
Public Function Search (ByVal Criteria As String) As String
    If Application(Criteria) Is Nothing Then
        Application(Criteria) = 1
    Else
        Application(Criteria) = CInt(Application(Criteria)) + 1
    End If
    Search = Application(Criteria)
End Function
```

Notice that the implementation is very similar to the way Session State is managed. In fact, besides replacing all of the references to the `Session` object with a reference to the `Application` object, only one other change was made. The `EnableSession` attribute does not appear here. Because this `WebMethod` only uses the `Application` object, enabling the session for this `WebMethod` is unnecessary.

The method starts by checking whether a variable, with a key identical to criteria that was passed into the `WebMethod`, has already been stored in the `Application` object. Based on the outcome, the method either initializes the variable with the value of 1 or increments that variable by 1.

The following is a `WebMethod` that retrieves a specific search count from the `Application` object:

```
<WebMethod()> _
Public Function GetCount(ByVal Criteria As String) As Integer
    If Application(Criteria) Is Nothing Then
        GetCount = 0
    Else
        GetCount = CInt(Application(Criteria))
    End If
End Function
```

If you are familiar with traditional ASP or ASP.NET, you will have noticed that this is identical to the way the `Application` object is accessed within traditional ASP and ASP.NET Web forms.

Maintaining State with the `Cache` Object

A new option for maintaining state in ASP.NET is caching of data with the `Cache` object.

The `Cache` object works in a similar way to the other state management objects covered in this chapter in that it too stores data in key-value pairs. The `Cache` object closely resembles the `Application` object because state can be maintained throughout the life of the application and is private to each application. The downside is that any data stored there will be lost if the application is recycled.

The following syntax can be used in a regular ASP.NET page to store data in the `Cache` object:

```
Cache("Key") = Value
```

The following syntax can be used in a regular ASP.NET page to retrieve data from the `Cache` object:

```
Value = Cache("Key")
```

Up to now, this looks identical to the `Application` object. So what is the added value of the `Cache` object?

The cache object provides more sophisticated functionality, allowing more advanced applications to take advantage of file and key dependencies, cache expiration, and scavenging.

File and key dependencies allow developers to specify an external file or another cached item to be validated against. The validity of a cache item is based on whether the external file has been modified (or deleted) or if the dependant cache item has been changed. If a dependency changes, the cache item is invalidated and removed from the cache.

An example of how file and key dependencies could be used is an application that has any form of dynamic information (financial information, weather, and so on) that is generated periodically and cached in an XML file. The application processes and displays the data. Keeping it up-to-date is of utmost importance. A cache item can be inserted containing this information, and a dependency on the file from which the data was read can be created. When the file is updated, the data is removed from the cache and the application can reread it and reinsert the updated copy of the data.

Cache expiration allows developers to give cached information a limited lifetime. The lifetime of a cache item can be defined as explicit (a time is specified) or relative to an item's last use (a time span is specified).

After an item has expired, it is removed from the cache. Any future attempts to retrieve a cached item after it has been removed will result in a null value being returned unless the item is reinserted into the cache.

An example of how cache expiration could be used is in a stock ticker application that receives stock prices every two minutes. Between the intervals there is no need to retrieve the information from its original source since this information is readily available in the cache.

Scavenging is the automated cleanup process of infrequently used or less important information.

When entering a piece of information into the Cache, you can specify how ASP.NET should scavenge the data. That is, you can specify the cost of creating the item and the relative rate at which the item should be accessed. As soon as ASP.NET recognizes that a certain cached item has not been accessed for a lengthy amount of time, or is less expensive to create than other cached items, it will remove this item of this cache.

An example of how scavenging could be used is an application performing lengthy calculations to speed up the process allowing for frequently calculated information to be cached. As the cache grows, the less expensive items will be disposed of, while the more expensive items can be retained in memory for continued use.

Within ASP.NET, the Cache object is exposed as a property of the Page object. Accessing the Cache object from a Web Service is a little different to the Application and Session objects, in that the Cache object cannot be accessed directly. To receive information from the Cache class, the Cache property of the HttpContext object will be used. The Web Service object exposes an HttpContext property.

Because the Cache object's Add method is overloaded, we will start from the simplest method call and work up from there.

The following is the syntax that can be used to insert an object into the cache:

```
Me.Context.Cache.Insert(<key>, <value>)
```

The term *key* identifies the item cached. The value of the key is defined by the developer and is identical to the key attribute of the Session and Application objects (receives a string value).

The *value* term specifies the item to be cached. This, too, is identical to that of the Session and Application object in that it can receive any object type.

An important issue to keep in mind when using the Cache object (and any of the other state objects) is the chance that this object may not yet exist in memory or may have been removed. Before attempting to retrieve a value from the Cache object, check that the value is not Nothing.

The following is common syntax for retrieving data from the Cache object:

```
If Me.Context.Cache.Item("key") Is Nothing Then
    ' Do Something!
Else
    CacheSearch = Me.Context.Cache.Item("key")
End If
```

As you can see, the retrieval is also a little different from that of the Session and Application objects.

Next let's take a look at how a file and key dependency can be specified for a cached item.

The following is the syntax that can be used to insert an object into the cache while specifying a dependant file:

```
Me.Context.Cache.Insert(<key>,
                        <value>,
                        <dependencies>)
```

The *dependencies* parameter specifies the file or cache key of a dependant cache item. If there are no dependencies, this parameter should be set to Nothing.

```
Me.Context.Cache.Insert("CalculatedInfo", Source, _
        New CacheDependency(Server.MapPath("financial.xml")))
```

A cached item can have single or multiple dependencies. These dependencies can include one or more files or cached item keys.

Cache expiration can prove to be very useful. Unused information can be removed from memory so resources are conserved.

The following is the syntax that can be used to insert an object into the cache while specifying cache expiration:

```
Me.Context.Cache.Insert(<key>,
                        <value>,
                        <dependencies>,
                        <absoluteExpiration>,
                        <slidingExpiration>)
```

The *absoluteExpiration* property specifies the time at which the cached item expires and is removed from the cache. (This property is a `DateTime` variable type.)

The *slidingExpiration* property indicates the interval between the time the cached item was last accessed and when that object expires. If the value is set to 5 minutes, the cached item expires and is removed from the cache 5 minutes after it is last accessed. (This property is a `TimeSpan` variable type.)

The following is an example of how to set an absolute cache expiration time:

```
Me.Context.Cache.Insert("CalculatedInfo", Source, null, _
                DateTime.Now.AddMinutes(90), _
                TimeSpan.Zero)
```

In this example, the *absoluteExpiration* parameter is set using the `DataTime.Now.AddMinutes(90)` call, which specifies the expiration time of the cached item as 90 minutes after the item is inserted into the cache. The *slidingExpiration* parameter is set to `Timespan.Zero`, which indicates that there is no relative expiration policy on this cached item.

The following is an example of how to set a relative expiration policy:

```
Me.Context.Cache.Insert("CalculatedInfo", Source, null, _
                DateTime.MaxValue, _
                TimeSpan.FromMinutes(90))
```

In this example, the *absoluteExpiration* parameter is set using the `DataTime.MaxValue`, which specifies that there is no absolute expiration policy of this cached item. The *slidingExpiration* parameter is set to `Timespan.FromMinutes(90)`, which indicates that the cached item should expire after 90 minutes.

Last, but definitely not least, we will look at the *priority* property that enables scavenging.

The following is the syntax that can be used to insert an object into the cache while specifying the *priority*:

```
Me.Context.Cache.Insert(<key>,
                <value>,
                <dependencies>,
                <absoluteExpiration>,
                <slidingExpiration>,
                <priority>,
                <onRemoveCallback>)
```

The *priority* parameter indicates the relative cost of the cached item. The cost is specified by the use of the CacheItemPriority enumeration.

The *onRemoveCallback* parameter is a delegate that can be provided to the Cache object so that the application can be notified if and when a cached item is removed from the cache.

The following is an example of how to set a priority:

```
Me.Context.Cache.Insert("CalculatedInfo", Source, null, _
                    DateTime.MaxValue, _
                    TimeSpan.Zero, _
                    CacheItemPriority.High, _
                    Nothing)
```

The *priority* has been set to CacheItemPriority.High so that this piece of information is removed last from the cache.

Some of the other CacheItemPriority values include the following:

- NotRemovable Cache items with this priority level will not be removed from the cache as the server frees system memory.

- High Cache items with this priority level are the least likely to be deleted from the cache as the server frees system memory.

- AboveNormal Cache items with this priority level are less likely to be deleted as the server frees system memory than those assigned a Normal priority.

- Default The default value for a cached item's priority is Normal.

- BelowNormal Cache items with this priority level are more likely to be deleted from the cache as the server frees system memory than items assigned a Normal priority.

- Low Cache items with this priority level are the most likely to be deleted from the cache as the server frees system memory.

Note that, as we have seen, not all of the parameters need to be passed into the call. Each type of parameter has its own null value for specifying if the specific policy is not implemented.

Custom State Management

Up to now, this chapter has covered the built-in functionality needed for state management provided from within the .NET framework.

Custom state management is a term given to user-defined mechanisms that are created to manage state outside of the functionality provided from within the .NET framework. Custom state management is a solution that needs to be developed from scratch. One of the advantages of using the built-in state management functionality is that it suits a vast majority of application state management needs. In contrast, custom state management that is developed for one application may not match the needs of another.

Some of the custom state management scenarios that have been developed include persisting state to disk and managing state using a database. They were created due to a lack of required functionality before .NET.

Managing State as a Web Service

Using a Web Service as a data store has similar advantages to the out-of-process state management options. Because the Web Service used to manage the state would exist in a separate process, or even on a separate machine, the state would be preserved, even if the ASP.NET service was recycled. A major advantage of using a Web Service to manage state is that the state is available to other applications that are not running within Microsoft Internet Information Server.

The major downside with this mechanism is that there is no ready-built solution that can be used. This is a do-it-yourself technique, meaning that the code and logic would have to be developed entirely from scratch.

Summary

This chapter covered three mechanisms for state management: The `Session`, `Application` and `Cache` objects. The `Session` object, which is used for managing state per-user, can be managed in-process session state, out-of-process session state, or out-of process in an SQL Server database. The `Application` and `Cache` objects are for managing state across the entire application. The `Cache` object can be used for more sophisticated tasks of caching information.

10

Microsoft SOAP SDK

So far, Microsoft has put forward two SOAP SDKs. Version one used a whimsically named component named the Remote Object Proxy Engine, also called ROPE. In case you don't get the pun, SOAP plus ROPE is "soap on a rope." People latched onto the Microsoft Developer Network created sample. When Microsoft saw the popularity, they decided to create a more full featured, supported library. MSDN is not a product team and does not have the mission to create this type of software. Instead, the WebData team at Microsoft took over the project and created the Microsoft SOAP Toolkit v2. WebData also owns the MSXML parser, which explains how they got the SOAP toolkit. By the time this book is published, the toolkit will have a third version available that improves upon v2. The differences will not be as radical as those when the product switched from life as an MSDN sample to a supported product.

While this book does focus on .NET based Web Services, you or people in your organization will also have to extend existing applications. Just because you go to Web Services does not mean that you have to abandon your existing investments. This chapter covers the SOAP Toolkit and shows how you can use it.

- As a client, the toolkit provides ways to interact with a Web Service using its WSDL file, as well as methods to directly access and manipulate the XML of the SOAP message.

- As a server, you are given the same capabilities. The server also provides alternatives in how clients access the endpoint—through Active Server pages (ASP) or Internet Services API (ISAPI).

We will discuss the advantages of each individual interface and how to use them all.

We will first cover the client access scenarios. After that, we will cover server deployment and how to make the service available to others. This will include editing the WSDL files, creating custom type mappers for the server, and showing the differences between the ASP and ISAPI listeners. To explain all of this, we will recreate the client and server that were presented in Chapter 1, "Creating Your First Web Service," and Chapter 2, "Consuming Your First Web Service." The first half of the chapter covers the server, and the second half covers the client. Throughout, this chapter assumes that you have a good deal of experience using Visual Basic 6.0 and that you have done some work with ASP. You will need to follow along carefully. It will help out quite a bit if you grab the code from the companion Web site if you have not done so already.

Using the SOAP Toolkit on the Server

In this section, we will recreate the example server shown in Chapter 1. This will involve a bit more work than what we saw to build the example using ASP.NET. The SOAP Toolkit does not know how to serialize or deserialize properties contained in an object. Instead, you need to handle this transformation yourself. For passing arrays of complex types, you will need to handle the complete transformation yourself. We will look at this in detail. If you pass simple data back and forth, things are quite a bit easier.

The code to handle the first three functions (HelloWorld, GetRandomNumbers, and GetPerson) is pretty basic, and is shown in Listing 10.1. The infrastructure included with the SOAP Toolkit handles these three with minimal interaction from you.

LISTING 10.1   Code to implement HelloWorld, GetRandomNumbers, and GetPerson

```
Public Function HelloWorld() As String
    HelloWorld = "Hello World"
End Function

Public Function GetRandomNumbers(ByVal arraySize As Long, _
    ByVal min As Long, ByVal max As Long) As Long()

    Dim i As Long
    Dim retval() As Long
    ReDim retval(1 To arraySize) As Long
    For i = 1 To arraySize
        Randomize
        retval(i) = CLng((max - min + 1) * Rnd + min)
    Next i
```

LISTING 10.1   Continued

```
    GetRandomNumbers = retval
End Function

Public Function GetPerson() As Person
    Dim retval As New Person
    Dim aName As New Name
    retval.Birthday = "April 5, 1972"
    aName.First = "Scott"
    aName.Middle = "Christopher"
    aName.Last = "Seely"
    retval.theName = aName
    Set GetPerson = retval
End Function
```

The Person and Name objects follow the same general layout as they did in the first chapter. Person contains a Name and a Date. Name contains three strings. Both use Property Get/Let to change the values. Things get a lot more complicated with GetAuthorNames. As a result of this, this section will have more text focused on handling the difficult case and little text that handles the simple cases. For reference, to the client, it needs to look like the GetAuthorNames function has the following signature:

```
Public Function GetAuthorNames() as Name()
```

This Web Service is being built under the assumption that it is intended to be a Web Service and not just another COM object. Using the SOAP Toolkit, you can choose to simply expose a COM object as a Web Service. This statement is important when looking at the code that makes GetPerson and GetAuthorNames work.

Generating the WSDL and WSML files

The SOAP Toolkit includes a utility, wsdlgen.exe, that allows you to create the WSDL and WSML files. We covered WSDL in Chapter 3, "SOAP, WSDL, and UDDI Explained." WSML stands for Web Services Meta Language. It is a proprietary XML vocabulary that the SOAP toolkit uses to map WSDL information to its COM counterpart. We will look at the details of the WSML and WSDL files as we progress. They will need to be edited by hand before we are done.

Before we go much further, make sure you have the Ch10STKExSvr project from the companion Web site for this book. You will find it helpful to have this project on your machine so that you can follow along with this discussion.

`wsdlgen.exe`, also known as the WSDL Generator, will get everything started. For two of the operations, `GetRandomNumbers` and `HelloWorld`, the WSDL Generator will be all we need to expose these operations as Web Services. The tool has both a command line and GUI. We will focus on the GUI. The command-line use comes in handy when adding creation of the WSDL and WSML files to the end of any build scripts you may create. All features available from the GUI are available through the command line.

When using the SOAP Toolkit to create your Web Service, you will first want to do the following things in the Visual Basic 6.0 project:

1. Create your ActiveX DLL project and add any classes you want to expose as a Web Service.

2. For the classes you will expose, type in stubs defining the Web Method signature. You will have plenty of time to actually implement the methods.

3. Build the project. Rename the resulting binary to something like [*project name*]`_baseline.dll`.

4. In the project settings, make sure you have everything set up for binary compatibility. From within Visual Basic 6.0, select Project, [Project Name] Properties. Switch to the Component tab and select the Binary Compatibility radio button in the Version Compatibility group box. Then, select the DLL you renamed in the previous step as the file with which you will be compatible.

The last step is very important. The SOAP Toolkit uses the object's `IDispatch` interface to call the functions exposed by the COM object. It stores the ID of each function in the WSML file. If you do not set Binary Compatibility and choose a file that contains a type library, the IDs of the functions will change every time you rebuild the library. If you want to make things even more stable, you have the option of writing an IDL file and compiling it into a type library. If you have written IDL files in the past, this option may be better because it locks the interface. The downside to this is that IDL files are harder to create than just updating the WSDL and WSML files as needed.

After you have the stubbed out version in place and a stable type library (either as a `.tlb` or `.dll`), you will be ready to run the WSDL Generator. To handle the intended deployment, you should go ahead and create a virtual directory named `Ch10STKExSvr` on your local machine. You can do this by using `inetmgr.exe` and mapping the virtual directory to the same spot in which the DLL is sitting. Alternatively, you can create the directory in the `\inetpub\wwwroot` directory. To mark the directory as a Web application, open up `inetmgr` and navigate to `\(local computer)\Web Sites\Default Web Site\Ch10STKExSvr` and right-click the node. Select the Properties option from the pop-up menu. On the Directory tab under

Application Settings, click the Create button to mark the directory as a Web application. Then click OK to save the change. Assuming that you have installed the SOAP Toolkit (available at `http://msdn.microsoft.com`), select Start, Programs, Microsoft SOAP Toolkit, WSDL Generator. This will bring up the dialog shown in Figure 10.1.

FIGURE 10.1   Opening dialog for the WSDL Generator.

From this dialog, press Next. Name the service **Ch10STKExSvr**. For the local path, select the Ch10STKEx.dll file. When you are done, this next screen should be set up as shown in Figure 10.2.

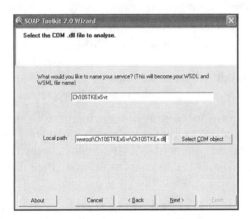

FIGURE 10.2   Selecting the file that contains the COM objects you want to expose.

Press Next and continue to the next screen. This is where you will select which objects and methods you want to expose on your object. By selecting a parent in the tree, all child nodes are automatically selected. Because the Web Service exposes all items, select the top node. The selection should look as shown in Figure 10.3.

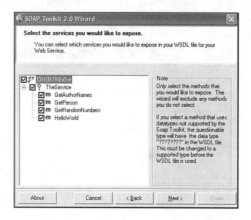

FIGURE 10.3 Exposing objects and related methods.

Now, you need to tell the WSDL Generator the name of the Web site that will be used to expose the WSDL and WSML files. You can also choose to expose the Web Service using an ISAPI or ASP listener. What's the difference?

The ISAPI listener assumes that you will completely hook into the default behavior of the SOAP Toolkit. All the types you use must be able to serialize and deserialize themselves using the built-in tools or using a fairly simple serializer/deserializer that you build yourself.

If you need to do any special processing or if you need to be able to read and write SOAP messages yourself, you need to use the ASP listener. This listener can be used to handle the default dispatch mechanisms, or you can use it to do your own dispatching. How you do things depends on what you need to do.

You should always create XSD information using the 2001 namespace. This namespace maps to the final XSD specification and is understood by all of the more popular open-source and commercial SOAP toolkits. By the time we are done, we will use both the ISAPI and ASP listeners to illustrate their uses. Figure 10.4 shows the selections for the initial WSDL file.

Next, select the default character set and location to place the generated files. The default setting for the WSDL character set, UTF-8, is just fine. You also need to pick a place for the generated files to be placed. I had the toolkit place them in the directory mapped to the Ch10STKExSvr virtual directory, as shown in Figure 10.5.

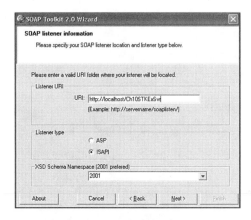

FIGURE 10.4   Exposing objects and related methods.

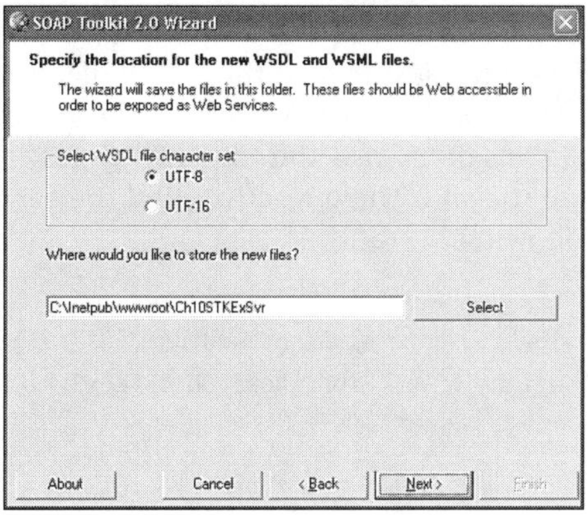

FIGURE 10.5   Generating the WSDL and WSML files.

Now press Next, and read any warning messages. You are now done. You should have received a warning message indicating that the SOAP Toolkit did not understand how to serialize some data types and that they will be marked with question marks (?) in the WSDL file. Now that we have generated the WSDL file, we will move on and take a look at some edits that you will need to make to it.

Common Edits to the WSDL and WSML Files

If you commonly pass complex types over your Web Service, get used to editing the WSDL and WSML files by hand. After you get things working, you will not want to use the tool to regenerate the files and lose any of your changes. The common edits include the following:

- Changing the endpoint
- Adding complex types to the types section
- Changing return types
- Adding portTypes, bindings, and service endpoints
- Mapping complex types to custom type mappers

The easiest of these items is changing the endpoint. When you initially deploy a Web Service for development on the local machine, it may make sense to set the service endpoint to point at `localhost`. Doing so allows for easy redeployment to other machines for single machine testing where the client and server run locally. Later, you will want to have the WSDL declare the path to the machine from either the intranet or Internet. Often, clients will keep a copy of the WSDL file locally to avoid an expensive round trip just to load the WSDL file. It will also be helpful for new clients to have a copy of the WSDL with the Web Service's actual endpoint for future reference. Regardless of the use, the edit is fairly easy to do. Open up the WSDL file and scroll to the end. There, you will find the `service` section. It will look something like the following:

```
<service name='Ch10STKExSvr' >
  <port name='TheServiceSoapPort' binding='wsdlns:TheServiceSoapBinding' >
    <soap:address location='http://localhost/Ch10STKExSvr/Ch10STKExSvr.WSDL' />
  </port>
</service>
```

Just go into the `soap:address` element and change the value of the `location` attribute to point at the correct endpoint. You can also alter this value to point to a trace utility such as the Microsoft SOAP Toolkit's Trace Utility. (This application was discussed in Chapter 5, "Troubleshooting Web Services/Consumers.")

We have complex types that declare the `Person`, `Name`, and an array of `Name` objects. These need to be added to the WSDL file. Listing 10.2 shows the types as they are declared by the wizard.

LISTING 10.2   The WSDL Generator Defined Types Section

```
<types>
    <schema targetNamespace='http://tempuri.org/type'
        xmlns='http://www.w3.org/2001/XMLSchema'
```

LISTING 10.2   Continued

```
        xmlns:SOAP-ENC='http://schemas.xmlsoap.org/soap/encoding/'
        xmlns:wsdl='http://schemas.xmlsoap.org/wsdl/'
        elementFormDefault='qualified'>
        <complexType  name ='ArrayOfint'>
            <complexContent>
                <restriction base='SOAP-ENC:Array'>
                    <attribute ref='SOAP-ENC:arrayType'
                        wsdl:arrayType='int[]'/>
                </restriction>
            </complexContent>
        </complexType>
    </schema>
</types>
```

This part does not even contain the question mark defined types. That part, shown in Listing 10.3, appears in the two message definitions that make use of the "unknown" types:

LISTING 10.3   The Messages Using Undefined Types

```
<message name='TheService.GetPersonResponse'>
    <part name='Result' type='xsd:???????'/>
</message>
<message name='TheService.GetAuthorNames'>
    <part name='Request' type='xsd:???????'/>
    <part name='Response' type='xsd:???????'/>
</message>
<message name='TheService.GetAuthorNamesResponse'>
</message>
```

To handle these items, we need to include type definitions. These definitions are not explicitly used by the SOAP Toolkit. Instead, we include them so that clients using the Web Service know how the data will be presented in the returned XML. This information allows the people creating clients to successfully interpret the returned data. Listings 10.4 and 10.5 contain the type definitions and message updates needed to make it easier for clients. This information is added to the types section of the Ch10STKExSvr.WSDL file.

LISTING 10.4   Types Needed to Define Name, Person, and Array of Name

```
<complexType name="Person">
    <sequence>
        <element minOccurs="0" maxOccurs="1" name="theName"
            type="typens:Name" />
        <element minOccurs="1" maxOccurs="1" name="birthDay"
            type="dateTime" />
    </sequence>
</complexType>
<complexType name="Name">
    <sequence>
        <element minOccurs="0" maxOccurs="1" name="First"
            type="string" />
        <element minOccurs="0" maxOccurs="1" name="Middle"
            type="string" />
        <element minOccurs="0" maxOccurs="1" name="Last"
            type="string" />
    </sequence>
</complexType>
<complexType name="ArrayOfName">
    <complexContent mixed="false">
        <restriction base="SOAP-ENC:Array">
            <attribute wsdl:arrayType="typens:Name[]"
                ref="SOAP-ENC:arrayType"
                xmlns:wsdl="http://schemas.xmlsoap.org/wsdl/" />
        </restriction>
    </complexContent>
</complexType>
```

LISTING 10.5   Updated Messages to Use New XSD Types

```
<message name='TheService.GetPersonResponse'>
    <part name='Result' type='typens:Person'/>
</message>
<message name='TheService.GetAuthorNames'>
</message>
<message name='TheService.GetAuthorNamesResponse'>
    <part name='Result' type='typens:ArrayOfName' />
</message>
```

You will notice that the types in the message now reflect the data needed for any clients. The SOAP Toolkit will also use this information to find custom type mappers in the WSML file. You will notice a radical change to the messages used for GetAuthorNames and GetAuthorNamesResponse. The reason is that the user needs to look at the message as though it was produced with no parts in the request and an array of names in the response. The actual signature of the GetAuthorNames function is as follows:

```
Public Sub GetAuthorNames(ByVal Request As ASPTypeLibrary.Request, _
                ByVal Response As ASPTypeLibrary.Response)
```

The two arguments, Request and Response, allow the GetAuthorNames function to directly read the HTTP message and write the HTTP response. Before looking at the hardest example of type mapping, we will look at the easy case. By the way, the two simple functions, GetRandomNumbers and HelloWorld, already work for the Web Service. Now, we are working on hooking up the other two.

We will first focus on adding the custom type mapper for the Person type. A custom type mapper implements the ISoapTypeMapper interface. This allows the type to read and write itself as XML. ISoapTypeMapper defines four functions—Init, varType, read, and write. Init gets called whenever the class gets loaded. In this function, you should create any objects you might need or capture any information tied to the object schema. The varType function has you return the type of variable the serializer handles. Typically, this will be vbObject. The read and write functions simply read and write the object as XML. We will spend our time looking at the write function (in the client side we will investigate the read portion).

The project contains a class called PersonMapper. PersonMapper only knows how to write a Person and the Name contained within. Listing 10.6 contains the code from the PersonMapper class that writes out a Person object.

LISTING 10.6 Function to Write a Person out as XML from PersonMapper class.

```
Private Sub ISoapTypeMapper_write( _
    ByVal pSoapSerializer As MSSOAPLib.ISoapSerializer, _
    ByVal bstrEncoding As String, _
    ByVal encodingMode As MSSOAPLib.enEncodingStyle, _
    ByVal lFlags As Long, _
    pvar As Variant)

    Dim aPerson As Person
    Dim aName As Name
```

LISTING 10.6   Continued

```
    ' pvar points to an existing Person object
    Set aPerson = pvar

    ' Grab the name embedded in the Person
    Set aName = aPerson.theName

    ' Write out the name first
    pSoapSerializer.startElement "theName"
        pSoapSerializer.startElement "First"

        ' m_stringMapper was captured in the Init function. It knows
        ' how to serialize strings.
        m_stringMapper.write pSoapSerializer, bstrEncoding, _
            encodingMode, lFlags, aName.First
        pSoapSerializer.endElement
        pSoapSerializer.startElement "Middle"
        m_stringMapper.write pSoapSerializer, bstrEncoding, _
            encodingMode, lFlags, aName.Middle
        pSoapSerializer.endElement
        pSoapSerializer.startElement "Last"
        m_stringMapper.write pSoapSerializer, bstrEncoding, _
            encodingMode, lFlags, aName.Last
        pSoapSerializer.endElement
    pSoapSerializer.endElement

    ' Write out the birthday
    pSoapSerializer.startElement "birthDay"

    ' m_dateMapper was captured in the Init function. It knows
    ' how to serialize dates.
    m_dateMapper.write pSoapSerializer, bstrEncoding, encodingMode, _
        lFlags, aPerson.Birthday
    pSoapSerializer.endElement
End Sub
```

To tell the SOAP Toolkit what to do when it needs to convert a `Person` from XML, a few entries need to be made in the WSML file. First, add the types section. Then, map the type declared there to the PROGID used to instantiate the type mapper. The SOAP Toolkit will handle everything else. Listing 10.7 shows the lines used to map the `PersonMapper` object to the `Person` XSD type.

LISTING 10.7   Using `PersonMapper` to Convert `Person` to XML

```
<using PROGID='Ch10STKEx.PersonMapper' cachable='0'
    ID='PersonMapperObject' />
<types>
    <type name='Person'
        targetNamespace='http://tempuri.org/type'
        uses='PersonMapperObject'/>
</types>
```

Now we have three of the four functions callable through our Web Service. We have one more left to go—GetAuthorNames.

The test case for this deployment is this: ASP.NET must be able to create proxy using the WSDL and it must be able to consume the Web Service without requiring the client application developer to write any code. To serialize an array of Name objects, the Web Service had to handle serialization of the objects on its own. For this reason, ASP is used to handle SOAP requests for the Web Service.

To handle any requests, the ASP code will read in the message, check to make sure that the caller wants the GetAuthorNames Web Method, and then hand control over to GetAuthorNames. Otherwise, the request will be handled by the SOAP Toolkit.

When the request comes through, the SOAP Toolkit does not have the intelligence to serialize an array of objects. It will not do this even if it knows how to serialize individual items of the same type. Instead, the server has to do this itself. The ASP code, shown in Listing 10.8, handles this by passing the Request and Response objects to the Visual Basic GetAuthorNames function.

LISTING 10.8   Giving the Response to the Web Method from `Ch10STKExSvr.asp`

```
Option Explicit
On Error Resume Next
Response.ContentType = "text/xml"
Dim SoapServer
Dim aSvc
If Not Application("Ch10STKExSvrInitialized") Then
  Application.Lock
  If Not Application("Ch10STKExSvrInitialized") Then
    Dim WSDLFilePath
    Dim WSMLFilePath
    WSDLFilePath = Server.MapPath("Ch10STKExSvr.wsdl")
    WSMLFilePath = Server.MapPath("Ch10STKExSvr.wsml")
    Set SoapServer = Server.CreateObject("MSSOAP.SoapServer")
```

LISTING 10.8 Continued

```
    If Err Then SendFault "Cannot create SoapServer object. " _
        & Err.Description
    SoapServer.Init WSDLFilePath, WSMLFilePath
    If Err Then SendFault "SoapServer.Init failed. " & Err.Description
    Set Application("Ch10STKExSvrServer") = SoapServer
    Application("Ch10STKExSvrInitialized") = True
  End If
  Application.UnLock
End If
If ( Request.ServerVariables("HTTP_SOAPACTION") = _
    """http://tempuri.org/action/TheService.GetAuthorNames""" ) Then
    ' Call out to the object ourself
    Set aSvc = Server.CreateObject("Ch10STKEx.TheService")
    aSvc.GetAuthorNames Request, Response
    If Err <> 0 Then
        Response.Write "<Error><num>" & Err.number & "</num>" & _
            "<desc>" & Err.Description & "</desc></Error>"
    End If
    Set aSvc = Nothing
Else
    Set SoapServer = Application("Ch10STKExSvrServer")
    SoapServer.SoapInvoke Request, Response, ""
End If
```

The ASP code should handle any errors and send SOAP `Fault` back if needed. To see how this is done, look at the `Ch10STKExSvr.asp` file in the `Ch10STKExSvr` project or generate an ASP listener using the WSDL Generator. My code is no different.

When this has been done, all you need to do is serialize the list of names to XML. When serializing arrays using SOAP-encoding, ASP.NET does best when arrays get serialized as separate top-level elements within the SOAP body. To do this, the code writes out the complete SOAP message. The SOAP Toolkit refers to this as the low-level SOAP interface. This means the code must write out the Envelope as well as any required XML namespaces, SOAP headers, or body elements. Listing 10.9 shows a complete listing of the `GetAuthorNames` function. The first part of the function initializes the array, followed by code that writes out the SOAP response.

LISTING 10.9 Handling the `GetAuthorNames` Request

```
Const TYPE_ATTR As String = "types"
Const TYPE_NS As String = "http://tempuri.org/type"
Const SOAP_ENC_NS As String = _
```

LISTING 10.9   Continued

```
            "http://schemas.xmlsoap.org/soap/encoding/"
Const SOAP_ENC As String = "SOAP-ENC"
Const XSD_NS As String = "http://www.w3.org/2001/XMLSchema"
Const XSI_NS As String = "http://www.w3.org/2001/XMLSchema-instance"
Const XSD As String = "xsd"
Const XSI As String = "xsi"

Public Sub GetAuthorNames(ByVal Request As ASPTypeLibrary.Request, _
                ByVal Response As ASPTypeLibrary.Response)

    ' Declare all the types we need
    Dim serializer As New MSSOAPLib.SoapSerializer
    Dim aName As Variant
    Dim retval(1 To 3) As Name
    Dim id As Long
    Dim index As Long
    Dim arrayLBound As Long
    Dim arrayUBound As Long
    Dim arraySize As Long
    Const MethodName As String = "GetAuthorNames"

    For index = 1 To 3
        Set retval(index) = New Name
    Next index

    retval(1).First = "Scott"
    retval(1).Middle = "Christopher"
    retval(1).Last = "Seely"

    retval(2).First = "Eric"
    retval(2).Middle = ""
    retval(2).Last = "Smith"

    retval(3).First = "Deon"
    retval(3).Middle = ""
    retval(3).Last = "Schaffer"

    id = 1

    ' Get the bounds of the array.
    arrayLBound = LBound(retval)
```

LISTING 10.9   Continued

```
arrayUBound = UBound(retval)
arraySize = arrayUBound - arrayLBound + 1

' Initialize the serializer and tell it to write
' out to the Response object.
serializer.Init Response

' Write out the envelope and the namespaces used by the
' response
serializer.startEnvelope
serializer.SoapNamespace XSD, XSD_NS
serializer.SoapNamespace XSI, XSI_NS
serializer.SoapNamespace TYPE_ATTR, TYPE_NS
serializer.SoapNamespace SOAP_ENC, SOAP_ENC_NS

' Start the Body and setup the reference to the array
' of references to the names.
serializer.startBody
serializer.startElement "GetAuthorNamesResponse", TYPE_NS, , _
    TYPE_ATTR
serializer.startElement "GetAuthorNamesResult"
serializer.SoapAttribute "href", , "#id" & id
serializer.endElement
serializer.endElement

' This is the array of name references.
serializer.startElement "Array", SOAP_ENC_NS, , SOAP_ENC
serializer.SoapAttribute "id", , "id" & id
serializer.SoapAttribute "arrayType", SOAP_ENC_NS, _
    TYPE_ATTR & ":Name[" & (arraySize) & "]"

' Write out the references
For index = 1 To arraySize
    serializer.startElement "Item"
    serializer.SoapAttribute "href", , "#id" & (id + index)
    serializer.endElement
Next index
serializer.endElement


' Now, write out the names
id = id + 1
```

LISTING 10.9   Continued

```
For Each aName In retval
    serializer.startElement "Name", TYPE_NS, , TYPE_ATTR
    serializer.SoapAttribute "id", , "id" & id
    serializer.SoapAttribute "type", XSI_NS, _
        TYPE_ATTR & ":Name", XSI
    serializer.startElement "First"
    serializer.SoapAttribute "type", XSI_NS, _
        XSD & ":string", XSI
    serializer.writeString aName.First
    serializer.endElement
    serializer.startElement "Middle"
    serializer.SoapAttribute "type", XSI_NS, _
        XSD & ":string", XSI
    serializer.writeString aName.Middle
    serializer.endElement
    serializer.startElement "Last"
    serializer.SoapAttribute "type", XSI_NS, _
        XSD & ":string", XSI
    serializer.writeString aName.Last
    serializer.endElement
    serializer.endElement
    id = id + 1
Next aName

' Close up the Body and the Envelope.
serializer.endBody
serializer.endEnvelope

End Sub
```

Listing 10.10 shows the SOAP message this code creates. Looking at this message, you should be able to see what all the previous methods do. SoapNamespace adds the namespace and identifier to the currently active element. SoapAttribute adds the attribute to the currently active element. Besides being able to correctly create and close a header, body, and envelope, the toolkit also can create arbitrary elements.

LISTING 10.10   SOAP Message Created by GetAuthorNames

```
<?xml version="1.0" encoding="UTF-8" standalone="no" ?>
<SOAP-ENV:Envelope
    xmlns:SOAP-ENV="http://schemas.xmlsoap.org/soap/envelope/"
```

LISTING 10.10   Continued

```
    xmlns:xsd="http://www.w3.org/2001/XMLSchema"
    xmlns:xsi="http://www.w3.org/2001/XMLSchema-instance"
    xmlns:types="http://tempuri.org/type"
    xmlns:SOAP-ENC="http://schemas.xmlsoap.org/soap/encoding/">
    <SOAP-ENV:Body>
        <types:GetAuthorNamesResponse>
            <GetAuthorNamesResult href="#id1" />
        </types:GetAuthorNamesResponse>
        <SOAP-ENC:Array id="id1" SOAP-ENC:arrayType="types:Name[3]">
            <Item href="#id2" />
            <Item href="#id3" />
            <Item href="#id4" />
        </SOAP-ENC:Array>
        <types:Name id="id2" xsi:type="types:Name">
            <First xsi:type="xsd:string">Scott</First>
            <Middle xsi:type="xsd:string">Christopher</Middle>
            <Last xsi:type="xsd:string">Seely</Last>
        </types:Name>
        <types:Name id="id3" xsi:type="types:Name">
            <First xsi:type="xsd:string">Eric</First>
            <Middle xsi:type="xsd:string"></Middle>
            <Last xsi:type="xsd:string">Smith</Last>
        </types:Name>
        <types:Name id="id4" xsi:type="types:Name">
            <First xsi:type="xsd:string">Deon</First>
            <Middle xsi:type="xsd:string"></Middle>
            <Last xsi:type="xsd:string">Schaffer</Last>
        </types:Name>
    </SOAP-ENV:Body>
</SOAP-ENV:Envelope>
```

So, did all this work pay off? You bet. Ch10STKExTest contains the Visual Basic .NET console application that consumes the Web Service. The developer did not have to write any custom code to transform the XML into an array of Name. Listing 10.11 shows all the code I had to write to use every method the Web Service exposes.

LISTING 10.11   Visual Basic .NET Client

```
Sub Main()
    Dim svc As New localhost.Ch10STKExSvr()
    Try
```

LISTING 10.11   Continued

```
        System.Console.WriteLine(svc.HelloWorld())
        Dim rndNums() As Integer = svc.GetRandomNumbers(10, 3, 19)
        Dim aVal As Integer
        For Each aVal In rndNums
            System.Console.Write(aVal.ToString() & " ")
        Next
        System.Console.WriteLine()
        Dim aPerson As localhost.Person
        aPerson = svc.GetPerson()
        System.Console.WriteLine(aPerson.theName.First & " " & _
            aPerson.theName.Middle & " " & aPerson.theName.Last & _
            " " & aPerson.birthDay.ToString())
        System.Console.WriteLine()

        Dim theNames() As localhost.Name = svc.GetAuthorNames()
        Dim aName As localhost.Name
        For Each aName In theNames
            System.Console.WriteLine(aName.First & " " & _
                    aName.Middle & " " & aName.Last)
        Next
    Catch ex As Exception
        System.Console.WriteLine(ex.ToString())
    End Try
    System.Console.ReadLine()
End Sub
```

Now that the Web Service has been written, let's take a look at how to deploy it.

Deploying Your SOAP Web Service

When it comes time to deploy the Web Service, you need to do a few simple things. First, create a virtual directory on the Web Server and map that directory to the location of the WSDL, WSML, and (if you are using ASP) the ASP files. You then need to install the SOAP Toolkit on the server. Finally, install the COM object and register it using regsvr32.exe. The DLL containing the COM object needs to live in a directory that any clients will appear as. If you use some form of authentication, you will need to make sure that those users have access to the directory. Likewise, if the default IIS user will be accessing the file, he or she needs access to the directory in which the COM object resides. Most issues with accessing the Web Service through the SOAP Toolkit involve improperly set permissions.

Other than the previously mentioned items, you do not have to do anything special to deploy a COM object as a Web Service. Now that the server side is covered, let's look at the client side.

Using the SOAP Toolkit on the Client

The SOAP Toolkit allows for clients to use two interfaces to access data. The high-level interface reads in the WSDL file and, based on how you call the methods, just knows what to do. It also allows for low-level interaction where you craft the entire SOAP message and handle the response. You can also create custom type mappers to handle data that you want the high-level interface to be able to handle. As you may have guessed after reading the last section, a custom type mapper uses the low-level interface to make the high-level one easier to work with.

In this section, we will write four different functions that use the high-level interface, a customer type mapper, and the low level interface. All of this will be demonstrated in the VBCh10Test application.

Using the High-Level Interface

The high-level interface allows for you to interact with any Web Service that sends back simple data types or arrays of simple types. Anything else will require you to manipulate the XML by hand somewhere. To use the high-level interface, simply declare an instance of the MSSOAPLib.SoapClient COM object. Then, load up the WSDL file and call the functions as though the SoapClient object supported them. Under the covers, it maps those calls to the WSDL file, makes the calls, and interprets the results for you. Listing 10.12 shows some code that calls HelloWorld and displays the response in a message box.

LISTING 10.12   Calling HelloWorld Using the High-Level Interface Using Visual Basic 6.0.

```
Private Sub HelloWorld_Click()
    Dim soap As New MSSOAPLib.SoapClient
    soap.mssoapinit _
        "C:\Inetpub\wwwroot\Ch10STKExSvr\Ch10STKExSvr.WSDL", _
        "Ch10STKExSvr", "TheServiceSoapPort"
    MsgBox soap.HelloWorld

    Set soap = Nothing
End Sub
```

You can even get good results when you need to read back an array of integers. The GetRandomNumbers call works equally well. This one takes three arguments and returns a set of random numbers within the specified range. To get 10 random numbers between 0 and 10, you would call the Web Service using the code in Listing 10.14.

LISTING 10.14   Calling GetRandomNumbers Using the High-Level Interface

```
Private Sub GetRandomNumbers_Click()
    Dim soap As New MSSOAPLib.SoapClient
    Dim randomNumbers As Variant
    Dim message As String
    Dim i As Long

    soap.mssoapinit _
        "C:\Inetpub\wwwroot\Ch10STKExSvr\Ch10STKExSvr.WSDL", _
        "Ch10STKExSvr", "TheServiceSoapPort"

    randomNumbers = soap.GetRandomNumbers(10, 0, 10)

    For i = LBound(randomNumbers) To UBound(randomNumbers)
        message = message & randomNumbers(i) & vbCrLf
    Next i

    MsgBox message
    Set soap = Nothing
End Sub
```

Listing 10.14 reads a local copy of the WSDL file. The SOAP Toolkit documentation recommends that the WSDL file always be located on the same machine as the client application. You can load the WSDL over the Internet or LAN, but doing so involves longer delays in getting the file. Why is this a safe thing to do? Odds are very good that if the Web Service changes, your client will fail, regardless of how up-to-date the WSDL is. If you get the WSDL from the Web Service computer, the function may work, but the results may be unusable. By storing the WSDL on the client machine, the changes are still breaking ones. As a result, you are better off keeping the WSDL file on the client. A deployed Web Service should not change its interface. If it does, clients are expected to break. This will either force the creators of the clients to update the code or abandon the Web Service for something more stable.

When you need to use simple types that the toolkit understands natively, you do not need to do a lot of work. The toolkit ups the ante when you need to read in a custom type. If you will only read the type using one call, you will not save much time by creating a custom type mapper. On the other hand, if you call the function a lot, a custom type mapper can come in handy. To create one, you need to make your own WSML file and COM object. The WSML file only needs to indicate the type and the COM object that knows how to translate the type into a COM object. The COM library VBCh10TestMappers handles the mapping, and a customized version of Ch10STKExSvr.wsml tells the toolkit how to use the COM library. Listing 10.15 shows the WSML file.

LISTING 10.15   Edited WSML File

```
<?xml version='1.0' encoding='UTF-8' ?>
<servicemapping name='Ch10STKExSvr'>
  <service name='Ch10STKExSvr'>
    <using PROGID='VBCh10TestMappers.PersonMapper'
      cachable='0' ID='PersonMapperObject' />
    <types>
     <type name='Person'
           targetNamespace='http://tempuri.org/type'
           uses='PersonMapperObject'/>
    </types>
  </service>
</servicemapping>
```

The class mapping the XML to COM objects does not need to keep its dispatch IDs constant. Because the SOAP Toolkit only attaches to the ISoapTypeMapper interface, the toolkit already knows what it is looking for and can handle using the functionality simply through the PROGID. Listing 10.16 shows the three functions that have any code for the client side: Init, varType and read.

LISTING 10.16   Client-Side Custom Type Mapper

```
Dim m_stringMapper As ISoapTypeMapper
Dim m_dateMapper As ISoapTypeMapper

Private Sub ISoapTypeMapper_Init( _
    ByVal pFactory As MSSOAPLib.ISoapTypeMapperFactory, _
    ByVal pSchema As MSXML2.IXMLDOMNode, _
    ByVal xsdType As MSSOAPLib.enXSDType)

  Set m_stringMapper = pFactory.getMapper(enXSDstring, Nothing)
  Set m_dateMapper = pFactory.getMapper(enXSDdate, Nothing)
End Sub


Private Function ISoapTypeMapper_read( _
    ByVal pNode As MSXML2.IXMLDOMNode, _
```

LISTING 10.16 Continued

```
    ByVal bstrEncoding As String, _
    ByVal encodingMode As MSSOAPLib.enEncodingStyle, _
    ByVal lFlags As Long) As Variant

    Dim aPerson As New Person
    Dim aName As New Name
    Dim nameNode As MSXML2.IXMLDOMNode
    aPerson.Birthday = m_dateMapper.read( _
        pNode.selectSingleNode("birthDay"), _
        bstrEncoding, encodingMode, lFlags)
    Set nameNode = pNode.selectSingleNode("theName")
    aName.First = m_stringMapper.read( _
        nameNode.selectSingleNode("First"), _
        bstrEncoding, encodingMode, lFlags)
    aName.Middle = m_stringMapper.read( _
        nameNode.selectSingleNode("Middle"), _
        bstrEncoding, encodingMode, lFlags)
    aName.Last = m_stringMapper.read( _
        nameNode.selectSingleNode("Last"), _
        bstrEncoding, encodingMode, lFlags)
    aPerson.theName = aName

    Set ISoapTypeMapper_read = aPerson
End Function

Private Function ISoapTypeMapper_varType() As Long
    ISoapTypeMapper_varType = vbObject
End Function
```

To put this all together, the executable tells the mssoapinit method to look in the WSML file for any types it does not know how to handle. When the library sees a Person come over the wire, it will load up the specified type mapper and tell it to read the XML. The method returns a Variant that the client can then use to get at the actual binary data. Using the type mapper allows you to keep your code fairly simplistic. Listing 10.17 shows the client code that takes advantage of the WSML file.

LISTING 10.17 Using a Custom Type Mapper to Read a Complex Type

```
Private Sub GetPerson_Click()
    Dim soap As New MSSOAPLib.SoapClient
    Dim aPerson As Object
```

LISTING 10.17 Continued

```
    Dim message As String
    Dim i As Long

    soap.mssoapinit _
        "C:\Inetpub\wwwroot\Ch10STKExSvr\Ch10STKExSvr.WSDL", _
        "Ch10STKExSvr", "TheServiceSoapPort", _
        "Ch10STKExSvr.wsml"

    Set aPerson = soap.GetPerson
    message = aPerson.theName.First & " " & _
        aPerson.theName.Middle & " " & _
        aPerson.theName.Last & " " & vbCrLf & _
        aPerson.Birthday
    MsgBox message
    Set soap = Nothing

End Sub
```

So, how do you handle an array of complex data? You execute the function and then manipulate the XML result however you see fit. When the toolkit does not know how to map the data, you will always get back an instance of an IXMLDOMNodeList. Using it, you can see any data returned within the body result. You might think that the serialization we did might make this difficult. It doesn't. Instead, we have three objects that each contain three fields. Listing 10.18 shows how you would extract this information.

LISTING 10.18 Calling GetAuthorNames and Reading the IXMLDOMNodeList

```
Private Sub GetAuthorNames_Click()
    Dim soap As New MSSOAPLib.SoapClient
    Dim theNames As Variant
    Dim content As Variant
    Dim nameData As Variant
    Dim message As String
    Dim i As Long

    soap.mssoapinit _
        "C:\Inetpub\wwwroot\Ch10STKExSvr\Ch10STKExSvr.WSDL", _
        "Ch10STKExSvr", "TheServiceCustomHandlerPort"

    theNames = soap.GetAuthorNames
```

LISTING 10.18   Continued

```
For Each content In theNames
    For Each nameData In content
        message = message & nameData.Text & " "
    Next nameData
    message = message & vbCrLf
Next content
MsgBox message
Set soap = Nothing


End Sub
```

So, what would you do if you needed to access the Web Service the hard way? You would use the low-level interface.

Using the Low-Level Interface

The low-level interface allows you to control the creation of the SOAP message. The low-level interface comes in handy when a WSDL file does not exist or when you need to craft the message by hand due to incompatibilities in between toolkits. To create the message, you need to know all the details about what the server is expecting. In particular, you need the following information:

- The SOAPAction value (only if required for routing)

- Address to send the request to

- Name of the message

- Names of any parameters

- Order the service requires the parameters to appear in

- How to interpret any return values

After you have all this information, you can call the Web Service the hard way. Sometimes, you just have to use the low-level interface. We will look at calling HelloWorld by crafting the entire message through custom code.

To create the connection, you need to use two classes—SoapSerializer and SoapConnector. SoapConnector specifies the interface for something that can send and receive SOAP messages. In our case, we will instantiate an HttpConnector to send the request to an HTTP endpoint. We saw SoapSerializer in the server code. It's still responsible for knowing how to create the actual SOAP message. Finally, we will need to use SoapReader. SoapReader knows how to read a SOAP message, and we will use it to read the response. Listing 10.19 shows how to put all these classes together to send and receive a simple SOAP message.

LISTING 10.19   Calling `HelloWorld` Using the Low-Level Interface

```
Private Sub HelloWorldLowLevel_Click()
    Dim serializer As SoapSerializer
    Dim reader As SoapReader
    Dim connector As SoapConnector

    ' Create the connection to the endpoint
    Set connector = New HttpConnector
    connector.Property("EndPointURL") = _
        "http://localhost/Ch10STKExSvr/Ch10STKExSvr.WSDL"
    connector.Connect

    ' Set the SoapAction (the SOAP Toolkit uses this for
    ' routing messages)
    connector.Property("SoapAction") = _
        "http://tempuri.org/action/TheService.HelloWorld"
    connector.BeginMessage

    ' Create the message serializer
    Set serializer = New SoapSerializer
    serializer.Init connector.InputStream

    ' Write out the SOAP message
    serializer.startEnvelope , _
        "http://schemas.xmlsoap.org/soap/encoding/"
    serializer.startBody
    serializer.startElement "HelloWorld", _
        "http://tempuri.org/message/"
    serializer.endElement
    serializer.endBody
    serializer.endEnvelope

    ' Send the message to the endpoint
    connector.EndMessage

    ' Read the response
    Set reader = New SoapReader
    reader.Load connector.OutputStream
```

LISTING 10.19 Continued

```
    If Not reader.Fault Is Nothing Then
        ' Display any fault information
        MsgBox reader.faultstring.Text, vbExclamation
    Else
        ' Display the result
        MsgBox reader.RPCResult.Text
    End If
End Sub
```

If the data being returned is more complex, you will have more code that handles the `SoapReader.RPCResult` member to discover what XML came back. Likewise, a method that takes parameters or complex types will have more serialization code inside the construction of the method name. Whatever you need to do with SOAP, it should be possible using the low-level interface.

Summary

This chapter covered the SOAP Toolkit in a fair amount of detail. We saw a whirl-wind "re-do" of the content presented in Chapters 1 and 2. This time around, we covered the SOAP Toolkit instead of ASP.NET. You should have an understanding of how to read and write simple SOAP messages, transmit and receive complex types, and handle the raw SOAP message. Most of the code applies equally well on the client or the server. After all, SOAP messages still need to go from one point to the other, and someone needs to read and write them.

If you need to expose existing Visual Basic 6.0 code as a Web Service or add client capabilities to an existing application, you should be able to use this chapter to guide you.

11

Converting Legacy Applications to Web Services

Right now, I'm looking at the title of this chapter and thinking, "Wow, I can't believe that I'm calling pre-.NET applications legacy!" In the world of application development on Windows, any application written using Visual Studio 6.0 or earlier will be viewed as a legacy application within the next year or two. There already exists a feeling that we are in the middle of a large-scale paradigm shift as the industry starts to migrate over to .NET. The broad adoption of garbage collection technologies that started with Java has shown us that developers really like the idea of having the computer worry about resources. Yes, I know that garbage collection has been a computer science research project for many years. Java proved that it was ready for commercial deployment. .NET takes lessons learned from Java and many other languages and technologies to make things even better.

So, what do you do to convert your existing applications into Web Services? The most important thing to do is to recognize which applications you should not convert. For example, most developers do a good job abstracting out the data access layer. As an added bonus, the data access layer can be kept stateless with little effort. Parts that have stateless interfaces make for good candidates for Web Services.

Other good candidates include background tasks where jobs get submitted and the work gets performed sometime in the future. You can put a Web Service front end that puts the requests in a queue. The stateful backend can then handle the requests.

A good time to look at adding Web Services is at the start of a maintenance cycle. To increase scalability, you will look at breaking the systems apart. Some sub-systems may have clients hooked up to them that were not there when the application was first constructed. You may have new applications coming up that will need the backend.

In this chapter, we will look at the two common areas where most of you will have an opportunity to add Web Service capabilities to existing code:

- *Existing distributed applications*—Your objects get activated using COM+ or a similar environment.

- *Existing COM objects*—Use and modify existing code to work as a Web Service.

For the purposes of these two topics, we will discuss options for retrofitting existing applications with Web Service capabilities.

Besides this, we will also cover situations where you will want to migrate a Web Service or COM object to Visual Basic .NET to take advantage of the better serialization support.

This chapter will be fairly sparse on code. Chapter 10, "Microsoft SOAP SDK," explained how to handle all the situations you can run into with the SOAP Toolkit. Here, we will focus on identifying existing resources and what to do to prepare them to be used as a Web Service.

Adding Web Service Support to COM+ Applications

Existing COM+ applications can be easily converted into a Web Service if they have a stateless interface and if they only use simple types, such as dates, numbers of any form, strings, and arrays of these types. If you transmit byte arrays, the existing tools will even encode them as base64 data. Overall, the base64 encoding bloats the content by 30 percent but conserves on space, because each byte in the array will not have a separate tag, such as `<byte>value</byte>`. Contrast this with passing arrays of any other numeric type that does have some XML surrounding each value.

> **NOTE**
>
> base64 encoding was developed for e-mail to handle attachments. The data is encoded to guarantee that the data can travel over a text connection. A full discussion of base64 is outside the scope of this text. If you do need information on how it works, look at RFC 2045, section 6.8 (`http://www.ietf.org/rfc/rfc2045.txt`).

If your application exports special data types, you will need to create a custom type mapper for each data type. A custom type mapper knows how to translate to an object to and from XML. Chapter 10 covers the SOAP Toolkit in detail.

If your hardware uses Windows 2000 or earlier, the easiest way to turn a COM+ application into a Web Service is to use the Microsoft SOAP Toolkit v2. The toolkit comes with a WSDL Generator tool that reads a COM type library and turns that information into WSDL. To deploy the application, make sure that the IIS user has access to the COM+ application. The IIS user on a given computer is the anonymous account created during installation of IIS that is named IUSR_[machine name]. Place the WSDL and WSML files into the same directory and make sure that directory is mapped to a virtual directory on your Web server. That's all there is to it.

If you have Windows XP or Windows .NET Server and the .NET Frameworks installed, exposing the same application is even easier. To expose an existing COM+ application in this situation, you need to look no further than the property pages for the application. To demonstrate this, add the Ch11ComPlusEx example into the COM+. You will need to be running Windows XP or later, and you must have the .NET Framework SDK installed on your machine. We will step through the entire setup, just in case you have never installed a COM+ application.

1. Open up Component Services. You can access this via the Control Panel. Assuming you have the Category View enabled, select Performance and Maintenance, Administrative Tools, Component Services.

2. In the Component Services Console, expand the tree so that this node is exposed: Component Services, Computers, My Computer, COM+ Applications. Figure 11.1 shows the tree expanded to this point.

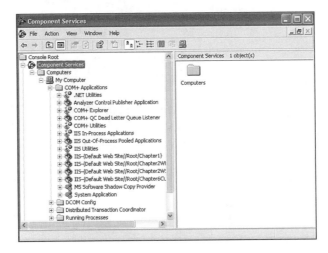

FIGURE 11.1   Getting ready to add an application to COM+.

3. Right-click the COM+ Applications node and select New, Application. This brings up the COM+ Application Installation Wizard.

4. Click Next, and then select Create an Empty Application.

5. Name the application `Ch11ComPlusEx`. Leave the default settings alone. Click Next twice and then click Finish.

Now that the application has been created, you need to add the `Ch11ComPlusEx` DLL to the application. If you have not copied the project from the companion Web site to your machine, do so now. Back in the Component Services Console, find `Ch11ComPlusEx` in the list of applications and perform the following steps:

1. Expand the `Ch11ComPlusEx` node and right-click Components. Select New, Component. This should put you in the Component Install Wizard.

2. Click Next, and then choose Install New Component(s).

3. Navigate to the directory where you stored the `Ch11ComPlusEx` project on your hard drive. Select `Ch11ComPlusEx.DLL` and click OK. The screen should be similar to the one shown in Figure 11.2.

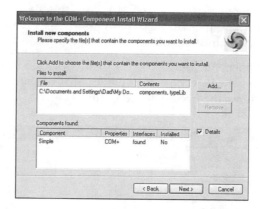

FIGURE 11.2   Getting ready to add an application to COM+.

4. Click Next, Finish. The component has been installed.

The last thing you need to do is allow others to connect to this COM+ application using SOAP.

1. Right-click the `Ch11ComPlusEx` application and select Properties.

2. Select the Activation tab.

3. In the SOAP group box, click the Uses SOAP check box. For the name of the SOAP VRoot, type in **Ch11ComPlusEx**. The tab should be setup as shown in Figure 11.3.

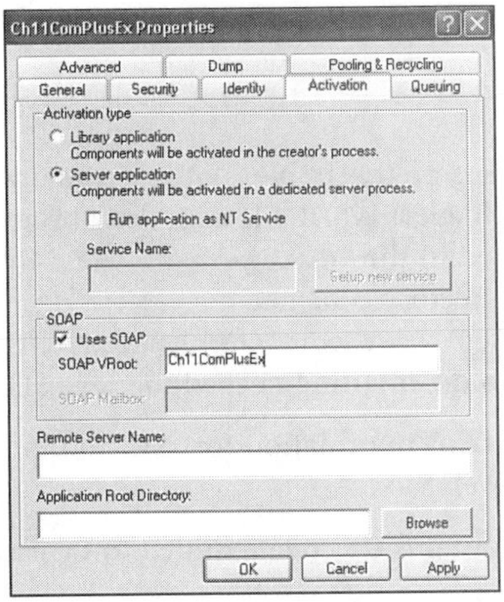

FIGURE 11.3   Enabling SOAP activation for the COM+ application.

4. Click OK and wait. It may take a little while for the SOAP VRoot to be created. A VRoot or virtual root is a logical mapping between an IIS directory and a location on a disk drive. For example, an HTTP request to the local machine might have the URL http://localhost/someDir. The part of the URL that is someDir is the virtual root and can be mapped to any directory that the computer can see, even if that directory is on a different computer.

These last steps create a COM Interop assembly and then constructs some code that will make the DLL usable through .NET Remoting. If the COM+ application was already a .NET Remoting endpoint, you could serialize and deserialize complex CLR objects. However, with traditional COM endpoints, this only works for the basic data types (number types, strings, dates, and byte arrays).

The COM object contains two functions—HelloWorld and Add. Listing 11.1 shows the complete implementation of these two functions.

LISTING 11.1   Code for the COM Object Exposed Using SOAP Activation via COM+

```
Public Function HelloWorld() As String
    HelloWorld = "Hello World"
End Function
```

LISTING 11.1   Continued

```
Public Function Add(ByVal a As Long, ByVal b As Long) _
    As Long

    Add = a + b
End Function
```

As you can see, the code is pretty simple. With minimal work on the COM+ application properties, we now have a WSDL file and virtual root ready to accept connections. The files are located in the `%WINDIR%\system32\Com\SOAPVRoots` directory. On my machine, the new directory is named `C:\WINDOWS\system32\Com\SOAPVRoots\Ch11ComPlusEx`. This directory has a few files in it that were created to do anything needed to make SOAP work.

- `web.config`   Contains information for .NET Remoting to be able to access the COM object as a Web Service.

- `default.aspx`   Contains C# code required to display a test page for the service.

- `default.disco`   Contains discovery information for the Web Service.

- `bin\[COM+ `*`Application Name`*`]SoapLib.dll`   The COM Interop assembly generated by COM+. This will not be generated when you use the same technique to expose COM+ applications that use managed code.

All of this machinery allows .NET Remoting to generate a WSDL file on demand. To see this file, navigate to the virtual root on your machine at `http://localhost/Ch11ComPlusEx/` and select the one link on the page. After you have the WSDL file, you can use it like any other to access the Web Service.

Reusing an Existing COM Object Within a Web Service

This section assumes that the COM object in question requires state or other things that, on the surface, make it a bad candidate for a Web Service. If all you need to do is write some type handling code or edit the WSDL file, you should be reading Chapter 10 right now. For COM objects that require state, you need to look at some ways of separating the COM object itself from the Web Service interface. You have a number of options, and all of them have different pros and cons associated with them.

You can place requests into a queue. This has the advantage of letting you process requests as they arrive and handle the requests fairly quickly. The downside to this is that you cannot send responses straight back to the user. Use this for services that require a large amount of coordination to complete. In this scenario, the Web Service may also need a method to check on the status of the request.

A COM object that uses ADO or some other technology to communicate will not work well with clients that do not understand that technology. Why? Imagine that the COM object does communicate with ADO. How are you going to serialize a recordset and specify that serialization such that a client understands what you are doing? You could use the ADO.NET approach. This serializes the XSD for the returned recordset. Unfortunately, doing this is time consuming and error prone. Instead, add another COM object or .NET project that accesses the original object. You can then add a stateless, easy-to-use Web Service interface on top of the original object. In the world of design patterns, this is called a façade. Visual Basic .NET may be the best way to accomplish this; it allows you to easily declare and use expressive data types with little or no effort on your part.

Keep in mind that many other options exist to reuse your existing code base. COM interop will often be a better solution than exposing a Web Service. Only expose the existing code as a Web Service to allow other platforms, languages, or Internet-based clients to access the code.

Migrating from Visual Basic 6 to Visual Basic .NET

The migration from Visual Basic 6 to Visual Basic .NET has been covered in many introductory texts on Visual Basic, so this section will not cover the basics. Instead, we will focus on deciding when it makes sense to move a Web Service based on the Microsoft SOAP Toolkit (STK) to Visual Basic .NET.

After doing a lot of work with the Microsoft SOAP Toolkit and .NET Web Services, I have come up with only one hard rule that tells me when to migrate the Web Service. If the Web Service needs to handle a good number of complex types, you will find that your time is better spent migrating the code to .NET. As a developer, you will want to get comfortable with .NET at some point in time, and your purchase of this book shows that you want to start writing for .NET now. The other reason to go with .NET instead of the STK is because writing custom type mappers and getting the WSDL and WSML files correct takes time and experience. Those of you who are just starting to write Web Services will want to lobby for .NET as a part of the overall solution.

If you must stay with Visual Basic 6 for practical reasons (boss mandates it, no experience with .NET, and so on), stick with it and get the code working. As Chapter 10 shows, you can do anything you need to do with the STK. It just takes more time—more time to write, deploy, and test. This is experience talking here.

Summary

Migration from Visual Basic 6.0 to Visual Basic .NET will not be much different than the migration for other technologies. Microsoft has gone out of its way to make sure that your old code will continue to work from .NET. This means that you do not need to be in a rush to migrate. Calls going from .NET to COM will cost more time than sticking with straight .NET or COM, but this does give you time to make the right decisions. If the application calls across this boundary one to ten times per second, you probably have no worries.

Use the information in this chapter to identify ways to expose existing code as a Web Service. Sometimes, you will be able to run the SOAP Toolkit's WSDL Generator and be done. Other times, you will write a front end using either .NET or the STK to access the code. Regardless of what you do, take some time to analyze what you need to accomplish and focus on that. You certainly have some code that will be valuable as a Web Service somewhere in your business.

PART III

Solving Real-World Problems

This section presents a number of case studies that show how Web Services can be used to solve problems that developers face in the course of their work. B2B and B2C services, as well as services that allow for platform integration, are discussed, as is the use of Web Services to create portals of various types.

IN THIS PART

CHAPTER 12

Business to Business XML Web Services

Now that you've learned the technical details about building Web Services, it's time to put them to use. In this and the next three chapters, you'll be building small applications that use Web Services as you might in the real world. XML Web Services aren't the right choice for every situation. However, I'll try to show you a few places where they do make sense.

In this chapter, we'll be talking about writing Web Services that allow one business to communicate with another. This is also known as a B2B (business-to-business) application. Our B2B application is one that exchanges data between two business applications in separate companies. Because both companies would typically be unwilling to open their systems up to each other, using an XML Web Service allows for data to move back and forth in an orderly and unobtrusive manner.

Choosing the Right Technology

As you've already learned, XML Web Services have a great deal of flexibility, but they aren't the right choice for every situation. While you could write all your applications using *only* XML Web Services, this would not be the best approach. For one, XML Web Services are not high performance components and would cause local applications to be too slow to be useful. Web Services don't provide the "stateful" programming environment that many developers require. They will provide information on demand, much like a Web site.

However, XML Web Services do make sense in a number of scenarios, some of which are documented here as examples.

Read-Only Access to Data

There are many cases in which users or applications require read-only access to data living on servers outside your company or organization. Directly integrating with the outside company is typically not allowed for security reasons, and even if you were integrating with them directly, there is always the problem of data conversion and formatting. All you really need is a copy of some piece of data at some point in time to allow your application to continue doing what it needs to do.

For example, if you go to get stock quotes, you are getting read-only data. You can use this data in a variety of ways in your own application, but your interaction with the stock quote provider is on a read-only basis. You may be requesting a single real-time quote, or you may be retrieving extensive financial data on a company through a service that aggregates this information from hundreds of companies.

In this situation, using an XML Web Service would be a great solution. The provider of the data can create a Web Service that responds to several types of inquiries, from a simple real-time stock quote to a request for information about a company. These types of inquiries are published as part of the Web Service, and companies needing this data can code their applications to use the Web Service to retrieve the data. The company providing the data benefits by making its data available to more customers, who might even be paying for the data. The companies using the data benefit by not having a huge consulting bill for writing custom integration software and, at the same time, getting the data from the provider for use in their applications.

Write-Only Access to Data

Some systems provide you write-only access to data. If you submit an order to a company, you are essentially writing the data into their system. You may have some options for modifying the order before you send it, but typically, after the order is sent, it's a done deal.

For example, many Web-based stores (including my own) do not stock inventory; instead, they have a distributor send the product directly to the end user. The distributor makes a little bit of money on every product, but they're really in it for the volume. As the store selling the product, I want to automate the process of sending the user's order to the distributor and not have to key the order in a second time to the distributor's order system.

An XML Web Service at the distributor could help alleviate these problems. With the proper authentication, the Web store could send a payload of data to the distributor to place an order. This would be done as soon as the end user confirmed the order. The Web store would then get status information back from the distributor indicating that the order was placed, back-ordered, or whatever status was provided. This information could then be presented to the end user as part of the Web store interface. The end result is that data duplication is kept to a minimum, the user's experience is not confused by forcing them to look in several places for status information, and the Web store is able to handle more orders than they might if they had to manually key in every order that came via the Web site.

Read/Write Access to Data

In many situations, you may need a combination of reading and writing data via a Web Service. In the Web store example, the distributor Web Service may return status information on all the products, including whether those products are in stock or on back-order. The Web Service at the store may then send back another packet to cancel the back-ordered items but leave the other items on order. That information would then be updated in the distributor's order database.

Designing the Web Service

To help you see how XML Web Services can work in this type of scenario, the rest of this chapter will show you how to build Web Services that allow two trading partners to interact. Our first fictitious company is called Jackson-Lauren Distributing Company (JLD), and it acts as distributor of a variety of products. JLD has a number of dealers around the country, including our second fictitious company, Elise's Emporium (EE). Elise's Emporium maintains a Web site that has a complete product listing, as well as information as to whether each product is in stock or back-ordered, based on information provided by JLD.

You'll be building the following software for both EE and JLD:

- A basic Web site to show products available from Elise's Emporium, including description, pricing, and availability

- A Web Service at JLD to allow customers to inquire about current stock level on an item

- A Web service at JLD to provide a full list of products available for order, allowing client stores to populate their databases on a routine basis

All the Web Services offered by JLD will include authentication to make sure that only customers use these services. We'll be handling security through the application and a SOAP header. You'll be supplying a username and password in this header, which is parsed by the .NET Framework and made available to your application. You could also add Secure Sockets Layer (SSL) to add an extra layer of protection for your data because if you don't, information is passing across the Internet unencrypted.

Building the JLD Database

For a database platform, we'll be using SQL Server 2000. If you're using a database other than SQL Server 7.0 or 2000, refer to the .NET documentation for information on how to configure your database connections.

To make this scenario more realistic, I've created two databases, one for each company. These tables will include just the fields that are relevant to our application. In real life, the tables you're building, such as the tblCustomers table on the JLD database, would have quite a bit more information.

To get started, create a database for the JLD application. In the sample code, this database is named WSCh12_JLD.

In the JLD database, we have to create the following tables:

- tblCustomers   Includes user and password information for each customer of JLD

- tblProducts   List of products, prices, and stock levels

The SQL script to create these tables is shown in Listing 12.1.

LISTING 12.1   JLDScript.sql—Script to Create Database Tables

```
CREATE TABLE [dbo].[tblCustomers] (
     [pkCustomerID] [int] IDENTITY (1, 1) NOT NULL ,
     [Name] [varchar] (80) NOT NULL ,
     [UserID] [varchar] (20) NOT NULL ,
     [Password] [varchar] (20) NOT NULL
) ON [PRIMARY]
GO


CREATE TABLE [dbo].[tblProducts] (
     [pkProductID] [int] NOT NULL ,
     [Name] [varchar] (80) NOT NULL ,
     [Description] [varchar] (240) NULL ,
     [RetailPrice] [money] NOT NULL ,
     [DealerPrice] [money] NOT NULL ,
     [Inventory] [int] NOT NULL
) ON [PRIMARY]
GO


ALTER TABLE [dbo].[tblCustomers] WITH NOCHECK ADD
     CONSTRAINT [PK_tblCustomers] PRIMARY KEY  CLUSTERED
        (
```

LISTING 12.1   Continued

```
            [pkCustomerID]
    )  ON [PRIMARY]
GO

ALTER TABLE [dbo].[tblProducts] WITH NOCHECK ADD
    CONSTRAINT [PK_tblProducts] PRIMARY KEY  CLUSTERED
    (
            [pkProductID]
    )  ON [PRIMARY]
GO
```

After you have built the database tables, you should add some test data. I'd suggest a couple of customers and between 5 and 10 products. Vary the stock levels and prices so that the store you build will look somewhat realistic.

Creating the Database Class

Database programming in ADO .NET requires a few more objects and more lines of code than you may be used to. If you have the code encapsulated inside another object, you can concentrate on the business logic you are trying to implement. The Database class you're going to build here is specifically designed to communicate with SQL Server (7.0 or 2000) and handle the most commonly used operations you'll need.

The code for the Database class is shown in Listing 12.2. You can add this class into your Web Service project. In the sample code, this file is called Database.vb.

LISTING 12.2   Database.vb—Class File for the Database Class

```
Imports System.Data.SqlClient
Imports System.Configuration

Public Class Database
  Private m_cnDB As SqlConnection


  '
  ' This constructor reads the application configuration
  ' file (Web.config for web applications) for a string
  ' called ConnectionString. If it's not there, an exception
  ' is thrown. Otherwise, the connection is made.
  '
  Public Sub New()
```

LISTING 12.2   Continued

```
Dim strConn As String
strConn = ConfigurationSettings.AppSettings("ConnectionString")
If strConn = "" Then
  Throw New Exception("Connection string not found " _
    & "in application configuration file.")
Else
  m_cnDB = New SqlConnection(strConn)
  m_cnDB.Open()
End If
End Sub


' This constructor accepts a connection string as input
' and makes a connection to that SQL Server.
'
Public Sub New(ByVal ConnectionString As String)
  m_cnDB = New SqlConnection(ConnectionString)
  m_cnDB.Open()
End Sub


' In case there are other objects that need the live
' connection, make it available through a read-only
' property.
'
Public ReadOnly Property Connection() As SqlConnection
Get
  Return m_cnDB
End Get
End Property


' Run a query that returns records in the form
' of a SqlDataReader.
'
Public Function GetDataReader(ByVal SQL As String, _
  Optional ByVal blnSkipRead As Boolean = False) As SqlDataReader

  Dim cmdQuery As New SqlCommand()
  Dim dr As SqlDataReader
  cmdQuery.Connection = m_cnDB
  cmdQuery.CommandText = SQL
```

LISTING 12.2 Continued

```
    cmdQuery.CommandType = CommandType.Text
    dr = cmdQuery.ExecuteReader
    If Not blnSkipRead Then dr.Read()
    Return dr
  End Function

  '
  ' Run a query that returns records in the form
  ' of a DataSet.
  '
  Public Function GetDataSet(ByVal SQL As String) As DataSet
    Dim da As New SqlDataAdapter(SQL, m_cnDB)
    Dim ds As New DataSet("Results")
    da.Fill(ds)
    Return ds
  End Function

  '
  ' Close the database connection.
  '
  Public Sub Close()
    m_cnDB.Close()
  End Sub
End Class
```

Starting at the top of the listing, you have a class-level private variable called m_cnDB. This variable will hold the SqlConnection object after it is created. The other methods in the class use this object to perform their database actions.

The class has two constructors—one that takes no arguments and one that takes a connection string. The one that doesn't take arguments reads the ConnectionString variable from the web.config file located in the Web application's directory. The ConnectionString is located in the AppSettings section, as follows:

```
... rest of Web.config file ...
  </system.web>
  <appSettings>
    <add key="ConnectionString"
        value="server=(local);database=WSCh12_JLD;UID=user;PWD=pass;" />
  </appSettings>

</configuration>
```

Using the web.config file to hold the ConnectionString makes it much easier to change when necessary. You don't have to recompile any objects; instead, you just edit this text file to change the connection information. Be sure to change the user ID and password as necessary.

After the database connection has been made, the calling object has three options for using it. The first is a property that returns the current SqlConnection object. This feature allows you to use a live SqlConnection object in controls that require it, while still keeping the logic encapsulated in the Database class. The second option returns a DataSet generated by a SQL statement, and the third option returns a SqlDataReader object. Because of a restriction in the SqlConnection object, you can only have one SqlDataReader open at any time.

When the caller is done using the Database object, a Close method closes the connection.

You'll be using the Database class throughout the Web Service to handle all database interaction.

Creating the SecurityToken **Class**

Because JLD doesn't want just anyone to be able to get wholesale pricing information, a username and password will be required to obtain information via this Web Service. The username and password will be sent for each request of this Web Service. You could make these additional parameters on the call to the Web Service, but instead, you'll be creating a SOAP header that will take care of this information. If the header values are not provided, the Web Service will not run. There is a great deal more involved with SOAP, so we'll just be focusing on this one aspect for now. Refer to the MSDN documentation for more information on what SOAP provides.

The data put into the SOAP header will be stored in a class called SecurityToken. The code for the SecurityToken class is shown in Listing 12.3.

LISTING 12.3   SecurityToken.vb—Class File for SecurityToken Class

```
Public Class SecurityToken
  Inherits System.Web.Services.Protocols.SoapHeader
  Public UserName As String
  Public Password As String

  Public Function Verify(ByVal db As Database) As Boolean
    Dim ds As DataSet

    Try
```

LISTING 12.3   Continued

```
      ds = db.GetDataSet("sp_RetrieveCustomer '" & UserName _
        & "', '" & Password & "'")
      Return (ds.Tables.Count > 0)
    Catch e As Exception
      Return False
    End Try

  End Function

End Class
```

We start the class by declaring two public properties—UserName and Password. The application calling this Web Service will supply data for each of these properties. The second piece of code you need to write is the Verify routine, which checks the supplied username and password against the database. It calls a stored procedure called sp_RetrieveCustomer, which is essentially a query saved to the database. If you're not familiar with stored procedures, refer to the SQL Server Books Online that will show you how to create one. The code for this stored procedure is as follows:

```
CREATE PROCEDURE dbo.sp_RetrieveCustomer
@UserID varchar(20),
@Password varchar(20)
AS
SELECT COUNT(*) As Result
FROM tblCustomers
WHERE Upper(UserID) = Upper(@UserID)
AND Upper(Password) = Upper(@Password)
```

This stored procedure accepts the username and password and determines if there is a customer matching that combination in the database. In this stored procedure, the Upper function is converting both the database field and the input data to uppercase letters, effectively making it non-case–sensitive. If you want your application to use case-sensitive passwords, you can remove the call to the Upper function here.

Building the Web Service

With the helper objects complete, it's time to write the code for the Web Service. This code will go into your .asmx file, which is called CustomerService.asmx in the sample code. The code for the Web Service is shown in Listing 12.4.

LISTING 12.4   `CustomerService.asmx`— Creating the CustomerService Web Service

```
Imports System.Web.Services
Imports System.Web.Services.Protocols

<WebService(Namespace:="http://www.jld.ncs")> _
Public Class CustomerService
  Inherits System.Web.Services.WebService
  Public SecurityHeader As SecurityToken

#Region " Web Services Designer Generated Code "

    Public Sub New()
        MyBase.New()

        'This call is required by the Web Services Designer.
        InitializeComponent()
        SecurityHeader = New SecurityToken()
        'Add your own initialization code after the InitializeComponent() call

    End Sub

    'Required by the Web Services Designer
    Private components As System.ComponentModel.IContainer

    'NOTE: The following procedure is required by the Web Services Designer
    'It can be modified using the Web Services Designer.
    'Do not modify it using the code editor.
    <System.Diagnostics.DebuggerStepThrough()> Private Sub InitializeComponent()
        components = New System.ComponentModel.Container()
    End Sub

    Protected Overloads Overrides Sub Dispose(ByVal disposing As Boolean)
        'CODEGEN: This procedure is required by the Web Services Designer
        'Do not modify it using the code editor.
        If disposing Then
            If Not (components Is Nothing) Then
                components.Dispose()
            End If
        End If
        MyBase.Dispose(disposing)
    End Sub
```

LISTING 12.4   Continued

```vbnet
#End Region
  <WebMethod(), SoapHeaderAttribute("SecurityHeader", _
    Direction:=SoapHeaderDirection.In, Required:=True)> _
  Public Function GetInventoryLevel(ByVal intProductID As Integer) As Integer

    Dim db As New Database()
    Dim ds As DataSet
    Dim dr As DataRow
    If Not SecurityHeader.Verify(db) Then
      Throw New Exception("Invalid authentication token.")
      Exit Function
    End If
    ds = db.GetDataSet("sp_RetrieveProduct " & intProductID.ToString())
    If ds.Tables(0).Rows.Count > 0 Then
      dr = ds.Tables(0).Rows(0)
      Return Integer.Parse(dr("Inventory"))
    Else
      Throw New Exception("Invalid product ID.")
    End If
    db.Close()

  End Function

  <WebMethod(), SoapHeaderAttribute("SecurityHeader", _
    Direction:=SoapHeaderDirection.In, Required:=True)> _
  Public Function GetProducts() As DataSet
    Dim db As New Database()
    Dim ds As DataSet

    If Not SecurityHeader.Verify(db) Then
      Throw New Exception("Invalid authentication token.")
      Exit Function
    End If

    ds = db.GetDataSet("sp_RetrieveProducts")
    Return ds
    db.Close()

  End Function
End Class
```

The first thing to do is to include the `System.Web.Services.Protocols` assembly, which provides access to the special features of SOAP that you'll need for the security features you'll be using with this Web Service.

In the declaration of the class, you use the `WebService` directive just before the `Class` keyword. This identifies the class as a Web Service to the .NET Framework. In this example, a fake URL is used as the namespace name, but in practice, you would put the real URL here.

When you start declaring the class, you need a public variable of type `SecurityToken`. This variable will be filled by the .NET Framework after the security token has been read from the SOAP header sent by the calling application. You'll see how this is done in the section "Building the Product List Page," when we call the Web Service from another application.

In Listing 12.4, the code between the `#Region` and `#End Region` markers is automatically generated, so don't type it into the page. However, you do need to add this line (shown in boldface in the previous listing) following the call to `InitializeComponent`:

```
SecurityHeader = New SecurityToken()
```

This creates a new instance of the `SecurityToken` class so that security verification can take place. Because the variable is declared at the class level, you only need to instantiate this object once for the life of the Web Service.

The first method you need to write is the `GetInventoryLevel` method. After authenticating the username and password against the database, this method accepts a product ID number and returns the current stock level for that item. It uses the `sp_RetrieveProduct` stored procedure, shown in the following code:

```
CREATE PROCEDURE dbo.sp_RetrieveProduct
@ProductID int
AS
SELECT *
FROM tblProducts
WHERE pkProductID = @ProductID
```

This stored procedure may seem a bit trivial, but it's a good habit to get into because stored procedures give you performance benefits whenever you use them.

The data returned from this stored procedure is put into a `DataSet` object, but in this case, the only value we need is the current stock represented in the `Inventory` field. If no rows are returned, an exception is generated indicating that the product ID doesn't exist in the database.

NOTE

If you wanted to, you could create a stored procedure that returned just that single value. However, returning a few extra bytes of data generally won't hurt, and it reduces the number of stored procedures you have to manage.

The second method you need to write returns the current list of products in the database. This method follows the same pattern as the last—authenticate the username and password and then retrieve the data. In this case, the returned data is sent back as a DataSet instead of just a single value. The calling application will be able to read this data from the Web Service into a DataSet locally and manipulate it. The stored procedure being called here, named sp_RetrieveProducts, is as follows:

```
CREATE PROCEDURE dbo.sp_RetrieveProducts
AS
SELECT *
FROM tblProducts
ORDER BY Name
```

Because we're using the SOAP header here to pass a username and password, the normal test page generated by Visual Studio .NET for a Web Service will display but not allow you to test the method. If you want to test this code now, you can do the following:

1. Change the WebMethod declaration above each method declaration to look as follows:

   ```
   <WebMethod()> _
   Public Function GetProducts() As DataSet
   ```

2. Comment out the lines that call the Verify method on the SecurityToken object.

Making these two changes will allow you to test the Web Service prior to building the Web site in the next section. When the test page comes up, you can use any of the methods exposed by the Web Service. For the GetProduct method, you can use any of the product ID values stored in the database that you created.

Building Elise's Emporium

The next step is building the Web site that will use the Web Service to display information to customers. At the Elise's Emporium Web site, the data from JLD generally takes too long to download each time someone wants a product listing. In addition, most distributors only update their product databases once a day. For those reasons, the data will be downloaded once a day and be stored in a local database. The Web site can read from the local copy of the database for the Web pages that need that information. The download could be done with a Windows Service application (which you can also create in Visual Studio .NET), but we will download the data a bit more frequently for this application. If the last download was more than ten minutes ago, the Web page will download a new copy of the data.

For the inventory level on a particular product, the ability to check actual stock levels will be available when a user clicks a link on the product detail page. Users on the site would be informed that getting real-time availability may take a little extra time, because the Web Service does not run particularly fast.

To get started with this application, you'll want to create a new ASP.NET Web Application. The sample code uses the name `WSCh12_EE`, but feel free to change that as you see fit. The key step is to reference the Web Service you created in the previous application for the JLD company. If you have both applications on the same machine, the reference will show up in your Solution Explorer (after you've added it as a Web Reference) as CustomerService on the localhost machine. For this application, I renamed localhost to be JLD to cut down on the typing. Just right-click localhost in the Web References and select Rename from the pop-up menu. Because many of the Web references you add will have extremely long names, this is a nice way to avoid some extra typing.

For this code to function properly, you need to make a copy of the `Database.vb` file from the JLD project and add it to this project. You should also add the `appSettings` section to the `web.config` file in this new application to point to your database server, just as you did in the first part of the chapter.

Creating the Database

The first step is to build the Elise's Emporium database. For this application, the database name is `WSCh12_EE` and was created in SQL Server 2000. This database has two tables—one for the product listings and one to store the last update of the data. This field could be stored in the Web server's `Cache` object, but the data is presumably used by other non-Web applications. For that reason, storing the timestamp directly in the database is the best approach.

For this application, the sample database was named `WSCh12_EE`. The database script to build the tables and two of the stored procedures is shown in Listing 12.5. The stored procedures here are exactly the same as the ones you created for the JLD database.

LISTING 12.5   `EE_Script.sql`—Script to Generate Elise's Emporium Database

```sql
enerate Elise's Emporium Database
CREATE TABLE [dbo].[tblProductTimestamp] (
     [LastDownload] [datetime] NOT NULL
) ON [PRIMARY]
GO

CREATE TABLE [dbo].[tblProducts] (
     [pkProductID] [int] NOT NULL ,
     [Name] [varchar] (80) NOT NULL ,
     [Description] [varchar] (240) NULL ,
     [RetailPrice] [money] NOT NULL ,
     [DealerPrice] [money] NOT NULL
) ON [PRIMARY]
GO

ALTER TABLE [dbo].[tblProductTimestamp] WITH NOCHECK ADD
     CONSTRAINT [PK_tblProductTimestamp] PRIMARY KEY  CLUSTERED
     (
            [LastDownload]
     ) ON [PRIMARY]
GO

ALTER TABLE [dbo].[tblProducts] WITH NOCHECK ADD
     CONSTRAINT [PK_tblProducts] PRIMARY KEY  CLUSTERED
     (
            [pkProductID]
     ) ON [PRIMARY]
GO

CREATE PROCEDURE dbo.sp_RetrieveProduct
@ProductID int
AS
SELECT *
FROM tblProducts
WHERE pkProductID = @ProductID
```

LISTING 12.5   Continued

```
GO

CREATE PROCEDURE dbo.sp_RetrieveProducts
AS
SELECT *
FROM tblProducts
ORDER BY Name
GO
```

The tblProducts table is missing a few things from the tblProducts table in the JLD database:

- No identity on the primary key

- No inventory field

The identity is unnecessary because the data is being supplied by the Web Service. The inventory field also is unnecessary because the application will request inventory via the other Web Service method as needed.

The new table here is a one column, one row table that holds the last date/time that the product list was updated. As was mentioned earlier, keeping this field in the database makes it easier for other applications to use the same data consistently. If the rumors about the next version of SQL Server end up being true, you'll be able to use .NET languages directly in SQL Server to handle updating the data instead of needing a "helper" application.

Building the Product List Page

Creating the product listing page is fairly straightforward. The page, when run in Internet Explorer, looks like Figure 12.1.

The data list is generated from a DataSet bound to a Repeater control. The Repeater control gives us good control over the formatting of the data without having to do it all manually. At the bottom of the page is a label control that your application will populate to help you determine where the data is coming from; that is, whether it is coming from the local database or from the Web Service.

The ASPX file for the list page is called EE_ViewProducts.aspx and is shown in Listing 12.6.

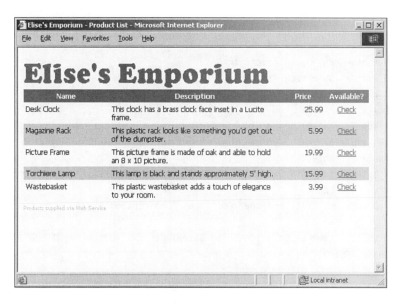

FIGURE 12.1 The product list page for Elise's Emporium.

LISTING 12.6 EE_ViewProducts.aspx—Page to List All Products in the Store

```
<%@ Page Language="vb" AutoEventWireup="false"
    Codebehind="EE_ViewProducts.aspx.vb" Inherits="WSCh12_EE.EE_ViewProducts"%>
<!DOCTYPE HTML PUBLIC "-//W3C//DTD HTML 4.0 Transitional//EN">
<HTML>
  <HEAD>
    <title>Elise's Emporium - Product List</title>
    <link href="styles.css" rel="stylesheet" type="text/css">
    <meta name=vs_targetSchema
      content="http://schemas.microsoft.com/intellisense/ie5">
  </HEAD>
  <body bgColor="#ffffcc">
    <asp:Label id="lblPageHeading"
      runat="server" Font-Names="Cooper Black"
      Font-Size="XX-Large" ForeColor="Teal">Elise's Emporium</asp:Label><br>
    <table cellpadding="4" cellspacing="0" width="100%">
    <asp:Repeater id="rptProducts" runat="server">
    <HeaderTemplate>
    <tr class="tableheading">
```

LISTING 12.6   Continued

```
    <td width="20%">Name</td>
    <td width="40%">Description</td>
    <td width="10%">Price</td>
    <td width="10%">Available?</td>
    </tr>
    </HeaderTemplate>
    <ItemTemplate>
    <tr class="tabletext">
    <td valign="top"><%# DataBinder.Eval(Container.DataItem, "Name") %></td>
    <td valign="top">
    <%# DataBinder.Eval(Container.DataItem, "Description") %>
    </td>
    <td valign="top" align="right"><%# DataBinder.Eval(Container.DataItem, _
      "RetailPrice") %></td>
    <td valign="top" align="center">
    <a href="EE_ProdAvail.aspx?id=<%# DataBinder.Eval(Container.DataItem, _
      "pkProductID") %>" target=_blank>Check</a>
    </td>
    </tr>
    </ItemTemplate>
    <AlternatingItemTemplate>
    <tr class="tabletext_gray">
    <td valign="top"><%# DataBinder.Eval(Container.DataItem, "Name") %></td>
    <td valign="top">
    <%# DataBinder.Eval(Container.DataItem, "Description") %>
    </td>
    <td valign="top" align="right"><%# DataBinder.Eval(Container.DataItem, _
      "RetailPrice") %></td>
    <td valign="top" align="center">
    <a href="EE_ProdAvail.aspx?id=<%# DataBinder.Eval(Container.DataItem, _
      "pkProductID") %>" target=_blank>Check</a>
    </td>
    </tr>
    </AlternatingItemTemplate>
    </asp:Repeater>
    </table>
    <asp:Label id="lblDataSource" runat="server"  CssClass="text_gray"/>
  </body>
</HTML>
```

The page starts with the normal page heading information and the Elise's Emporium title. The Repeater control is called rptProducts and includes a HeaderTemplate, ItemTemplate, and AlternatingItemTemplate. Using the ItemTemplate and AlternatingItemTemplate lets us easily switch the background color to gray for every other row. This makes it easier to scan the page quickly. The Name, Description, and RetailPrice fields are populated into each row, and the pkProductID field is substituted into the middle of a URL as follows:

```
http://localhost/WSCh12_EE/EE_ProdAvail.aspx?id=5
```

This creates a link to the second page you'll be building in the application. At the bottom of the page, the lblDataSource label will hold a piece of text indicating where the data for the page came from—the local database or the Web Service.

This page links to a style sheet for formatting most of the text on the page, and the style sheet is shown in Listing 12.7.

LISTING 12.7   styles.css—Style Sheet for the Product List Page

```
.tableheading
{
   COLOR: #FFFFFF;
   FONT-FAMILY: Tahoma, Arial;
   FONT-WEIGHT: bold;
   FONT-SIZE: 9pt;
   BACKGROUND-COLOR: Teal;
   TEXT-ALIGN: center;
}
.tabletext
{
   COLOR: #000000;
   FONT-FAMILY: Tahoma, Arial;
   FONT-SIZE: 9pt;
}
.tabletext_gray
{
   COLOR: #000000;
   FONT-FAMILY: Tahoma, Arial;
   FONT-SIZE: 9pt;
   BACKGROUND-COLOR: #CCCCCC;
}
.text_gray
{
  font-size: 7pt;
```

LISTING 12.7   Continued

```
  color: #cccccc;
  font-family: Tahoma, Arial;
}
.largetext
{
  font-size: 12pt;
  color: Black;
  font-family: Tahoma, Arial;
}
```

The VB .NET code behind this page is shown in Listing 12.8.

LISTING 12.8   EE_ViewProducts.aspx.vb—Code Behind for the Product List Page

```
Imports System.Data.SqlClient

Public Class EE_ViewProducts
  Inherits System.Web.UI.Page
  Protected WithEvents rptProducts As System.Web.UI.WebControls.Repeater
  Protected WithEvents lblDataSource As System.Web.UI.WebControls.Label
  Private CS As New JLD.CustomerService()
#Region " Web Form Designer Generated Code "

    'This call is required by the Web Form Designer.
    <System.Diagnostics.DebuggerStepThrough()>
    Private Sub InitializeComponent()

    End Sub

    Private Sub Page_Init(ByVal sender As System.Object, ➥
      ByVal e As System.EventArgs) Handles MyBase.Init
        'CODEGEN: This method call is required by the Web Form Designer
        'Do not modify it using the code editor.
        InitializeComponent()
    End Sub

#End Region

  Private Sub Page_Load(ByVal sender As System.Object, ➥
    ByVal e As System.EventArgs) Handles MyBase.Load
    Dim ds As DataSet
```

LISTING 12.8   Continued

```
  Dim dr As DataRow
  Dim cmd As SqlCommand
  Dim db As New Database()
  ds = db.GetDataSet("sp_RetrieveProductTimestamp")
  If Int32.Parse(ds.Tables(0).Rows(0)("Interval")) > 10 Then
    CS.SecurityTokenValue = New JLD.SecurityToken()
    CS.SecurityTokenValue.UserName = "emporium"
    CS.SecurityTokenValue.Password = "mystore!"
    ds = CS.GetProducts()

    cmd = New SqlCommand()
    cmd.Connection = db.Connection
    cmd.CommandText = "sp_DeleteProducts"
    cmd.CommandType = CommandType.StoredProcedure
    cmd.ExecuteNonQuery()

    cmd.CommandText = "sp_InsertProduct"
    For Each dr In ds.Tables(0).Rows
      With cmd.Parameters
        .Add("@ProductID", dr("pkProductID"))
        .Add("@Name", dr("Name"))
        .Add("@Description", dr("Description"))
        .Add("@RetailPrice", dr("RetailPrice"))
        .Add("@DealerPrice", dr("DealerPrice"))
      End With
      cmd.ExecuteNonQuery()
      cmd.Parameters.Clear()
    Next

    cmd.CommandText = "sp_UpdateProductTimestamp"
    cmd.ExecuteNonQuery()
    lblDataSource.Text = "Products supplied via Web Service"

  Else
    ds = db.GetDataSet("sp_RetrieveProducts")
    lblDataSource.Text = "Products supplied via local database"
  End If
  rptProducts.DataSource = ds
  rptProducts.DataBind()
  db.Close()
End Sub
```

LISTING 12.8   Continued

```
End Class
```

When the page loads, this code gets the timestamp from the database using the sp_RetrieveProductTimestamp. This timestamp indicates the number of minutes since the last refresh of the data in the Elise's Emporium database. The stored procedure code is shown in Listing 12.9.

LISTING 12.9   sp_RetrieveProductTimestamp

```
CREATE PROCEDURE dbo.sp_RetrieveProductTimestamp
AS
DECLARE @Last datetime
SELECT @Last = LastDownload FROM tblProductTimestamp
IF @Last = NULL
  BEGIN
    SELECT 60 AS INTERVAL
  END
ELSE
  BEGIN
    SELECT DateDiff(mi, @Last, getdate()) As Interval
  END
GO
```

This stored procedure returns the number of minutes that have elapsed since the last refresh from the Web Service. However, there are cases in which there won't be a timestamp in the database yet. In that case, the stored procedure returns 60, which is a value that will trigger a refresh of data. If you're using a different time scheme, such as once every 24 hours, you can change the initial parameter to DateDiff to figure the number of hours, days, or nearly any other time interval. The calling code will make the determination as to whether to pull the data or not.

Back in the Page_Load subroutine, we start by calling this stored procedure, and, if the returned value is greater than 10 (minutes), we start the refresh procedure. The code creates an instance of the SecurityToken class, which is made available through the Web Service declared as the CS variable. The name SecurityTokenValue is automatically generated because this variable is a SOAP header for the Web Service. The username and password are populated into the SecurityToken and the data is retrieved into a DataSet from the GetProducts routine.

The next step is to clear out the database and get it ready to add new records. The sp_DeleteProducts stored procedure deletes all the products and removes the product timestamp value:

```
CREATE PROCEDURE sp_DeleteProducts
AS
DELETE FROM tblProducts
DELETE FROM tblProductTimestamp
GO
```

For each product that is in the DataSet, the sp_InsertProduct stored procedure is called. The stored procedure code is shown in Listing 12.10.

LISTING 12.10   The Stored Procedure for Adding a New Product to the Table

```
CREATE PROCEDURE dbo.sp_InsertProduct
@ProductID int,
@Name varchar(80),
@Description varchar(240),
@RetailPrice money,
@DealerPrice money
AS
INSERT INTO tblProducts
(pkProductID, Name, Description, RetailPrice, DealerPrice)
VALUES
(@ProductID, @Name, @Description, @RetailPrice, @DealerPrice)

GO
```

After all the rows are loaded from the DataSet into the database, the sp_UpdateProductTimestamp stored procedure is called. That code is as follows:

```
CREATE PROCEDURE dbo.sp_UpdateProductTimestamp
AS
DELETE FROM tblProductTimestamp
INSERT INTO tblProductTimestamp VALUES (getdate())
GO
```

The DELETE statement here is somewhat redundant, but it doesn't hurt anything to call it again. The last step is to bind the DataSet to the Repeater control, which dutifully displays all the rows for us.

In the case in which the data in the local database is still new enough, the application skips to the end and calls the sp_RetrieveProducts stored procedure, which is

the same as the one used on the JLD database. This generates a `DataSet` that is
bound to the `Repeater` control.

Determining Product Availability

The last part of the application is to let the user determine if a particular product is
available or on backorder. For this, we'll use a separate WebForm that will make its
own call to the Web Service. The ASPX file is shown in Listing 12.11.

LISTING 12.11   `EE_ProdAvail.aspx`—Web Page to Check Realtime Product Availability
in the JLD Database

```
<%@ Page Language="vb" AutoEventWireup="false"
    Codebehind="EE_ProdAvail.aspx.vb" Inherits="WSCh12_EE.EE_ProdAvail"%>
<!DOCTYPE HTML PUBLIC "-//W3C//DTD HTML 4.0 Transitional//EN">
<!DOCTYPE HTML PUBLIC "-//W3C//DTD HTML 4.0 Transitional//EN">
<HTML>
  <HEAD>
    <title>Elise's Emporium - Product Availability</title>
    <link href="styles.css" rel="stylesheet" type="text/css">
    <meta name=vs_targetSchema
     content="http://schemas.microsoft.com/intellisense/ie5">
  </HEAD>
  <body bgColor="#ffffcc">
  <asp:Label id="lblPageHeading" Font-Names="Cooper Black"
    Font-Size="XX-Large"
    ForeColor="Teal" Runat="server">Elise's Emporium</asp:Label><br>
  <asp:Label ID="lblAvailable" Runat="server" CssClass="largetext" />
  </body>
</html>
```

This page provides a place to put the result of calling the Web Service and the database call to get the product name. The code behind file is shown in Listing 12.12.

LISTING 12.12   `EE_ProdAvail.aspx.vb`—Code Behind for the Product Availability Web
Page

```
Public Class EE_ProdAvail
  Inherits System.Web.UI.Page
  Protected WithEvents lblAvailable As System.Web.UI.WebControls.Label

  Private CS As New JLD.CustomerService()
```

```
#Region " Web Form Designer Generated Code "

    'This call is required by the Web Form Designer.
    <System.Diagnostics.DebuggerStepThrough()>
    Private Sub InitializeComponent()

    End Sub

    Private Sub Page_Init(ByVal sender As System.Object, ➥
      ByVal e As System.EventArgs) Handles MyBase.Init
        'CODEGEN: This method call is required by the Web Form Designer
        'Do not modify it using the code editor.
        InitializeComponent()
    End Sub

#End Region

  Private Sub Page_Load(ByVal sender As System.Object, ➥
    ByVal e As System.EventArgs) Handles MyBase.Load
    Dim ds As DataSet
    Dim db As New Database()

    Dim intReturn As Integer
    ds = db.GetDataSet("sp_RetrieveProduct " & Request.QueryString("id"))

    CS.SecurityTokenValue = New JLD.SecurityToken()
    CS.SecurityTokenValue.UserName = "emporium"
    CS.SecurityTokenValue.Password = "mystore!"
    intReturn = CS.GetInventoryLevel(Int32.Parse(Request.QueryString("id")))
    If intReturn > 0 Then
      lblAvailable.Text = ds.Tables(0).Rows(0)("Name") & "<br>" _
        & intReturn.ToString & " unit(s) available."
    Else
      lblAvailable.Text = ds.Tables(0).Rows(0)("Name") & "<br>" _
        & "Product is currently on back order."
    End If
    db.Close()

  End Sub

End Class
```

As before, we fill in the authentication information for the SOAP header so that the Web Service will call properly. After that is done, the `GetInventoryLevel` method runs with the ID value passed via the `QueryString` from the previous page. If the result is positive, the product name (retrieved from the local database) and the inventory amount are shown to the user. If not, a message indicating that the product is backordered is stored in the `Label` control on the page.

Summary

The applications in this chapter were designed to show you how to integrate two separate systems from two different companies using an XML Web Service. Instead of spending lots of time and money trying to integrate a distributor with all its customers, a web service provides an easy, non-intrusive way to exchange data. Adding the security token and SSL to encrypt data along the way makes this a great way to exchange even private financial data between trading partners.

13

Business to Customer XML Web Services

XML Web Services are primarily designed for program-to-program data transfer. When we talk about Business-to-Customer, we are really talking about server-to-desktop applications. Many of the services that people use on the Web today could be integrated into applications using Web Services. For example, a ZIP code-to-city feature is common in most customer service and call center applications. However, everyone who needs this feature has to do their own development to make it work. Making a Web Service available, possibly for a fee, could be a potential money-maker for a company willing to set it up.

In this chapter, you'll be building a Windows application that integrates with a public Web Service that returns stock quotes. The Windows application will keep a database of stocks, along with "alert" prices that should trigger a message to the user. This saves the active trader from having to watch every stock value all day long. The Web Service is hosted at xmethods.com, which is an excellent source of information on publicly available Web Services.

Designing the Database

For this application, you'll use a Microsoft Access database to hold the stocks that you are tracking. The database is called Ch13.mdb and is placed somewhere accessible by the application you'll be building. Ch13.mdb contains one table called tblStocks, whose structure is as follows:

Field Name	Data Type	Length
StockID	Text	5
LowPriceAlert	Currency	

Field Name	Data Type	Length
HighPriceAlert	Currency	
CurrentPrice	Currency	
LastPriceAlert	Date/Time	

The only field that is required is the StockID, which is also the primary key for the table. All the fields in the table will be provided for each row based on the stocks that you choose to watch.

Designing the Application

The next step in this chapter is to build the stock monitoring application. In the Visual Studio .NET environment, create a new Windows Application and give it a useful name, such as **StockMonitor**. By default, Visual Studio .NET will add a form to the application, and you'll use this form to build your first window. The first window in this application is shown in Figure 13.1.

StockID	CurrentPrice	HighPriceAlert	LowPriceAlert	LastPriceUpdate
INTC	33.92	40	30	1/28/2002
MSFT	63.82	65	60	1/28/2002
SPY	113.86	115	105	1/28/2002

FIGURE 13.1   Stock viewing window.

After selecting a stock from the list, the user can edit or delete the stock from the Functions menu. The user can also create a new stock by choosing Add from the Functions menu. The secondary window that appears is shown in Figure 13.2.

FIGURE 13.2   Stock adding & editing window.

The list window is fully responsible for all database activity, as well as interaction with the Web Service that the application uses. The editing window is called by the list window and is signaled by the edit window with the new/modified data via an event.

Referencing the External Web Service

For this application, you'll be using a Web Service that is hosted at the xmethods.net Web site. This site has an ever-growing list of publicly available Web Services running on a variety of platforms. The Web Service that you'll be using for this application can be found at `http://services.xmethods.net/soap/urn:xmethods-delayed-quotes.wsdl?`.

To add this Web Service as a reference in your solution, perform the following steps:

1. Right-click References in the Solution Explorer window and select Add Web Reference from the pop-up menu.

2. The dialog that appears allows you to enter the URL to the Web Service that you want to use. Type the URL into the box on the top of the dialog.

3. When you press the Enter key, the left side of the window will open up the WSDL (Web Services Description Language) code for the Web Service, and the Add Reference button will be enabled at the bottom of the dialog. Click the Add Reference button to add this reference.

Creating the List Window

The list window uses a DataGrid control bound directly to the Access database table. In this particular form, three controls are used to bind the database to the DataGrid—an `OleDbConnection` object, an `OleDbDataAdapter` object, and a `DataSet` object. The form also includes a Timer control and a Menu control. In this section, you'll add code and set properties for all these controls.

This form is called `frmStockMonitor` and you should set the following properties of the form before getting started with the controls:

Property	Value
(*Name*)	frmStockMonitor
Text	Stock Monitor

The next control to add is the DataGrid, which is shown on the Toolbox's Windows Forms tab. Add the control to your form and set the following properties:

Property	Value
(*Name*)	grdStocks
AlternatingBackColor	224,224,224
BackColor	White
CaptionVisible	False
ReadOnly	True
RowHeadersVisible	False

As you add the database binding controls, other properties will be set for you. Place the control so that you have a margin on the top and left of the control. In the Resize event handler, you'll write code to resize this control to fill the form's area, and the margin will be based on the position of the upper-left corner of the control.

Periodically, this window will update the prices of the stocks being monitored. To do this, a Timer control can be set with an interval in milliseconds to refresh every 10 minutes, which would be 600000 milliseconds. This value goes into the Interval property. Add a Timer control and set the following properties:

Property	Value
(*Name*)	tmrInterval
Enabled	True
Interval	600000

If you want, you can change the interval to be a shorter length of time for testing purposes.

The last non-data control you need to add is the Menu control. Unlike previous versions of Visual Basic, there is no separate menu editor. After you add the Menu control to your form, you can edit the menu in place. The following are the menu choices and options you want to create for the menu:

Text	Name	Shortcut
&Functions		mnuFunc
&Add Stock...	Ctrl+A	mnuFuncAdd
&Edit Stock...	Ctrl+E	mnuFuncEdit
&Delete Stock		mnuFuncDel
-		mnuFuncSeparator
E&xit		mnuFuncExit

Now that all the non-data controls are created, you can add your data controls to bind the grid. The first control you want is the OleDbConnection control, which is on the Data tab of the Toolbox. The properties you need to set on this control are as follows:

Property	Value
(*Name*)	dbStocks
ConnectionString	* use wizard to create connection string

When you select the ConnectionString property, you'll have the option to create a new connection string to point to your Access database.

The next step is to create an OleDbDataAdapter control to handle changes to the database that you will be making by way of the DataSet object. Create the OleDbDataAdapter control, name it **daStocks**, and then right-click it to select Configure Data Adapter from the pop-up menu. Using a wizard, the Data Adapter will generate the SQL statements to insert, delete, and update records based on the SQL SELECT statement you write. Use the following SQL statement or a variation:

```
SELECT StockID, CurrentPrice, HighPriceAlert, LowPriceAlert, LastPriceUpdate
FROM tblStocks ORDER BY StockID
```

After you enter this statement and continue through the configuration wizard, the insert, update, and delete statements will be generated automatically for you.

The final step is to generate a DataSet object. If you right-click the configured data adapter object, you can select Generate DataSet from the pop-up menu. In the dialog that appears, you can choose to create a new DataSet object and to link it to the tblStocks table the data adapter is providing. You can rename the DataSet to **dsStocks**, which is what is used in the example code.

The final step in binding is to tie the DataSet to the DataGrid control. This can be done in several ways. You can bind the DataSet at design time by changing the DataSource property of the DataGrid to point to the DataSet you created. The other way you can do it is through code, which you'll see in the code in the next section.

Adding the List Window Code

Now that you have the window designed, it's time to add the code behind the scenes. There are many graphical effects that you might want to add, but for reasons of simplicity, the number of "bonus" features has been kept to a minimum. This application is designed to let you focus on working with the Web Service in a typical client application.

Listing 13.1 shows the code for the list window that you need to write. Most of the code in your form is automatically generated and is omitted here for clarity. Much of the generated code deals with the database controls that you already added to the form.

LISTING 13.1   frmListStocks.frm—Code for the List Window

```
Public Class frmStockMonitor
  Inherits System.Windows.Forms.Form
  Private SS As
➥    New StockService.netxmethodsservicesstockquoteStockQuoteService()
  Private WithEvents frmEdit As frmEditStock
```

LISTING 13.1   Continued

```
  Private Sub tmrInterval_Tick(ByVal sender As System.Object,
➡      ByVal e As System.EventArgs) Handles tmrInterval.Tick
    UpdatePrices()
  End Sub


  Private Sub frmStockMonitor_Load(ByVal sender As System.Object,
➡      ByVal e As System.EventArgs) Handles MyBase.Load
    daStocks.Fill(dsStocks.Tables(0))
    grdStocks.SetDataBinding(dsStocks.Tables(0), "")
    UpdatePrices()
  End Sub


  Private Sub UpdatePrices()
    Dim dr As DataRow
    For Each dr In dsStocks.Tables(0).Rows
      dr("CurrentPrice") = SS.getQuote(dr("StockID").ToString())
      dr("LastPriceUpdate") = Now()
    Next dr
    daStocks.Update(dsStocks.Tables(0))
  End Sub


  Private Sub frmStockMonitor_Resize(ByVal sender As Object,
➡      ByVal e As System.EventArgs) Handles MyBase.Resize
    grdStocks.Height = Height - (grdStocks.Top * 2)
    grdStocks.Width = Width - (grdStocks.Left * 2)
    grdStocks.PreferredColumnWidth = grdStocks.Width / 5
  End Sub


  Private Sub mnuFuncEdit_Click(ByVal sender As System.Object,
➡      ByVal e As System.EventArgs) Handles mnuFuncEdit.Click
    Dim dr As DataRow
    dr = dsStocks.Tables(0).Rows(grdStocks.CurrentCell.RowNumber)
    frmEdit = New frmEditStock(dr("StockID"), dr("LowPriceAlert"),
➡        dr("HighPriceAlert"))
  End Sub


  Private Sub mnuFuncAdd_Click(ByVal sender As Object,
➡      ByVal e As System.EventArgs) Handles mnuFuncAdd.Click
    frmEdit = New frmEditStock()
  End Sub
```

LISTING 13.1   Continued

```
  Private Sub mnuFuncExit_Click(ByVal sender As Object,
➡    ByVal e As System.EventArgs) Handles mnuFuncExit.Click
    Me.Close()
  End Sub

  Private Sub frmEdit_EditComplete(ByVal strStock As String,
➡    ByVal dblLowPrice As Double, ByVal dblHighPrice As Double)
➡    Handles frmEdit.EditComplete
    Dim dr As DataRow
    For Each dr In dsStocks.Tables(0).Rows
      If dr("StockID") = strStock Then
        dr("LowPriceAlert") = dblLowPrice
        dr("HighPriceAlert") = dblHighPrice
        UpdatePrices()
        Exit For
      End If
    Next
  End Sub

  Private Sub frmEdit_AddComplete(ByVal strStock As String,
➡    ByVal dblLowPrice As Double, ByVal dblHighPrice As Double)
➡    Handles frmEdit.AddComplete
    Dim dr As DataRow = dsStocks.Tables(0).NewRow
    dr("StockID") = strStock
    dr("LowPriceAlert") = dblLowPrice
    dr("HighPriceAlert") = dblHighPrice
    dsStocks.Tables(0).Rows.Add(dr)
    UpdatePrices()
  End Sub

  Private Sub mnuFuncDel_Click(ByVal sender As System.Object,
➡    ByVal e As System.EventArgs) Handles mnuFuncDel.Click
    If MessageBox.Show("Delete this stock?", "Stock Monitor", _
      MessageBoxButtons.YesNo, MessageBoxIcon.Exclamation) = DialogResult.Yes Then
      dsStocks.Tables(0).Rows(grdStocks.CurrentCell.RowNumber).Delete()
      daStocks.Update(dsStocks)
    End If
  End Sub
End Class
```

Starting at the top, we have some form-level variables that are declared. The SS variable is a reference to the StockService Web Service that has been referenced in the project already. The `frmEdit` variable refers to the stock editing form that you will create in the next section. This form will be raising events to the list window, so the variable is declared using the `WithEvents` keyword.

The first event handler, `tmrInterval_Tick`, in the listing is the `Tick` event of the Timer control. When the timer expires, the stock prices are updated via the `UpdatePrices` subroutine. This subroutine is also called when the window initially loads, shown in the `Load` event handler, `frmStockMonitor_Load`, next in the listing.

The `Load` event has two tasks—bind the DataGrid to the DataSet and update the prices via the Web Service. The binding is done by first filling the DataSet from the `DataAdapter` and then by setting the binding to the grid. After this is done, the `UpdatePrices` subroutine gets the latest prices for each stock in the table.

This update is done in the `UpdatePrices` subroutine, which loops through each row in the DataSet and gets the current price for each stock symbol from the Web Service. The Web Service being used has a `getQuote` method that accepts a stock symbol and returns the last price for the stock. This price is then stored in the DataSet, and when all prices have been retrieved, the DataSet is stored in the database.

The database has the ability to store a high and low price, as well, and if the new price comes back exceeding the high price or under the low price, this routine could generate some sort of message. This feature hasn't been implemented, but it would be easy to add in this routine.

The `Resize` event of the form is managed by the `frmStockMonitor_Resize` subroutine. This event is used to resize the DataGrid to fill the form. This is done by using the upper-left corner of the DataGrid as a reference point. The margins are generated on the top and left by resizing the grid to fill the remaining space. You can modify this routine to enforce a minimum size if you wanted, but that's outside the scope of the chapter.

The rest of the code that you need to create next deals with the interaction between the list window and the editing window. The Add and Edit menu choice handlers both create new instances of the edit window; however, the Edit menu choice also passes along the stock to be edited and its low and high price alert values. Those values are passed into one of the constructors, and the Add menu choice calls a different constructor that doesn't require any arguments.

After the edits are complete in the editor window, either the `AddComplete` or `EditComplete` event is raised and intercepted by the list window. In both cases, the stock information and low/high price values are retrieved from the event data. For a new record, the new stock is added to the DataSet. For a changed record, the existing record is found and updated with the new data. In both cases, the DataSet is then saved to the database by way of the `SqlDataAdapter` object on the form. Having the edit window transmit the data back to the list window eliminates the need to have database code in both windows and makes the code somewhat easier to follow.

The last event code you need to write, other than the trivial Exit menu choice code, is the code to delete a stock. After confirming the delete with the user, the stock is removed from the DataSet. The DataSet is saved to the database and the record is removed automatically. While this works fine for our simple database, most more complex databases would include related tables for that stock. Deleting the primary key while still having related records would cause referential integrity errors, so don't count on the database to do everything for you automatically.

Designing the Stock Editing Window

The last part of this application requires that you to build an editing window to add and edit stocks in the database. This window is shown in Figure 13.3.

FIGURE 13.3   Stock editing window.

Because the bulk of the code for managing stocks is kept in the list window, this window doesn't have much code in it. To get started, you need to add some controls and set some properties on them. For the form, you need to set the following properties:

Property	Value
(*Name*)	frmEditStock
Text	### Stock

The title of the window will be changed at runtime, depending on whether the window is being used to add a new stock or to edit an existing one. The three pound signs are just there as a visual placeholder.

Next, you need three Label controls and three TextBox controls, as well as two Button controls. For the code you'll write later in the chapter, the following names are used for the controls:

- txtTicker   Ticker Symbol box

- txtLowPrice   Low Price Alert box

- txtHighPrice   High Price Alert box

- btnOK   OK button

- btnCancel   Cancel button

You can arrange the controls as you see fit, but be sure to clear the Text property of each of the TextBox controls so they initially are empty.

With the controls on the form, it's time to add the code to make this window work. The complete listing (including all the hidden code) is shown in Listing 13.2. The code you need to add is highlighted in bold in this listing.

LISTING 13.2   frmEditStock.frm—The Editor Window Code

```
Public Class frmEditStock
  Inherits System.Windows.Forms.Form
  Public Event EditComplete(ByVal strStock As String,
➥     ByVal dblLowPrice As Double, ByVal dblHighPrice As Double)
  Public Event AddComplete(ByVal strStock As String,
➥     ByVal dblLowPrice As Double, ByVal dblHighPrice As Double)
  Private blnNew As Boolean = False

  Public Sub New()
    MyBase.New()
    InitializeComponent()
    Me.Text = "Add New Stock"
    txtLowPrice.Text = "0.00"
    txtHighPrice.Text = "0.00"
    blnNew = True
    Me.Show()
  End Sub


  Public Sub New(ByVal strTicker As String,
➥     ByVal dblLowPrice As Double, ByVal dblHighPrice As Double)
    MyBase.New()
    InitializeComponent()
```

LISTING 13.2 Continued

```
   Me.Text = "Edit Stock"
   txtTicker.Text = strTicker
   txtLowPrice.Text = dblLowPrice.ToString
   txtHighPrice.Text = dblHighPrice.ToString
   Me.Show()
 End Sub

 Private Sub btnCancel_Click(ByVal sender As System.Object,
➥    ByVal e As System.EventArgs) Handles btnCancel.Click
   Me.Close()
 End Sub

 Private Sub btnOK_Click(ByVal sender As System.Object,
➥    ByVal e As System.EventArgs) Handles btnOK.Click
   If blnNew Then
     RaiseEvent AddComplete(txtTicker.Text,
➥       CDbl(txtLowPrice.Text), CDbl(txtHighPrice.Text))
   Else
     RaiseEvent EditComplete(txtTicker.Text,
➥       CDbl(txtLowPrice.Text), CDbl(txtHighPrice.Text))
   End If
   Me.Close()
 End Sub

End Class
```

This window will use events to notify its parent when the user has finished either adding a new stock or editing an existing one. This is done through two public events declared in the declarations section of the form. Each event has the same parameters; however, the events are named differently because the action that the list form needs to take is different for an addition versus an edit.

You also declare a Boolean variable to store whether or not the record is being edited. This will determine which event is raised when the user clicks the OK button.

The next code you need is the constructor, or New subroutine, for the form. Normally, the constructor is stored in the "Windows Form Designer" generated code. However, because we'll have two constructors, you need to move the default constructor (the one with no parameters) out of the #Region tag. You'll also create a second constructor that is used to edit a stock. The one with no parameters is used for adding new stocks. Each of these routines populates the boxes on the form, either with the data passed to it from the list window or with default values.

The user is then able to make changes to the values in the form, at which point he or she decides to close the window. Clicking the Cancel button simply closes the window, but clicking the OK button needs to signal the list window of the new or modified stock. The code in the OK button handler takes care of this task. Based on the value in the flag variable, the new data is either sent via the `AddComplete` or `EditComplete` events back to the list window. This routine should have some validation in a real world application; however, it's been omitted here for clarity.

Summary

The application in this chapter was designed to help get you thinking about how Web Services can be integrated into traditional client/server applications. With the wide variety of services that are expected to start appearing from companies all over the world, it's a waste of resources to try to build these features on your own. Using the various directories, including the various directory projects currently going on, you'll be able to get Web Services to accomplish many tasks that you wouldn't have been able to do before now.

14

Platform Integration

As you've already learned, web Services are an excellent way to integrate different platforms without having to create custom layers of code to do it. Because Web Services are based on open standards, any platform that supports the protocols can use Web Services to use data.

In this chapter, you'll be creating Web Services that provide product information from the Northwind Traders database. You'll then integrate those Web Services into an application designed for use with the Microsoft Mobile Internet Toolkit, which provides support for WAP and WML-enabled phones and devices. As Web Services become more mainstream, many mobile devices will be taking advantage of Web Services all over the world and the Internet.

Assembling the Tools

To build this application, you need to get a few components. Even if you don't have a WAP-enabled or WML-enabled phone, there are simulators available that will make your development job easier and let you keep your airtime bills to a minimum.

The first software package you need is the Microsoft Mobile Internet Toolkit, which is available from Microsoft as a free download. At the time of writing, the Toolkit was available at
`http://www.microsoft.com/downloads/release.asp?ReleaseID=35406`.

The second tool that you need is a WAP/WML emulator. The one that I used and was recommended in a number of discussion forums is the Openwave SDK, available from openwave.com at `http://developer.openwave.com/download/license_50.html`.

Be sure to reboot when the installation programs ask to do so. This will help ensure that the controls and libraries are installed properly.

This application also uses SQL Server as the back-end database, but you can use whatever database you want. You'll just need to make the appropriate database call changes when you start writing the code.

Building the Web Services

The first task is to build the Web Services that your mobile application will use. You'll be creating three Web Services with two methods each that access the sample Northwind Traders database. While you would typically not build Web Services for this purpose, they serve a useful purpose here to show you another method in which Web Services can be integrated into different types of applications.

To get started, create a new Web Service project in your choice of languages. For this project, we'll be using Visual Basic .NET, as has been done throughout these projects.

Adding the Database Class

The first task is to add the `Database` class to get access to SQL Server without having to write a lot of extra data access code. This class makes it easy to connect to and retrieve data from the selected database.

This class should be added to the Web Service project, because that is where you'll be accessing the database. In other cases, this class would belong in a shared assembly so it could be used among multiple projects. This class's code was covered in Chapter 12, "Business to Business XML Web Services," but Listing 14.1 provides it here for reference.

LISTING 14.1   Database.vb

```
Imports System.Data.SqlClient
Imports System.Configuration

Public Class Database
  Private m_cnDB As SqlConnection

    '
    ' This constructor reads the application configuration
    ' file (Web.config for web applications) for a string
    ' called ConnectionString. If it's not there, an exception
    ' is thrown. Otherwise, the connection is made.
    '
    Public Sub New()
```

LISTING 14.1 Continued

```
  Dim strConn As String
  strConn = ConfigurationSettings.AppSettings("ConnectionString")
  If strConn = "" Then
    Throw New Exception("Connection string not found " _
      & "in application configuration file.")
  Else
    m_cnDB = New SqlConnection(strConn)
    m_cnDB.Open()
  End If
End Sub


'
' This constructor accepts a connection string as input
' and makes a connection to that SQL Server.
'
Public Sub New(ByVal ConnectionString As String)
  m_cnDB = New SqlConnection(ConnectionString)
  m_cnDB.Open()
End Sub


'
' In case there are other objects that need the live
' connection, make it available through a read-only
' property.
'
Public ReadOnly Property Connection() As SqlConnection
Get
  Return m_cnDB
End Get
End Property


'
' Run a query that returns records in the form
' of a SqlDataReader.
'
Public Function GetDataReader(ByVal SQL As String, _
  Optional ByVal blnSkipRead As Boolean = False) As SqlDataReader

  Dim cmdQuery As New SqlCommand()
  Dim dr As SqlDataReader
  cmdQuery.Connection = m_cnDB
```

LISTING 14.1   Continued

```
      cmdQuery.CommandText = SQL
      cmdQuery.CommandType = CommandType.Text
      dr = cmdQuery.ExecuteReader
      If Not blnSkipRead Then dr.Read()
      Return dr
   End Function

   '
   ' Run a query that returns records in the form
   ' of a DataSet.
   '
   Public Function GetDataSet(ByVal SQL As String) As DataSet
      Dim da As New SqlDataAdapter(SQL, m_cnDB)
      Dim ds As New DataSet("Results")
      da.Fill(ds)
      Return ds
   End Function

   '
   ' Close the database connection.
   '
   Public Sub Close()
      m_cnDB.Close()
   End Sub
End Class
```

The class has two constructors—one that takes no arguments, and one that takes a
connection string. The one that doesn't take arguments reads the ConnectionString
variable from the web.config file located in the web application's directory. The
ConnectionString is located in the AppSettings section, as shown in the following:

```
... rest of Web.config file ...
   </system.web>
   <appSettings>
     <add key="ConnectionString"
        value="server=(local);database=Northwind;UID=sa;PWD=;" />
   </appSettings>

</configuration>
```

Creating the Products Service

Because the point of this chapter is to show how to integrate the Web Services with various platforms, these web methods are straightforward and similar to ones you've built before. The code you need to add to your Web Service file is highlighted in bold in Listing 14.2.

LISTING 14.2   Products.asmx

```
Imports System.Web.Services

<WebService(Namespace:="http://www.nwind.ncs/")> _
Public Class NorthwindProducts
  Inherits System.Web.Services.WebService

  Private db As Database

#Region " Web Services Designer Generated Code "

    Public Sub New()
      MyBase.New()

      'This call is required by the Web Services Designer.
      InitializeComponent()

      'Add your own initialization code after the InitializeComponent() call
      db = New Database()
    End Sub

    'Required by the Web Services Designer
    Private components As System.ComponentModel.IContainer

    'NOTE: The following procedure is required by the Web Services Designer
    'It can be modified using the Web Services Designer.
    'Do not modify it using the code editor.
    <System.Diagnostics.DebuggerStepThrough()> Private Sub InitializeComponent()
        components = New System.ComponentModel.Container()
    End Sub

    Protected Overloads Overrides Sub Dispose(ByVal disposing As Boolean)
        'CODEGEN: This procedure is required by the Web Services Designer
        'Do not modify it using the code editor.
        If disposing Then
```

LISTING 14.2   Continued

```
            If Not (components Is Nothing) Then
                components.Dispose()
            End If
        End If
        MyBase.Dispose(disposing)
    End Sub

#End Region

  <WebMethod(Description:="Returns all products from database, sorted by name.")> _
  Public Function GetList() As DataSet
    Return db.GetDataSet("SELECT ProductID, ProductName FROM Products "
➥        & "ORDER BY ProductName")
  End Function


  <WebMethod(Description:="Returns product details for selected product.")> _
  Public Function GetDetails(ByVal ProductID As Integer) As DataSet
    Return db.GetDataSet("SELECT * FROM Products WHERE ProductID = "
➥        & ProductID.ToString())
  End Function


End Class
```

After instantiating the Database object in the New constructor method, it connects to the database specified in the web.config file for the application. When that is done, the Web Service has a live database connection. Depending on the latency between calls, you may want to open the connection and have a timeout value so that it is shut down when it is not in use.

The first method returns a simple list. Based on the way the list will be displayed in the mobile device, only the product name will be visible, so only that field along with the primary key is required. This data is returned as a DataSet so that it can be bound to the mobile data control you'll learn about.

The second method returns the details for a particular product ID. The form will be showing some of the fields from the table, but not all. If you want, you can modify this query to only return the requested fields.

After you build this application, you can test this Web Service by exercising both methods. The first method will return a list of all the products, from which you can choose a product ID to feed into the second method. When you're sure that the Web Service is working fine, you can move on to the second part of this project.

Creating the Customers Service

The next service you need to build is used to retrieve customers and customer details. This service also has two methods—one to retrieve the list and one to retrieve the details of a particular record. One difference between this service and the last is the fact that the customer ID is a string instead of a number. The code is shown in Listing 14.3, with the code you need to write shown in boldface.

LISTING 14.3   Customers.asmx

```
Imports System.Web.Services

<WebService(Namespace:="http://www.nwind.ncs/")> _
Public Class NorthwindCustomers
  Inherits System.Web.Services.WebService

    Private db As Database

#Region " Web Services Designer Generated Code "

    Public Sub New()
      MyBase.New()

        'This call is required by the Web Services Designer.
        InitializeComponent()

        'Add your own initialization code after the InitializeComponent() call
        db = New Database()
    End Sub

    'Required by the Web Services Designer
    Private components As System.ComponentModel.IContainer

    'NOTE: The following procedure is required by the Web Services Designer
    'It can be modified using the Web Services Designer.
    'Do not modify it using the code editor.
    <System.Diagnostics.DebuggerStepThrough()>
    Private Sub InitializeComponent()
        components = New System.ComponentModel.Container()
    End Sub

    Protected Overloads Overrides Sub Dispose(ByVal disposing As Boolean)
        'CODEGEN: This procedure is required by the Web Services Designer
        'Do not modify it using the code editor.
```

LISTING 14.3   Continued

```
        If disposing Then
            If Not (components Is Nothing) Then
                components.Dispose()
            End If
        End If
        MyBase.Dispose(disposing)
    End Sub

#End Region

  <WebMethod(Description:="Returns all customers, sorted by name.")> _
  Public Function GetList() As DataSet
    Return db.GetDataSet("SELECT CompanyName, 'customers.aspx?id='"
➡        & " + CustomerID As CustomerLink FROM Customers ORDER BY CompanyName")
  End Function

  <WebMethod(Description:="Returns details for selected customer.")> _
  Public Function GetDetails(ByVal CustomerID As String) As DataSet
    Return db.GetDataSet("SELECT * FROM Customers WHERE CustomerID = '"
➡        & CustomerID.ToUpper() & "'")
  End Function

End Class
```

After initializing the service, the two methods are ready for business. The GetList method returns a DataSet with the customer name and a link to the customer that will be used later. The GetDetails method returns the details for a customer, given the customer ID. In this case, we change the customer ID to an uppercase string, because that's how it is in the database. If you want to force case sensitivity, simply remove the ToUpper() call in the GetDetails method.

Creating the Orders Service

The third Web Service you'll be creating works with the Orders table to provide information about the orders placed by a particular customer. The code for the service is shown in Listing 14.4.

LISTING 14.4   Orders.asmx

```
Imports System.Web.Services

<WebService(Namespace:="http://www.nwind.ncs/")> _
```

LISTING 14.4   Continued

```vbnet
Public Class NorthwindOrders
  Inherits System.Web.Services.WebService

  Private db As Database

#Region " Web Services Designer Generated Code "

    Public Sub New()
      MyBase.New()

      'This call is required by the Web Services Designer.
      InitializeComponent()

      'Add your own initialization code after the InitializeComponent() call
      db = New Database()
    End Sub

    'Required by the Web Services Designer
    Private components As System.ComponentModel.IContainer

    'NOTE: The following procedure is required by the Web Services Designer
    'It can be modified using the Web Services Designer.
    'Do not modify it using the code editor.
    <System.Diagnostics.DebuggerStepThrough()>
    Private Sub InitializeComponent()
        components = New System.ComponentModel.Container()
    End Sub

    Protected Overloads Overrides Sub Dispose(ByVal disposing As Boolean)
        'CODEGEN: This procedure is required by the Web Services Designer
        'Do not modify it using the code editor.
        If disposing Then
            If Not (components Is Nothing) Then
                components.Dispose()
            End If
        End If
        MyBase.Dispose(disposing)
    End Sub

#End Region
```

LISTING 14.4   Continued

```
<WebMethod(Description:="Returns all orders from database by customer ID.")>
Public Function GetList(ByVal CustomerID As String) As DataSet
    Return db.GetDataSet("SELECT CONVERT(varchar, OrderDate, 101) "
➥      & " As OrderDateConverted, " _
        & "'orders.aspx?oid=' + convert(varchar, OrderID) As OrderLink "
➥      & "FROM Orders WHERE CustomerID = '" _
        & CustomerID.ToUpper & "' ORDER BY OrderDate ASC")
End Function

<WebMethod(Description:="Returns details for selected order.")> _
Public Function GetDetails(ByVal OrderID As Integer) As DataSet
    Return db.GetDataSet("SELECT CONVERT(varchar, OrderDate, 101) "
➥        & "As OrderDateConverted, "
        & "CONVERT(varchar, ShippedDate, 101) As ShippedDateConverted " _
        & "FROM Orders WHERE OrderID = " & OrderID.ToString())
End Function

End Class
```

As in the Customers service, the customer ID is uppercased to allow any lowercase requests to be handled without generating errors. In this case, the GetList requires a customer ID to be entered to select the orders, which are returned with the order ID and the date. The order ID is actually embedded into a URL so that when it is put into the mobile device's List control, it is clickable and will pass the correct data to the orders page.

After the order ID has been obtained, the customer ID is not necessary for the next request, which is to retrieve the details about the order. In this case, the method retrieves the other fields from the Orders table, not the Order Details table. If you wanted the line items in the order, it's a simple next step to add to this application. The SQL query actually converts the dates being retrieved to the following format:

MM/DD/YYYY

This could be done in the Web page, as well, but it's just as easy to do it right in the query.

After you get all the Web Service code entered, be sure to build and test each service and each method. It's easier to find the bugs here before getting into the next portion of the chapter. With the Web Services created and tested, it's time to build the mobile application to wrap these services with a user interface.

Building the Mobile Application

The next step is to build the mobile application. One of the best parts about the Mobile Internet Toolkit is that you don't have to learn all the nuances of WAP and WML, because the server controls will determine what type of device is viewing the page and generate the appropriate code. You simply have to worry about what you want the application to do. While there isn't space to cover everything in the Mobile Internet Toolkit, you'll at least get an idea of how the pages function and how they make building mobile applications significantly easier than doing it by hand.

Creating the Main Menu

After you have the Mobile Internet Toolkit installed, you'll get a new type of project that you can create—the Mobile Web Application. It appears in the New Project dialog, as shown in Figure 14.1.

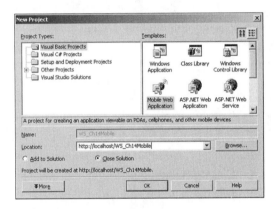

FIGURE 14.1   The new project dialog box.

The sample code's project name is WS_Ch14Mobile, but you can name yours whatever you want. When you click OK, Visual Studio .NET will create the project in your Web server and present you with a blank .aspx page. The first page you'll be building is a menu to the customer and product viewers. The order viewer will be accessible from a customer viewer. This page will have two links on it, as well as a title on the page created using a label control. To build the page, perform the following steps:

1. Set the ID property of the form to **frmMenu**.

2. Add a Label control to the form and give it the ID value of **lblTitle**. Set the Text property to **Northwind Traders**, and you may want to change the font to bold.

3. Add a Link control to the form. Give it the ID property of **lnkCustomers**. Set the Text property to **Customer Viewer** and set the NavigateURL property to **customers.aspx**.

4. Add a second Link control to the form. Give it an ID property of **lnkProducts**. Set the Text property to **Product Catalog** and set the NavigateURL property to **products.aspx**.

When you're done adding the controls, the page will look like Figure 14.2 in design view.

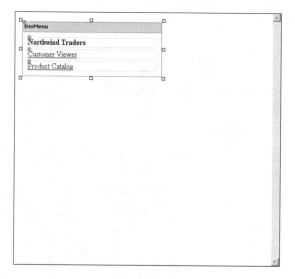

FIGURE 14.2   The main menu of the mobile application.

The link controls will let the user go to each of the other viewers. No back-end code is required for this page to work properly, so you're done coding the page. Be sure to save your work to prevent any unexpected problems.

You can test this page in a regular Web browser; however, to fully test it, it should be run in the simulator. Depending on the simulator you use, the steps to select the URL may be different. Using the Openwave 5.0 simulator, this page looks like Figure 14.3 when it is running. You should also remember that the links you built in this page are pointing to pages that don't exist yet.

The user can navigate to the links using either the up/down buttons or the number keys on the phone. Of course, clicking any of the links at this point will earn you an error because the pages don't exist yet.

FIGURE 14.3   The main menu as seen in the OpenWave simulator.

Creating the Customer Viewer

The next page you need to build is the customer list page. Because of the inherent limits in the mobile device, there will only be room for the company name, and even that may wrap onto more than one line. The first page will show a list of links to each of the customer records, and the user's device will allow him or her to scroll through the data. Selecting an item will bring up the contact name, phone, and fax number for the customer. The user will also be able to link to the orders placed by the customer from the customer details viewer.

For this portion of the application, you'll need two forms—one for the customer list, and one for the customer detail page. The order viewer will be taken care of using a separate .aspx page. To build this page, do the following:

1. Create a new Mobile Web Form in your project and name it **customers.aspx**.

2. Change the ID property of the form to **frmList**.

3. Add a Label control to the form and give it the ID value of **lblTitle**. Set the Text property to **Customer List**, and you may want to change the font to bold.

4. Add a List control to the form and give it the ID value of **lstCustomers**. Set the DataTextField value to **CompanyName**, and set the DataValueField value to **CustomerLink**. These two fields will let the list control read the fields from the

DataSet that you'll bind to the control. You should also set the ItemsAsLinks property to **True**. This will make the List control use the value for each item as a URL, and the text for each item will be the text shown to the user.

5. Add a second form to the .aspx file and set its ID property to **frmDetails**. This form will be placed just below the first one you created. Don't worry, you'll only see one at a time when the page is running.

6. Add four Label controls and a Link control to the form. These controls will be used to show the customer details. The Text property of each should be deleted. The names are as follows:

   - **lblCompanyName** (the example uses a bold font for this)
   - **lblContactName**
   - **lblPhone**
   - **lblFax**

   The Link control should be named **lnkOrders** and its Text property should be set to **View Orders**. You will populate the NavigateURL property at runtime.

When you are done adding the controls, the .aspx page will look like Figure 14.4 in design view.

FIGURE 14.4   The customer viewer menu.

The next step is to add the code behind the page. The code for this page is shown in Listing 14.5.

LISTING 14.5   customers.aspx

```
Public Class pgCustomers
  Inherits System.Web.UI.MobileControls.MobilePage
  Protected WithEvents lblTitle As System.Web.UI.MobileControls.Label
  Protected WithEvents frmList As System.Web.UI.MobileControls.Form
  Protected WithEvents lstCustomers As System.Web.UI.MobileControls.List
  Protected WithEvents lblPhone As System.Web.UI.MobileControls.Label
  Protected WithEvents lblContactName As System.Web.UI.MobileControls.Label
  Protected WithEvents lblCompanyName As System.Web.UI.MobileControls.Label
  Protected WithEvents frmDetails As System.Web.UI.MobileControls.Form
  Protected WithEvents lblFax As System.Web.UI.MobileControls.Label
  Protected WithEvents lnkOrders As System.Web.UI.MobileControls.Link
  Private C As New NTCustomers.NorthwindCustomers()


#Region " Web Form Designer Generated Code "

  'This call is required by the Web Form Designer.
  <System.Diagnostics.DebuggerStepThrough()> Private Sub InitializeComponent()

  End Sub

  Private Sub Page_Init(ByVal sender As System.Object,
➥     ByVal e As System.EventArgs) Handles MyBase.Init
      'CODEGEN: This method call is required by the Web Form Designer
      'Do not modify it using the code editor.
      InitializeComponent()
  End Sub

#End Region

  Private Sub Page_Load(ByVal sender As System.Object,
➥     ByVal e As System.EventArgs) Handles MyBase.Load
    If Request.QueryString("ID") <> "" Then
      Dim ds As DataSet = C.GetDetails(Request.QueryString("ID"))
      Dim dr As DataRow = ds.Tables(0).Rows(0)
      lblCompanyName.Text = dr("CompanyName")
      lblContactName.Text = dr("ContactName")
      lblPhone.Text = "Phone: " & dr("Phone")
```

LISTING 14.5   Continued

```
      lblFax.Text = "Fax: " & dr("Fax")
      lnkOrders.NavigateUrl = "orders.aspx?id=" & Request.QueryString("ID")
      Me.ActiveForm = frmDetails
   Else
      Dim ds As DataSet = C.GetList
      lstCustomers.DataSource = ds
      lstCustomers.DataBind()
   End If
End Sub

End Class
```

If this page is called with no value in the query string variable named ID, the page assumes it is being asked to list the customer data using the frmList page. For this, it uses the GetList method of the NorthwindCustomers service and binds this data to the List control.

After the user selects an item from the list, the link will contain a value for the ID and the other part of the Page_Load routine will run, filling the Label controls with the details for the customer. The NavigateURL property of the Link control will become

orders.aspx?id=#

The # will be replaced by the customer ID being viewed.

With the code complete, it's time to test this page in the simulator. When you select Customer Viewer from the main menu, you'll see the customer list, as shown in Figure 14.5. Remember that the links on the page are still pointing to other pages you haven't created yet.

FIGURE 14.5   The customer list, as seen in the simulator.

The limitations of the mobile device are evident here because of the long company names being used. However, you can scroll through the list and select a customer to view. When you do so, the page shown in Figure 14.6 will appear.

FIGURE 14.6   The customer details, as seen in the simulator.

If everything worked fine, you can move on to the next step—the order list and detail page.

Creating the Order Viewer

The next page is only accessible from the customer detail page, because it's necessary to have a customer ID to select an order. You could modify this page to list orders by date, regardless of customer, but considering the large number of orders in the sample database, this might not be the best approach.

The order viewer initially lists the orders, sorted by date, for a selected customer. The order date is shown, but you could show the order number if that was more useful for your business application. Selecting an order brings up information on when that order was placed and when it was shipped. A logical extension would be to show the line items for the order, but this would be difficult, given the page size restrictions on most mobile devices.

This page is similar in structure to the Customer Viewer, with some naming changes and a few less controls on the detail view. Perform the following steps to create the Order Viewer:

1. Create a new Mobile Web Form in your project and name it **orders.aspx**.

2. Change the ID property of the form to **frmList**.

3. Add a Label control to the form and give it the ID value of **lblTitle**. Set the Text property to **Order List**, and you may want to change the font to bold.

4. Add a List control to the form and give it the ID value of **lstOrders**. Set the DataTextField value to **OrderDateConverted**, and set the DataValueField value

to **OrderLink**. These two fields will let the list control read the fields from the DataSet that you'll bind to the control. You should also set the ItemsAsLinks property to **True**. This will make the List control use the value for each item as a URL, and the text for each item will be the text shown to the user.

5. Add a second form to the .aspx file and set its ID property to **frmDetails**. This form will be placed just below the first one you created. Don't worry, you'll only see one at a time when the page is running.

6. Add three Label controls to the form. These controls will be used to show the order details. The Text property of each should be deleted. The names are as follows:

- **lblDetailsTitle** (set the Text to **Order Details**)

- **lblOrderDate**

- **lblShippedDate**

When you are done adding the controls, the .aspx page will look like Figure 14.7 in design view.

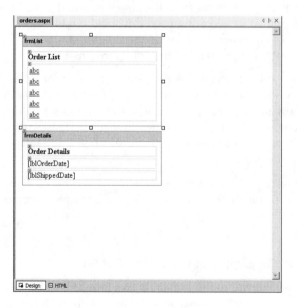

FIGURE 14.7   Order viewer in design mode.

The next step is to add the code behind the page. The code for this page is shown in Listing 14.6.

LISTING 14.6 orders.aspx

```
Public Class pgOrders
  Inherits System.Web.UI.MobileControls.MobilePage
  Protected WithEvents lstOrders As System.Web.UI.MobileControls.List
  Protected WithEvents lblTitle As System.Web.UI.MobileControls.Label
  Protected WithEvents frmList As System.Web.UI.MobileControls.Form
  Protected WithEvents lblShippedDate As System.Web.UI.MobileControls.Label
  Protected WithEvents lblOrderDate As System.Web.UI.MobileControls.Label
  Protected WithEvents lblDetailTitle As System.Web.UI.MobileControls.Label
  Protected WithEvents frmDetails As System.Web.UI.MobileControls.Form
  Private O As New NTOrders.NorthwindOrders()

#Region " Web Form Designer Generated Code "

    'This call is required by the Web Form Designer.
    <System.Diagnostics.DebuggerStepThrough()> Private Sub InitializeComponent()

    End Sub


    Private Sub Page_Init(ByVal sender As System.Object,
➡       ByVal e As System.EventArgs) Handles MyBase.Init
        'CODEGEN: This method call is required by the Web Form Designer
        'Do not modify it using the code editor.
        InitializeComponent()
    End Sub

#End Region

  Private Sub Page_Load(ByVal sender As System.Object,
➡     ByVal e As System.EventArgs) Handles MyBase.Load
    If Request.QueryString("oID") <> "" Then
      Dim ds As DataSet = O.GetDetails(CInt(Request.QueryString("oID")))
      Dim dr As DataRow = ds.Tables(0).Rows(0)
      lblOrderDate.Text = "Ordered: " & dr("OrderDateConverted")
      lblShippedDate.Text = "Shipped: " & dr("ShippedDateConverted")
      Me.ActiveForm = frmDetails
    Else
      Dim ds As DataSet = O.GetList(Request.QueryString("ID").ToUpper())
      lstOrders.DataSource = ds
      lstOrders.DataBind()
    End If
```

LISTING 14.5   Continued

```
  End Sub

End Class
```

This page is called using a particular customer ID, sent via the query string variable called *ID*. When the page views order details, that order ID will be sent via the *oID* variable.

If this page is called with no value in the query string variable named *oID*, the page assumes it is being asked to list the customer data using the frmList page. For this, it uses the GetList method of the NorthwindOrders service and binds this data to the List control.

After the user selects an item from the list, the link will contain a value for the ID and the other part of the Page_Load routine will run, filling the Label controls with the details for the customer. The NavigateURL property of the Link control will become

```
orders.aspx?oid=#
```

The # will be replaced by the order ID being viewed.

With the code complete, it's time to test this page in the simulator. When you select View Orders from the details view of a customer, you'll see the order list, as shown in Figure 14.8.

FIGURE 14.8   The order list, as seen in the simulator.

The user can scroll up and down the list to see the orders placed by this customer. Selecting an order transfers the user to the order detail view, which is shown in Figure 14.9.

The last part of the application is to build the product catalog viewer, which is accessed from the main menu of the application.

FIGURE 14.9   Order details, as seen in the simulator.

Creating the Product Catalog

The last step in this application is to build the product catalog viewer. This page
follows the same design pattern as the customer viewer that you did earlier. Initially,
you'll see a list of products. Clicking on a product will bring up some of the important details of that product. Perform the following steps to create the product
catalog:

1. Create a new Mobile Web Form in your project and name it **products.aspx**.

2. Change the ID property of the form to **frmList**.

3. Add a Label control to the form and give it the ID value of **lblTitle**. Set the
   Text property to **Product List**, and you may want to change the font to bold.

4. Add a List control to the form and give it the ID value of **lstProducts**. Set the
   DataTextField value to **ProductName**, and set the DataValueField value to
   ProductID. These two fields will let the list control read the fields from the
   DataSet that you'll bind to the control.

5. Add a second form to the .aspx file and set its ID property to **frmDetails**.

6. Add four Label controls to the form. These controls will be used to show the
   product details. The Text property of each should be deleted. The names are as
   follows:

   - **lblProductName** (set font to bold)

   - **lblPrice**

   - **lblQuantityPerUnit**

   - **lblUnitsInStock**

When you are done adding the controls, the .aspx page will look like Figure 14.10 in
design view.

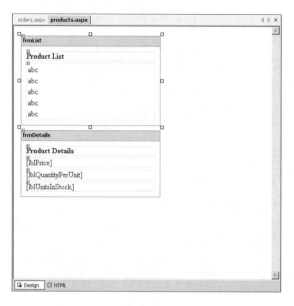

FIGURE 14.10   The product viewer in design mode.

The next step is to add the code behind the page. The code for this page is shown in Listing 14.7.

LISTING 14.7   products.aspx

```
Imports System.Data

Public Class pgProducts
    Inherits System.Web.UI.MobileControls.MobilePage
    Protected WithEvents frmList As System.Web.UI.MobileControls.Form
    Protected WithEvents lstProducts As System.Web.UI.MobileControls.List
    Protected WithEvents lblTitle As System.Web.UI.MobileControls.Label
    Protected WithEvents frmDetails As System.Web.UI.MobileControls.Form
    Protected WithEvents lblProductName As System.Web.UI.MobileControls.Label
    Protected WithEvents lblPrice As System.Web.UI.MobileControls.Label
    Protected WithEvents lblQuantityPerUnit As System.Web.UI.MobileControls.Label
    Protected WithEvents lblUnitsInStock As System.Web.UI.MobileControls.Label
    Private S As New NTProducts.NorthwindProducts()
#Region " Web Form Designer Generated Code "

    'This call is required by the Web Form Designer.
    <System.Diagnostics.DebuggerStepThrough()>
    Private Sub InitializeComponent()
```

LISTING 14.7   Continued

```
    End Sub

    Private Sub Page_Init(ByVal sender As System.Object,
➡        ByVal e As System.EventArgs) Handles MyBase.Init
            'CODEGEN: This method call is required by the Web Form Designer
            'Do not modify it using the code editor.
            InitializeComponent()
    End Sub

#End Region

    Private Sub Page_Load(ByVal sender As System.Object,
➡      ByVal e As System.EventArgs) Handles MyBase.Load
        Dim ds As DataSet = S.GetList
        lstProducts.DataSource = ds
        lstProducts.DataBind()
    End Sub

    Protected Sub lstProducts_ItemCommand(ByVal sender As Object,
➡        ByVal e As System.Web.UI.MobileControls.ListCommandEventArgs)
➡        Handles lstProducts.ItemCommand

        Dim ds As DataSet = S.GetDetails(CInt(e.ListItem.Value))
        Dim dr As DataRow = ds.Tables(0).Rows(0)
        lblProductName.Text = dr("ProductName").ToString()
        lblPrice.Text = "Price: " & CDbl(dr("UnitPrice")).ToString("C")
        lblQuantityPerUnit.Text = "Qty: " & dr("QuantityPerUnit").ToString()
        If dr("UnitsInStock") > 0 Then
          lblUnitsInStock.Text = "Stock: " & dr("UnitsInStock").ToString()
➡            & " units"
        Else
          lblUnitsInStock.Text = "Out of Stock"
        End If
        Me.ActiveForm = frmDetails
    End Sub
End Class
```

This page is initially called with no parameters on the query string, and the
Page_Load event fills the List control with the records sent back from the
NorthwindProducts service. Because the products' ID values match with the order,
they are placed into the list.

After the user selects an item, the ItemCommand event is triggered, and the value of the product is passed through the e variable. This code then creates a new DataSet using the GetDetails method of the NorthwindProducts service.

With the code complete, it's time to test this page in the simulator. When you select View Orders from the details view of a customer, you'll see the product list, as shown in Figure 14.11.

FIGURE 14.11   The product list, as seen in the simulator.

The user can scroll up and down the list to see the products in the catalog. Selecting a product opens the product detail view, shown in Figure 14.12.

FIGURE 14.12   Product details, as seen in the simulator.

Summary

The goal of this chapter was to show you how to integrate Web Services with different platforms. In Chapter 13, "Business to Customer XML Web Services," you already did some of this by using a Web Service located on a different operating system (Apache Web Server on Linux, at the time of writing). In this chapter, you integrated your Web Services with the Mobile Internet Toolkit, which provides wireless and handset users views into the same data that you can get from a Web page. As WAP/WML-enabled handsets become more powerful and faster, many analysts predict that more Web browsing will be done on handsets than on desktop computers. Learning this toolkit and some of the techniques covered in this chapter will serve you well in the future.

15

Portals

Now that you've learned how to build and use Web Services, you'll be building an application that ties together a variety of Web Services into a single portal application built using ASP.NET. This application will be able to do the following:

• Allow new users to register automatically

• Retrieve the weather for a particular ZIP code

• Retrieve information about a user's stocks

• Retrieve news headlines from a variety of news sources

• Allow the user profile to be edited to change the information being displayed in the portal page

The profile information will be stored in Microsoft SQL Server 2000, but you can use any database you want. This application uses a total of four Web Services that were available at the time of writing through the XMethods site (xmethods.net). By using publicly available services, you eliminate the need to "reinvent the wheel" for your portal. You can focus instead on the user interface and how the Web Services interact with the user's portal desktop. When the portal is running, it looks something like Figure 15.1.

After the user logs into the portal, the page shown in Figure 15.2 will appear.

The main portal page includes sections for the local weather, the stocks the user wishes to track, and the current headlines. At the top of the page, the user can choose to log out of the system or edit his/her profile, which allows the ZIP code and/or the stocks to be changed. You could also add an additional page to allow passwords to be changed, but this is left for you to complete.

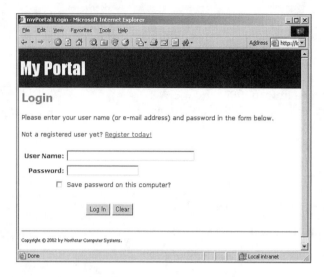

FIGURE 15.1   User interface for the portal application.

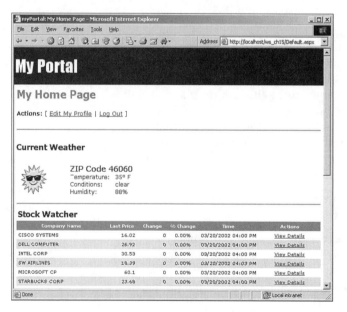

FIGURE 15.2   The user's home page for the portal application.

In the process of building this page, you'll also work with the following features of .NET:

- Forms Authentication security
- File I/O
- Web user controls
- Validation controls

These technology components, as well as the others you've already learned, will help you build a better application for the potential users of the system.

Designing the Database

The database for this application consists of two tables—tblUsers and tblUserStocks. The tblUsers table contains the usernames, passwords, and ZIP codes of the registered users of the system. The tblUserStocks table contains one row for each stock that any user wants to track. Because the application will be getting stock data for each stock individually, this table structure works out nicely for quickly looping through the table data. In the sample code, the database is named WSCh15 and was built in SQL Server 2000. When you've created your database, you can use the script shown in Listing 15.1 to create the tables.

LISTING 15.1   Tables.sql—Tables for the Web Portal

```
if exists (select * from dbo.sysobjects where id =
object_id(N'[dbo].[tblUserStocks]')
and OBJECTPROPERTY(id, N'IsUserTable') = 1)
drop table [dbo].[tblUserStocks]
GO


if exists (select * from dbo.sysobjects where id =
object_id(N'[dbo].[tblUsers]')
and OBJECTPROPERTY(id, N'IsUserTable') = 1)
drop table [dbo].[tblUsers]
GO


CREATE TABLE [dbo].[tblUserStocks] (
    [pkStockID] [varchar] (10) NOT NULL ,
    [fkUserID] [int] NOT NULL
) ON [PRIMARY]
GO
```

LISTING 15.1   Continued

```
CREATE TABLE [dbo].[tblUsers] (
     [pkUserID] [int] IDENTITY (1, 1) NOT NULL ,
     [UserName] [varchar] (20) NOT NULL ,
     [Password] [varchar] (20) NOT NULL ,
     [ZipCode] [varchar] (5) NOT NULL
) ON [PRIMARY]
GO
```

Besides the tables, there are also several stored procedures that cut down on the amount of raw SQL code required in the application. The first, sp_GetUser, returns the information for the user specified by a username and password. If this stored procedure doesn't return any records, it means that the user and/or password are incorrect, and an appropriate message is displayed to the user.

The sp_GetUserByID routine is used to retrieve a user's profile information, based on the primary numeric key value. This is used on the portal viewer page, as well as the profile editor page, to retrieve the key information from the database about this particular user.

The sp_GetUserStocks routine brings back all the stock records for a particular user ID. The primary key of the tblUserStocks table is the ticker symbol. No primary key was defined on this table because we are not checking for duplicate stock symbols. In all actuality, a duplicate symbol won't hurt anything in the system, so it's not a concern at this point.

The script to generate the stored procedures is shown in Listing 15.2.

LISTING 15.2   StoredProcs.sql— Generating the Stored Procedures for the Web Portal

```
if exists (select * from dbo.sysobjects
where id = object_id(N'[dbo].[sp_GetUser]')
and OBJECTPROPERTY(id, N'IsProcedure') = 1)
drop procedure [dbo].[sp_GetUser]
GO

if exists (select * from dbo.sysobjects
where id = object_id(N'[dbo].[sp_GetUserByID]')
and OBJECTPROPERTY(id, N'IsProcedure') = 1)
drop procedure [dbo].[sp_GetUserByID]
GO
```

LISTING 15.2 Continued

```
if exists (select * from dbo.sysobjects
where id = object_id(N'[dbo].[sp_GetUserStocks]')
and OBJECTPROPERTY(id, N'IsProcedure') = 1)
drop procedure [dbo].[sp_GetUserStocks]
GO

SET QUOTED_IDENTIFIER OFF
GO
SET ANSI_NULLS OFF
GO

CREATE PROCEDURE dbo.sp_GetUser
@UserName varchar(20),
@Password varchar(20)
AS
SELECT *
FROM tblUsers
WHERE Upper(UserName) = Upper(@UserName)
AND Upper(Password) = Upper(@Password)

GO
SET QUOTED_IDENTIFIER OFF
GO
SET ANSI_NULLS ON
GO

SET QUOTED_IDENTIFIER OFF
GO
SET ANSI_NULLS OFF
GO

CREATE PROCEDURE dbo.sp_GetUserByID
@UserID int
AS
SELECT *
FROM tblUsers
WHERE pkUserID = @UserID
GO
SET QUOTED_IDENTIFIER OFF
GO
SET ANSI_NULLS ON
```

LISTING 15.2   Continued

```
GO

SET QUOTED_IDENTIFIER ON
GO
SET ANSI_NULLS ON
GO

CREATE PROCEDURE dbo.sp_GetUserStocks
@UserID int
AS
SELECT * FROM tblUserStocks
WHERE fkUserID = @UserID
ORDER BY pkStockID

GO
SET QUOTED_IDENTIFIER OFF
GO
SET ANSI_NULLS ON
GO
```

You may want to create a user ID and password that the Web application will use to access the application database. If you're in a testing mode, you can use the **sa** username with a blank password, but be sure that your SQL Server is set up to allow mixed (or SQL) authentication. The next step is to set up the application configuration file.

Configuring the Application

When you're finished setting up the database, you should create a new ASP.NET Web Application on your test server. In the sample code, the Web application is called WS_Ch15. When that is done, you'll need to make a few server changes to allow this application to work. One of the Web Services that you'll use returns a long stream of XML, which will need to be converted for use with the Web page. One of the easier ways to do this is to write the string to a text file and then read it into the DataSet using the ReadXML function. To do this, however, the ASP.NET worker process (the user ID is ASPNET) needs to have access to write to the server at some location. Find a directory to use and give the ASPNET user ID Full Control over that directory using NTFS permissions.

The next step is to set up the web.config file for the application. Listing 15.3 shows the settings you should put into this file to configure the security properly.

LISTING 15.3   web.config—Security Settings

```
<?xml version="1.0" encoding="utf-8" ?>
<configuration>

  <system.web>

    <!-- DYNAMIC DEBUG COMPILATION
         Set compilation debug="true" to insert
         debugging symbols (.pdb information)
         into the compiled page. Because this
         creates a larger file that executes
         more slowly, you should set this value
         to true only when debugging and to
         false at all other times. For more information,
         refer to the documentation about
         debugging ASP.NET files.
    -->
    <compilation defaultLanguage="vb" debug="true" />

    <!-- CUSTOM ERROR MESSAGES
         Set customErrors mode="On" or "RemoteOnly" to
         enable custom error messages, "Off" to disable.
         Add <error> tags for each of the errors you want to handle.
    -->
    <customErrors mode="RemoteOnly" />

    <!-- AUTHENTICATION
         This section sets the authentication policies of
         the application. Possible modes are "Windows",
         "Forms", "Passport" and "None"
    -->
    <authentication mode="Forms">
      <forms name="Users"
        path="/" loginUrl="login.aspx" protection="All" timeout="20" />
    </authentication>

    <!-- AUTHORIZATION
         This section sets the authorization policies
         of the application. You can allow or deny access
         to application resources by user or role.
         Wildcards: "*" mean everyone, "?" means anonymous
```

LISTING 15.3   Continued

```
                (unauthenticated) users.
      -->
      <authorization>
        <deny users="?" />
      </authorization>


      <!-- APPLICATION-LEVEL TRACE LOGGING
           Application-level tracing enables trace log
           output for every page within an application.
           Set trace enabled="true" to enable application
           trace logging.  If pageOutput="true", the
           trace information will be displayed at the bottom
           of each page.  Otherwise, you can view the
           application trace log by browsing the "trace.axd"
           page from your web application
           root.
      -->
      <trace enabled="false" requestLimit="10" pageOutput="false"
         traceMode="SortByTime" localOnly="true" />



      <!-- SESSION STATE SETTINGS
           By default ASP.NET uses cookies to identify which
           requests belong to a particular session.
           If cookies are not available, a session can be tracked
           by adding a session identifier to the URL.
           To disable cookies, set sessionState cookieless="true".
      -->
      <sessionState
            mode="InProc"
            stateConnectionString="tcpip=127.0.0.1:42424"
            sqlConnectionString="data source=127.0.0.1;user id=sa;password="
            cookieless="false"
            timeout="20"
      />


      <!-- GLOBALIZATION
           This section sets the globalization settings of the application.
      -->
      <globalization requestEncoding="utf-8" responseEncoding="utf-8" />

   </system.web>
```

LISTING 15.3 Continued

```
<location path="login.aspx">
  <system.web>
    <authorization><allow users="?" /></authorization>
  </system.web>
</location>
<location path="profile.aspx">
  <system.web>
    <authorization><allow users="?" /></authorization>
  </system.web>
</location>
<appSettings>
    <add
        key="ConnectionString"
      value="server=(local);database=WSCh15;uid=sa;pwd=;" />
</appSettings>
</configuration>
```

The first section that is marked in this file indicates that this application will be handling security via Forms. Security in ASP.NET applications can be handled in four different ways—no security, form (or user-defined), Microsoft Passport, and Windows authentication. Because using Microsoft Passport isn't practical for most developers, and because most public web sites don't use Windows authentication, forms authentication is probably going to be the most likely choice for most applications that make their way to the Web.

The name attribute is the name of the cookie that will be used for authentication. You won't have to access that cookie directly; instead, there are functions in the FormsAuthentication object (part of System.Web.Security namespace) that makes your job easier. The loginURL parameter specifies what page to use to let the user log into the application. The application will use the cookie to determine if the user has logged in; if not, the user will automatically go to the login page.

The next section in the configuration file that's marked removes access to anonymous users for the site. The question mark refers to anonymous users in this case, so telling the application to deny access to all anonymous users has the effect of locking everyone out who does not authenticate using the login page that you'll build. The problem with that is twofold: users still need access to the login page, and new users need to be able to register using the profile page.

These concerns are covered by the <location> tags at the end of the document. You can think of the <location> tags as overrides. Each of these tags specifies that one page (login.aspx and profile.aspx) can be accessed by unauthenticated users.

The last section is the database connection string, which you should change to fit your server and Web configuration. With the configuration complete, it's time to write some code.

Adding the Business Objects

This application requires the use of several classes, which will be added to the single ASP.NET application instead of being placed in a separate project. The first class is the Database class, which you've used in previous projects. Because the code for this class has been covered in previous chapters, we'll omit the listing here. If you need to refer to the code, look at Listing 12.2.

The second class is called MyStockData and this class will be used in conjunction with the stock information service that the application uses. The code for this class is shown in Listing 15.4.

LISTING 15.4   MyStockData.vb—The Class for the Stock Information Service

```
Imports WS_Ch15.StockService
Public Class MyStockData
  Private _CompanyName As String
  Private _LastTradeAmount As Decimal
  Private _StockChange As Decimal
  Private _ChangePercent As String
  Private _LastTradeDateTime As DateTime
  Private _StockSymbol As String
  Public Sub New(ByVal QD As QuoteData)
    _CompanyName = QD.CompanyName
    _LastTradeAmount = QD.LastTradeAmount
    _StockChange = QD.StockChange
    _ChangePercent = QD.ChangePercent
    _LastTradeDateTime = QD.LastTradeDateTime
    _StockSymbol = QD.StockSymbol
  End Sub

  Public ReadOnly Property CompanyName() As String
  Get
    Return _CompanyName
  End Get
  End Property

  Public ReadOnly Property LastTradeAmount() As String
  Get
```

LISTING 15.4   Continued

```
   Return _LastTradeAmount.ToString()
End Get
End Property

Public ReadOnly Property StockChange() As String
Get
  Return _StockChange.ToString()
End Get
End Property

Public ReadOnly Property ChangePercent() As String
Get
  Return _ChangePercent
End Get
End Property

Public ReadOnly Property LastTradeDateTime() As String
Get
  Return _LastTradeDateTime.ToString("MM/dd/yyyy hh:mm tt")
End Get
End Property

Public ReadOnly Property StockSymbol() As String
Get
  Return _StockSymbol
End Get
End Property
End Class
```

This object really has one function—to take the data from the QuoteData object passed into it and to store the data in private member variables. When the data is shown in a control that supports data binding, the properties on the object will return the actual data. For binding purposes, if the object you're using does not have properties, the binding will not work properly. You'll see more how to use this later in the application.

Creating the Web User Controls

One of the nicest features about writing ASP.NET applications is the ability to create Web User Controls, which are stored in .ascx files. You can think of these as "smart includes." In classic ASP, server-side includes were one method for bringing in common code and HTML to multiple pages. However, you couldn't pass or change parameters, such as the page title or other pieces of information.

However, Web User Controls have this ability and more. You can create complex code in these controls and then use them as part of Web forms that you create simply by registering them in the page.

To get started, add a new Web User Control to your project and name it **header.ascx**. The Web User Control has both the front-end (stored in the .ascx file) and the code-behind (stored in the .ascx.vb or .ascx.cs file). The front-end code for the header is shown in Listing 15.5.

LISTING 15.5   header.ascx—Front-End Code for the Page Header

```
<%@ Control AutoEventWireup="false"
    Codebehind="header.ascx.vb" Inherits="WS_Ch15.header"
TargetSchema="http://schemas.microsoft.com/intellisense/ie5" %>
<!DOCTYPE HTML PUBLIC "-//W3C//DTD HTML 4.0 Transitional//EN" >
<html>
  <head>
    <title>myPortal:
      <% = Title %>
    </title>
    <meta http-equiv="Content-Type" content="text/html; charset=iso-8859-1">
    <link href="styles.css" rel="stylesheet" type="text/css">
  </head>
  <body topmargin="0" leftmargin="0">
    <table width="100%" bgcolor="#000084" cellspacing="0" cellpadding="0">
      <tr bgcolor="#000084">
        <td valign="middle">
        <a href="default.aspx"><img src="pics/myportal.gif" vspace="10" width="148"
          height="40" border="0" alt="Logo - Click for home page"></a></td>
        <td valign="middle"><img src="/pics/spacer.gif" alt=""
            height="60" width="1" vspace="10"></td>
      </tr>
    </table>
    <table width="100%" cellpadding="4">
      <tr>
        <td valign="top">
          <p class="pageheading"><% = Title %></p>
```

For the most part, this user control is just a portion of HTML used to build the page. The difference is in the code that's marked, which is used to print the value of a variable called `Title`. This variable is defined as a public member of the user control, which means it can be set when the header control is referenced in other pages.

The code behind this page is shown in Listing 15.6.

LISTING 15.6   `header.ascx.vb`— Code behind for the Page Header

```
Public MustInherit Class header
    Inherits System.Web.UI.UserControl

    Public Title As String

    Private Sub Page_Load(ByVal sender As System.Object, ➥
      ByVal e As System.EventArgs) Handles MyBase.Load
        'Put user code to initialize the page here
    End Sub


End Class
```

Most of the code for this particular control doesn't change, except for the addition of a public variable called `Title`. By adding the public variable, you've essentially created a parameter that lets pages control what this control does. This is just a simple example of this functionality, but it's a helpful feature to have.

The second user control you need to add takes care of the footer of the page. The front-end of the control is shown in Listing 15.7.

LISTING 15.7   `footer.ascx`—Front-End Code for the Page Footer

```
<%@ Control Language="vb" AutoEventWireup="false"
      Codebehind="footer.ascx.vb" Inherits="WS_Ch15.footer"
TargetSchema="http://schemas.microsoft.com/intellisense/ie5" %>
<hr noshade>
<span class="copyright">Copyright &copy;
  <% = Year(Now) %>
  by Northstar Computer Systems.</span> </td></tr>
  </table>
  </body>
</html>
```

This particular control doesn't need to have any code in its code-behind file. This file uses the `Year` function and the `Now` function to show the current year in the copyright line. This ensures that the page's date is always current. The rest of the HTML takes care of closing out the table opened in the header control, as well as closing out the page using </body> and </html> tags.

The last file you need for the controls to work is the style sheet, stored in styles.css. The code for this page is shown in Listing 15.8.

LISTING 15.8   styles.css—Style Sheet for the Control

```
.copyright {
     font-family : Tahoma, Arial, Helvetica;
     font-size : 7pt;
     color : Black;
     margin-top: 0px;
}
.pageheading {
     font-family : Tahoma, Arial, Helvetica;
     font-size: large;
     color: #666666;
     text-decoration : none;
     font-weight : bold;
}
.subheading {
     font-family : Tahoma, Arial, Helvetica;
     font-size: medium;
     color: #000084;
     text-decoration : none;
     font-weight : bold;
}
.largetext {
     font-family : Verdana, Arial, Helvetica;
     font-size: small;
     color: Black;
     font-weight: bold;
     text-decoration : none;
}
.text {
     font-family : Verdana, Arial, Helvetica;
     font-size: x-small;
     color: Black;
     text-decoration : none;
}

.errortext {
```

LISTING 15.8   Continued

```
    font-family : Verdana, Arial, Helvetica;
    font-size: x-small;
    font-weight: bold;
    color: Red;
    text-decoration : none;
}

.tableheading {
    background-color: #5A7394;
    font-family: Verdana, Arial, Helvetica;
    font-size: xx-small;
    font-weight: bold;
    color: White;
    padding : 3px 3px 3px 3px;
    vertical-align : top;
}
.tabletext {
    font-family : Verdana, Arial, Helvetica;
    font-size: xx-small;
    color: Black;
    vertical-align : top;
    padding : 3px 3px 3px 3px;
}
.tabletext_gray {
    font-family : Verdana, Arial, Helvetica;
    font-size: xx-small;
    color: Black;
    vertical-align : top;
    background-color : #DDDDDD;
    padding : 3px 3px 3px 3px;
}
```

These styles are all used in various pages throughout this application.

Building the Web Pages

The next step in the application is to build the Web pages. There are several pages required for this application, but we make the best use of the profile editor by using it for both adding users and editing existing users.

Creating the Login Page

Because the Web pages are interconnected via the security scheme and the users table, it's probably best to start with the login page's code first. The page is named login.aspx, and the front-end code is shown in Listing 15.9.

LISTING 15.9   login.aspx—Front-End Code for the Login Page

```
<%@ Page language="vb" AutoEventWireup="false" Inherits="WS_Ch15.Login" Tar-
getSchema="http://schemas.microsoft.com/intellisense/ie5"
CodeBehind="login.aspx.vb" %>
<%@ Register TagPrefix="Portal" Tagname="Header" Src="header.ascx" %>
<%@ Register TagPrefix="Portal" Tagname="Footer" Src="footer.ascx" %>
<Portal:Header id="PageHeader" runat="server" Title="Login" /></P>
<asp:label id="lblMessage" runat="server" class="text">
Please enter your user name (or e-mail address) and password in the form below.</p>
</asp:label>
<P class="text">Not a registered user yet?
 <a href="profile.aspx">Register today!</a></P>
<form runat="server">
  <table cellspacing="5">
    <tr class="text">
      <td align="right"><b>User Name:</b></td>
      <td>
        <asp:textbox id="txtUserName" columns="40"
          maxlength="100" runat="server" />
      </td>
    </tr>
    <tr class="text">
      <td align="right"><b>Password:</b></td>
      <td>
        <asp:textbox id="txtPassword" textmode="Password"
          columns="20" maxlength="20" runat="server" />
      </td>
    </tr>
    <tr class="text">
      <td align="right"><asp:CheckBox id="chkSavePassword"
        runat="server" /></td>
      <td class="text">Save password on this computer?</td>
    </tr>
    <tr class="text">
```

LISTING 15.9   Continued

```
    <td colspan="2"> </td>
  </tr>
  <tr class="text">
    <td colspan="2" align="middle">
      <input type="submit" id="btnLogin" runat="server"
        value="Log In">
      <input type="reset" id="btnReset" runat="server"
        value="Clear">
    </td>
  </tr>
</table>
</form>
<Portal:Footer id="PageFooter" runat="server" />
```

For the most part, this page is a standard data entry form, with the exception of the highlighted code. The code marked in this listing is used to register and use the Web User Controls in the page. The Register directives name the controls and provide links to the source code for each control. When registered, the controls can be used by specifying the type of control, the ID with which they are accessed, and that they should "runat" the server. In the Header control, the Title is also specified as an attribute of the tag. This attribute maps directly to the public variable that you created as part of the Header control. At the bottom of the page, the Footer tag is referenced and is displayed on the page. Because the footer doesn't have any public variables, no additional declarations are required here.

The code behind this login page is shown in Listing 15.10.

LISTING 15.10   login.aspx.vb—Code Behind for the Login Page

```
Imports System.Data.SqlClient
Imports System.Web.Security

Public Class Login
  Inherits System.Web.UI.Page
  Protected WithEvents lblMessage As System.Web.UI.WebControls.Label
  Protected WithEvents txtUserName As System.Web.UI.WebControls.TextBox
  Protected WithEvents txtPassword As System.Web.UI.WebControls.TextBox
  Protected WithEvents chkSavePassword As System.Web.UI.WebControls.CheckBox
  Protected WithEvents btnLogin As System.Web.UI.HtmlControls.HtmlInputButton
  Protected WithEvents btnReset As System.Web.UI.HtmlControls.HtmlInputButton
```

LISTING 15.10   Continued

```
Private Sub Page_Load(ByVal sender As System.Object, ➥
  ByVal e As System.EventArgs) Handles MyBase.Load
  Dim strUserID As String
  If (Page.IsPostBack) Then
    Dim db As New Database()
    Dim dr As SqlDataReader = db.GetDataReader("sp_GetUser '" ➥
      & txtUserName.Text & "', '" & txtPassword.Text & "'", True)
    If dr.Read() Then
      strUserID = dr("pkUserID")
      dr.Close()
      FormsAuthentication.RedirectFromLoginPage(strUserID, ➥
        chkSavePassword.Checked)
    Else
      dr.Close()
      lblMessage.Text = ➥
        "ERROR: The user name and/or password you entered were incorrect."
      lblMessage.CssClass = "errortext"
    End If
  End If
End Sub
End Class
```

After the server-side controls have been declared, the next code takes care of the case in which the user has entered data in the form and clicked the Login button. The username and password go into a stored procedure call to verify that the user name/password combination exists. The GetDataReader normally reads the first record to "prime" the reader so you don't have to do a read to get the first record. In this case, we tell the GetDataReader to omit that initial read so that the code here can check the result of the Read method. If it returns a false, no records were returned and the user name/password combination was invalid. In this case, the lblMessage control's text is changed and the style class is changed to be errortext, which is a bold red font.

If the username and password are good, the routine reads the user ID value, closes the data reader, and stores the ID value as the value of the authentication cookie. This gives us easy access to that ID value in other pages in the system. The RedirectFromLoginPage has two functions—set the authentication cookie and mark it as persistent or not, and to send the user on his/her way to the page that was originally requested.

Creating the Profile Editor

The next page you need to build is the profile editor, which is used for both creating new users and editing existing users. When it is being used in "new user" mode, it looks like Figure 15.3.

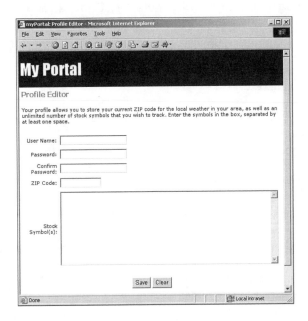

FIGURE 15.3 Profile editor screen for the portal application.

In profile editor mode, only the ZIP code and stock boxes are available, because the application does not allow the username to be changed. Changing the password is tricky, because ASP.NET does not allow password text fields to be assigned values. This is probably due to security concerns, but I couldn't find any documentation on the actual reasoning. Typically, I would create a form that has an Old Password and then New Password and Confirm Password boxes. This bypasses the issue by making the user type in the old and new passwords, eliminating the need to populate the boxes.

The HTML code for this page is shown in Listing 15.11.

LISTING 15.11 `profile.aspx` —HTML Code for the Profile Editor

```
<%@ Page Language="vb" AutoEventWireup="false"
  Codebehind="profile.aspx.vb" Inherits="WS_Ch15.profile"%>
<%@ Register TagPrefix="Portal" Tagname="Header" Src="header.ascx" %>
<%@ Register TagPrefix="Portal" Tagname="Footer" Src="footer.ascx" %>
```

LISTING 15.11   Continued

```
<Portal:Header id="PageHeader" runat="server" Title="Profile Editor" />
<p class="text">Your profile allows you to store your current ZIP code for the
  local weather in your area, as well as an unlimited number of stock symbols
  that you wish to track. Enter the symbols in the box, separated by at least one
  space.
</p>
<form runat="server" ID="frmUser">
  <asp:ValidationSummary id="valSummary" runat="server"
    CssClass="errortext"
    HeaderText=
      "ERROR: The following problems were found and need to be corrected:">
  </asp:ValidationSummary>
  <table cellspacing="5">
    <tr class="text" id="trUserName" runat="server">
      <td align="right" class="boldtext">User Name:</td>
      <td>
        <asp:textbox id="txtUserName" columns="20" maxlength="20"
          runat="server" Text='<%# dr("UserName") %>' />
        <asp:RequiredFieldValidator id="valReqUserName" runat="server"
          ErrorMessage="User name is a required field."
          ControlToValidate="txtUserName" Display="None">
        </asp:RequiredFieldValidator>
      </td>
    </tr>
    <tr class="text" runat="server" id="trPassword">
      <td align="right" class="boldtext">Password:</td>
      <td>
        <asp:textbox id="txtPassword" textmode="Password"
          columns="20" maxlength="20" runat="server"
          Text='<%# dr("Password") %>' />
        <asp:RequiredFieldValidator id="valReqPassword" runat="server"
          ErrorMessage="Password is a required field."
          ControlToValidate="txtPassword" Display="None">
        </asp:RequiredFieldValidator>
      </td>
    </tr>
    <tr class="text" runat="server" id="trConfirmPassword">
      <td align="right" class="boldtext">Confirm Password:</td>
      <td>
        <asp:textbox id="txtConfirmPassword" textmode="Password"
          columns="20" maxlength="20" runat="server"
```

LISTING 15.11   Continued

```
          Text='<%# dr("Password") %>' />
      <asp:RequiredFieldValidator id="valReqConfirm" runat="server"
         ErrorMessage="Please confirm the password you entered."
         ControlToValidate="txtConfirmPassword" Display="None">
      </asp:RequiredFieldValidator>
      <asp:CompareValidator id="valCompConfirm" runat="server"
         ErrorMessage="The passwords you entered do not match."
         ControlToValidate="txtConfirmPassword"
         ControlToCompare="txtPassword" Display="None">
      </asp:CompareValidator>
    </td>
  </tr>
  <tr class="text">
    <td align="right" class="boldtext">ZIP Code:</td>
    <td>
      <asp:textbox id="txtZIP" columns="10" maxlength="50"
         runat="server"  Text='<%# dr("ZipCode") %>' />
      <asp:RequiredFieldValidator id="valReqZip" runat="server"
         ErrorMessage="ZIP code is a required field."
         ControlToValidate="txtZIP" Display="None">
      </asp:RequiredFieldValidator>
    </td>
  </tr>
  <tr class="text">
    <td align="right" class="boldtext">Stock Symbol(s):</td>
    <td>
      <asp:textbox id="txtStocks" TextMode="MultiLine" Wrap="True"
         Rows="10" Columns="60" runat="server" />
    </td>
  </tr>
  <tr class="text">
    <td colspan="2"> </td>
  </tr>
  <tr class="text">
    <td colspan="2" align="middle">
      <input type="submit" id="btnSave" runat="server" value="Save"
         NAME="btnSave"> <input type="reset" id="btnReset" value="Clear">
    </td>
  </tr>
  </table>
</form>
<Portal:Footer id="PageFooter" runat="server" />
```

To handle validation on this page, you can use the various validation controls included with .NET. If you're building this page in the development environment, you may need to add the controls by right-clicking your Toolbox and selecting the Customize menu choice. In my installation, these controls were not included in the Toolbox at startup.

The following are the basic validation rules:

- Username, password, password confirmation, and ZIP code are required.

- Password and password confirmation must match.

- The stock box is optional.

Each of the validation controls handles one of these rules. Each field marked as required has a required field validator linked to it. For the password boxes, a CompareValidator makes sure that the boxes match.

When all the validation is complete, a ValidationSummary control displays all the errors in a single list instead of individual nagging prompts, as many sites often do. The ValidationSummary control can be configured to display a message box in addition to putting the text on the page, but when it does, the error is consolidated into a single message.

The one validation we are not doing is verifying that the user ID does not already exist. This could be done using a custom validation control, which can also be added to the page. If you decide to add this code, you may also want to validate that the e-mail address does not already exist either.

The code behind this page is shown in Listing 15.12.

LISTING 15.12   profile.aspx.vb—Code Behind for the Profile Editor

```
Imports System.Data.SqlClient
Imports System.Web.Security

Public Class profile
  Inherits System.Web.UI.Page
  Protected WithEvents txtUserName
      As System.Web.UI.WebControls.TextBox
  Protected WithEvents txtPassword As System.Web.UI.WebControls.TextBox
  Protected WithEvents txtConfirmPassword As System.Web.UI.WebControls.TextBox
  Protected WithEvents txtZIP As System.Web.UI.WebControls.TextBox
  Protected WithEvents txtStocks As System.Web.UI.WebControls.TextBox
  Protected WithEvents btnSave As System.Web.UI.HtmlControls.HtmlInputButton
  Protected WithEvents trUserName As System.Web.UI.HtmlControls.HtmlTableRow
  Protected WithEvents trPassword As System.Web.UI.HtmlControls.HtmlTableRow
```

LISTING 15.12   Continued

```
  Protected WithEvents trConfirmPassword
➥     As System.Web.UI.HtmlControls.HtmlTableRow
  Protected dr As SqlDataReader
  Protected WithEvents valReqUserName
➥     As System.Web.UI.WebControls.RequiredFieldValidator
  Protected WithEvents valReqPassword
➥     As System.Web.UI.WebControls.RequiredFieldValidator
  Protected WithEvents valReqConfirm
➥     As System.Web.UI.WebControls.RequiredFieldValidator
  Protected WithEvents valCompConfirm
➥     As System.Web.UI.WebControls.CompareValidator
  Protected WithEvents valReqZip
➥     As System.Web.UI.WebControls.RequiredFieldValidator
  Protected WithEvents valSummary
➥     As System.Web.UI.WebControls.ValidationSummary
  Private db As Database
#Region " Web Form Designer Generated Code "

  'This call is required by the Web Form Designer.
  <System.Diagnostics.DebuggerStepThrough()> Private Sub InitializeComponent()

  End Sub

  Private Sub Page_Init(ByVal sender As System.Object,
➥     ByVal e As System.EventArgs) Handles MyBase.Init
    'CODEGEN: This method call is required by the Web Form Designer
    'Do not modify it using the code editor.
    InitializeComponent()
  End Sub

#End Region

  Private Sub Page_Load(ByVal sender As System.Object,
➥     ByVal e As System.EventArgs) Handles MyBase.Load
    db = New Database()
    Dim strStocks As String
    If Not Page.IsPostBack Then
      If User.Identity.Name <> "" Then
        trUserName.Visible = False
        trPassword.Visible = False
        trConfirmPassword.Visible = False
        dr = db.GetDataReader("sp_GetUserByID " & User.Identity.Name)
```

LISTING 15.12   Continued

```
        Page.DataBind()
        dr.Close()
        dr = db.GetDataReader("sp_GetUserStocks " & User.Identity.Name, True)
        Do While dr.Read()
          strStocks += dr("pkStockID") + " "
        Loop
        txtStocks.Text = strStocks
        dr.Close()
      Else
        trUserName.Visible = True
        trPassword.Visible = True
        trConfirmPassword.Visible = True
      End If
    End If
  End Sub


  Private Sub btnSave_ServerClick(ByVal sender As System.Object,
➥    ByVal e As System.EventArgs) Handles btnSave.ServerClick
    Dim strLoop As String
    If User.Identity.Name = "" Then
      If Page.IsValid Then
        db.Execute("INSERT INTO tblUsers (UserName, Password, ZipCode) "
➥          & "VALUES " _
          & "('" & txtUserName.Text & "', '" & txtPassword.Text
➥          & "', '" & txtZIP.Text & "')")
        Dim dr As SqlDataReader =
➥          db.GetDataReader("sp_GetUser '" & txtUserName.Text & "', '"
➥            & txtPassword.Text & "'")
        FormsAuthentication.SetAuthCookie(dr("pkUserID"), False)
        dr.Close()

        For Each strLoop In txtStocks.Text.Split(" ")
          db.Execute("INSERT INTO tblUserStocks (pkStockID, fkUserID) "
➥            & "VALUES ('" & strLoop & "', " & User.Identity.Name & ")")
        Next
        Response.Redirect("default.aspx")
      End If
    Else
      If Page.IsValid Then
        db.Execute("UPDATE tblUsers SET ZipCode = '" & txtZIP.Text
➥          & "' WHERE pkUserID = " & User.Identity.Name)
```

LISTING 15.12   Continued

```
        db.Execute("DELETE FROM tblUserStocks WHERE fkUserID = "
➥         & User.Identity.Name)
        For Each strLoop In txtStocks.Text.Split(" ")
            db.Execute("INSERT INTO tblUserStocks (pkStockID, fkUserID) "
➥             & "VALUES ('" & strLoop & "', " & User.Identity.Name & ")")
        Next
        Response.Redirect("default.aspx")
      End If
    End If
    db.Close()
  End Sub
End Class
```

Because this page is used for both adding and editing, we can use the
User.Identity.Name object to tell us if the user is logged in or not. Remember the
user ID that we stored in the authentication cookie? That's the value that will be in
the User.Identity.Name field. If the user is not logged in, User.Identity.Name will
be an empty string. This gives us an easy way to tell which mode we're in. Note that
this page will not run properly if you're not logged in, because it uses the
User.Identity.Name to update profile information.

If the user is just starting out and isn't logged in, we only run code in this portion of
the page if the page is valid. This property is set by the validation controls on the
form. If any errors exist, this property will be set to False. When we know that the
data meets our validation rules, the new user is inserted into the table, and then the
new user ID number is retrieved and stored in the authentication cookie using the
SetAuthCookie method. The SetAuthCookie method works in a similar way to
RedirectFromLoginPage, just without the redirection to another page. Calling
SetAuthCookie saves the user from having to log in after they register.

After the user ID has been retrieved, the stock text box is split wherever a space is
found, and each row is inserted into the tblUserStocks table.

In cases where we are editing a user's profile, we have to populate the form and
update the ZIP and the stock table. If you go back to the previous listing, you will see
the controls on the page look like the following:

```
<asp:textbox id="txtConfirmPassword"
  textmode="Password"
  columns="20"
  maxlength="20"
  runat="server"
  Text='<%# dr("Password") %>' />
```

The Text property is being bound to an object named dr, which happens to be a SqlDataReader. When we call Page.DataBind(), the controls on the ASP.NET page are bound to the properties of the SqlDataReader and the data currently there is filled into the box. If the DataBind method is never called, this code is ignored. This saves us the trouble of populating these fields manually. We still have to fill the stock list, but that is easily done using another SqlDataReader object and a simple loop.

When we're ready to save the data, we write an UPDATE SQL statement instead of an INSERT. Other than that, the update code is basically the same as the new record.

Writing the Portal Page

The next page you need to create is the portal page itself. This page requires the use of four Web Services that were available at the time of writing. If any of these services go away, you can find new ones at XMethods.net. The four services that should be added as Web References are

- *NewsService*—http://www.xmlme.com/WSCustNews.asmx?WSDL

- *StockService*—
http://ws.cdyne.com/delayedstockquote/delayedstockquote.asmx?wsdl

- *WeatherService*—http://www.vbws.com/services/
weatherretriever.asmx?WSDL

- *ZipCodeService*—http://www.alethea.net/webservices/ZipCode.asmx?WSDL

The HTML code for the page is somewhat lengthy due to the two Repeater controls being used for data formatting. The HTML code is shown in Listing 15.13.

LISTING 15.13   default.aspx—HTML Code for the Portal Page

```
<%@ Register TagPrefix="Portal" Tagname="Footer" Src="footer.ascx" %>
<%@ Register TagPrefix="Portal" Tagname="Header" Src="header.ascx" %>
<%@ Page Language="vb" AutoEventWireup="false"
    Codebehind="default.aspx.vb" Inherits="WS_Ch15.HomePage"%>
<Portal:Header id="PageHeader" runat="server" Title="My Home Page" />
<p class="text"><b>Actions:</b> [
<a href="profile.aspx">Edit My Profile</a> | <a href="logout.aspx">
    Log Out</a> ]</p>
<hr noshade>
<p class="subheading">Current Weather</p>
<table cellspacing="4" cellpadding="4" id="tblWeather" runat="server">
  <tr>
    <td valign="center">
      <img id="imgGraphic" runat="server">
```

LISTING 15.13   Continued

```
      </td>
    <td valign="top">
      <asp:Label id="lblCityState" runat="server" class="largetext" />
      <table cellpadding="0" cellspacing="0">
        <tr>
          <td class="text">Temperature:</td>
          <td class="text"><asp:Label id="lblTemperature"
              runat="server" class="text" /></td>
        </tr>
        <tr>
          <td class="text">Conditions:</td>
          <td class="text"><asp:Label id="lblConditions"
              runat="server" class="text" /></td>
        </tr>
        <tr>
          <td class="text">Humidity:</td>
          <td class="text"><asp:Label id="lblHumidity"
              runat="server" class="text" /></td>
        </tr>
      </table>
    </td>
  </tr>
</table>

<ASP:Repeater id="rptStocks" runat="server">
  <HeaderTemplate>
    <hr noshade>
    <table cellpadding="4" cellspacing="0" width="100%">
    <tr>
      <td colspan="2" class="subheading">Stock Watcher</td>
    </tr>
    <tr class="tableheading">
      <td width="30%" align="center">Company Name</td>
      <td width="10%" align="center">Last Price</td>
      <td width="10%" align="center">Change</td>
      <td width="10%" align="center">% Change</td>
      <td width="20%" align="center">Time</td>
      <td width="20%" align="center">Actions</td>
    </tr>
  </HeaderTemplate>
  <ItemTemplate>
    <tr class="tabletext">
```

LISTING 15.13   Continued

```
      <td><%# DataBinder.Eval(Container.DataItem, "CompanyName") %></td>
      <td align="right">
      <%# DataBinder.Eval(Container.DataItem, "LastTradeAmount") %></td>
      <td align="right">
      <%# DataBinder.Eval(Container.DataItem, "StockChange") %></td>
      <td align="center">
      <%# DataBinder.Eval(Container.DataItem, "ChangePercent") %></td>
      <td align="center">
      <%# DataBinder.Eval(Container.DataItem, "LastTradeDateTime") %></td>
      <td align="center">
      <a href="http://quote.yahoo.com/q?d=v1&s=<%# DataBinder.Eval
      (Container.DataItem, "StockSymbol") %>" target=_blank>View 
       Details</a>
      </td>
    </tr>
  </ItemTemplate>
  <AlternatingItemTemplate>
    <tr class="tabletext_gray">
      <td><%# DataBinder.Eval(Container.DataItem, "CompanyName") %></td>
      <td align="right"><%# DataBinder.Eval(Container.DataItem,
         "LastTradeAmount") %></td>
      <td align="right"><%# DataBinder.Eval(Container.DataItem,
      "StockChange") %></td>
      <td align="center"><%# DataBinder.Eval(Container.DataItem,
      "ChangePercent") %></td>
      <td align="center"><%# DataBinder.Eval(Container.DataItem,
         "LastTradeDateTime") %></td>
      <td align="center">
      <a href="http://quote.yahoo.com/q?d=v1&s=<%# DataBinder.Eval
      (Container.DataItem, "StockSymbol") %>" target=_blank>
       View Details</a>
      </td>
    </tr>
  </AlternatingItemTemplate>
  <FooterTemplate>
    </table>
  </FooterTemplate>
</ASP:Repeater>

<ASP:Repeater id="rptArticles" runat="server">
  <HeaderTemplate>
    <hr noshade>
```

LISTING 15.13   Continued

```
  <table cellpadding="4" cellspacing="0" width="100%">
  <tr>
    <td colspan="2" class="subheading">News Headlines</td>
  </tr>
  <tr class="tableheading">
    <td width="60%" align="center">Article Title</td>
    <td width="30%" align="center">Date/Time</td>
    <td width="10%" align="center">Actions</td>
  </tr>
</HeaderTemplate>
<ItemTemplate>
  <tr class="tabletext">
    <td valign="top">
    <%# DataBinder.Eval(Container.DataItem, "headline_text") %><br>
    <i><%# DataBinder.Eval(Container.DataItem, "source") %></i>
    </td>
    <td valign="top" align="center">
    <%# DateTime.Parse(DataBinder.Eval(Container.DataItem,
    "harvest_time")).ToString("MM/dd/yyyy hh:mm tt") %>
    </td>
    <td valign="top" align="center">
    <a href="<%# DataBinder.Eval(Container.DataItem, "url") %>"
       target=_blank>View</a>
    </td>
  </tr>
</ItemTemplate>
<AlternatingItemTemplate>
  <tr class="tabletext_gray">
    <td valign="top">
    <%# DataBinder.Eval(Container.DataItem, "headline_text") %><br>
    <i><%# DataBinder.Eval(Container.DataItem, "source") %></i>
    </td>
    <td valign="top" align="center">
    <%# DateTime.Parse(DataBinder.Eval(Container.DataItem,
    "harvest_time")).ToString("MM/dd/yyyy hh:mm tt") %>
    </td>
    <td valign="top" align="center">
    <a href="<%# DataBinder.Eval(Container.DataItem, "url") %>"
       target=_blank>View</a>
    </td>
  </tr>
</AlternatingItemTemplate>
```

LISTING 15.13   Continued

```
  <FooterTemplate>
    </table>
  </FooterTemplate>
</ASP:Repeater>



<Portal:Footer id="PageFooter" runat="server" />
```

There are three distinct sections on this page—the weather display, the stock ticker display, and the headline viewer. The code behind will make this clearer, because each section is populated via a separate function. The code-behind is shown in Listing 15.14.

LISTING 15.14   `default.aspx.vb`—Code Behind for the Portal Page

```
Imports System.Data.SqlClient
Imports System.IO

Public Class HomePage
    Inherits System.Web.UI.Page
    Protected WithEvents lblCityState As System.Web.UI.WebControls.Label
    Protected WithEvents lblTemperature As System.Web.UI.WebControls.Label
    Protected WithEvents lblConditions As System.Web.UI.WebControls.Label
    Protected WithEvents lblHumidity As System.Web.UI.WebControls.Label
    Protected WithEvents tblHeadlines As System.Web.UI.HtmlControls.HtmlTable
    Protected WithEvents imgGraphic As System.Web.UI.HtmlControls.HtmlImage
    Protected WithEvents rptArticles As Repeater
    Protected WithEvents rptStocks As Repeater
    Private RowCount As Integer = 0
    Private SS As StockService.DelayedStockQuote

    Private Sub Page_Load(ByVal sender As System.Object,
        ByVal e As System.EventArgs) Handles MyBase.Load
        Dim db As New Database()
        Dim dr As SqlDataReader = db.GetDataReader("sp_GetUserByID "
            & User.Identity.Name)

        RetrieveWeather(dr("ZipCode"))
        RetrieveNews()
        dr.Close()
        RetrieveStocks(db)
```

LISTING 15.14   Continued

```
    End Sub

    Private Sub RetrieveWeather(ByVal ZipCode As String)
      Dim cs As New ZipCodeService.ZipCode()
      Dim ws As New WeatherService.WeatherRetriever()
      Dim wi As WeatherService.CurrentWeather = ws.GetWeather(ZipCode)
      Try
        lblCityState.Text = cs.ZipCodeToCityState(ZipCode)(0)
      Catch e As Exception
        lblCityState.Text = "ZIP Code " & ZipCode
      End Try
      imgGraphic.Src = wi.IconUrl
      lblTemperature.Text = wi.CurrentTemp.ToString("#0") & "&deg; F"
      lblConditions.Text = wi.Conditions
      lblHumidity.Text = (wi.Humidity * 100).ToString("#0") & "%"
      cs = Nothing
      ws = Nothing
      wi = Nothing
    End Sub

    Private Sub RetrieveNews()
      Dim ds As New DataSet()

      Dim ns As New NewsService.GetCustomNews()
      Dim strNews As String = ns.GetCustomNews("AP")
      Dim fn As String = Server.MapPath("news"
          & DateTime.Now.ToString("yyyymmdd-hhmmss") + ".xml")
      Dim sr As New StreamWriter(fn, False)
      sr.Write(strNews)
      sr.Close()
      ds.ReadXml(fn)
      File.Delete(fn)

      Dim dt As DataTable = ds.Tables(0)
      Dim i As Integer
      Dim dtLimited As DataTable

      If dt.Rows.Count > 10 Then
        dtLimited = ds.Tables(0).Clone()
        For i = 0 To 9
          dtLimited.ImportRow(dt.Rows(i))
        Next
```

LISTING 15.14   Continued

```
      rptArticles.DataSource = dtLimited.DefaultView
      rptArticles.DataBind()
    Else
      rptArticles.DataSource = ds.Tables(0).DefaultView
      rptArticles.DataBind()
    End If
  End Sub

  Private Sub RetrieveStocks(ByVal db As Database)
    Dim strStocks As String
    Dim alStockInfo As New ArrayList()
    Dim sd As StockService.QuoteData
    Dim md As MyStockData
    SS = New StockService.DelayedStockQuote()
    Dim dr As SqlDataReader = db.GetDataReader("sp_GetUserStocks "
      & User.Identity.Name, True)
    Do While dr.Read()
      sd = SS.GetQuote(dr("pkStockID"), "0")
      md = New MyStockData(sd)
      alStockInfo.Add(md)
    Loop
    If alStockInfo.Count = 0 Then
      rptStocks.Visible = False
    Else
      rptStocks.DataSource = alStockInfo
      rptStocks.DataBind()
    End If
    dr.Close()
  End Sub

End Class
```

The RetrieveWeather routine calls the WeatherService Web Service to retrieve the weather for the local area. It uses the ZipCodeService to get the name of the city and state, but if this service is not available (which it was occasionally while I was testing), the ZIP code is displayed by itself. If the data does come back, a graphic URL as well as the weather information is filled into the table, with a little formatting as necessary.

The RetrieveNews routine is next and it uses a service that was a little difficult to figure out. It appeared that if you put in a keyword (I used "Wall Street Journal") it would return articles that had that reference. However, there wasn't a good way to tell if the keywords you were using were actually getting good results, or it just ignored them. As time goes on, I'm sure the big news providers (CNN, MSNBC, CNBC) will create their own Web Services that you'll be able to use directly.

In the meantime, the data coming back from the `NewsService` is a large XML document. I chose to store that file on disk temporarily and then read it into the DataSet. There may be an easier way to do this all in memory, but the documentation I found was sketchy and didn't lend itself easily to doing this. After the data has been read into the DataSet, we have an additional problem. The document contains far more stories (around 30, at least) than we want to display. Because we are binding the data to the Repeater, we want to limit the rows we get back. The easiest way I found to do this was to create a copy of the DataSet and then add only the first ten rows into the copy. After this is done, the copy is bound to the Repeater control. If there are less than 10 stories, the DataSet is bound directly to the Repeater.

The last function, `RetrieveStocks`, is even more tricky. The object and service being used returns the data in an object called a `QuoteData` object. Unfortunately, the structure of this object does not bind properly to the Repeater control. You can add all the `QuoteData` objects to the `ArrayList`, but when the binding occurs, there were errors indicating that the object didn't have properties that the data binding engine could use. The easy solution is to create a wrapper that used read-only properties for each of the fields of the `QuoteData` object that you want to use. After doing this, the data binding works perfectly. The only downside of this particular service is that it works with a single stock at a time. This means that it can take a while to get all the data back. To help prevent your page from drawing too many resources, you may want to use output caching on the web page, with a 10–20 minute refresh rate.

NOTE

The Web Service providing the stock quotes allows you to get quotes in testing mode, using a license key (the zero in quotes) they made available. However, if you're planning to use this for commercial purposes, they require fees to be paid on a per-quote basis. The rest of the Web Services used were all freely available.

Building the Log Out Page

When the user is done admiring your work, he/she will want to log out of the system. The HTML for this page is shown in Listing 15.15, and the code behind is shown in Listing 15.16.

LISTING 15.15   `logout.aspx`—HTML Code for the Log Out Page

```
<%@ Page Language="vb" AutoEventWireup="false"
    Codebehind="logout.aspx.vb" Inherits="WS_Ch15.Logout"%>
<%@ Register TagPrefix="Portal" Tagname="Header" Src="header.ascx" %>
```

LISTING 15.15   Continued

```
<%@ Register TagPrefix="Portal" Tagname="Footer" Src="footer.ascx" %>
<Portal:Header id="PageHeader" runat="server" Title="Log Out" />
<p class="text">You have been logged out of
    the My Portal web site. <a href="login.aspx">
    Click here</a> to log in again.
</p>
<Portal:Footer id="PageFooter" runat="server" />
```

LISTING 15.16   `logout.aspx.vb`—Code Behind for the Log Out Page

```
Imports System.Web.Security
Public Class Logout
    Inherits System.Web.UI.Page


    Private Sub Page_Load(ByVal sender As System.Object,
➡        ByVal e As System.EventArgs) Handles MyBase.Load
        FormsAuthentication.SignOut()
    End Sub

End Class
```

The `SignOut` method of the `FormsAuthentication` object takes care of removing the authentication cookie that was placed on the user's machine, effectively logging them out. Attempting to go to any protected page at this point will send the user back to the initial login screen.

Summary

As you can see, there are many Web Services already available on the Internet, and more are sure to follow. When building your portals, take advantage of these services as much as possible. There's no sense rebuilding something that's already done, as long as it works. The key is to tie the portal information being brought back to the user's preferences, which is your job to gather. After you've done that, you can easily create useful services for your users without making them wander all over the Internet looking for good information.

16

Profiting From Your Web Services

IN THIS CHAPTER

- Creating Services that Fill a Need

- Decreasing Business Costs

- Revenue Models

- Marketing the Web Service

After you have identified a need, designed and constructed a Web Service solution, and found a group of people interested in using that solution, how do you make any money from it? Because Web Services are fairly new, no one has yet made their fortune through them. This chapter looks at a few of the revenue models that are being experimented with or examined. It is not meant only for hobbyists who are creating something of value for the outside world. Independent software vendors (ISVs), people with big ideas, and the curious also will benefit from a quick read of this chapter.

Trying to make money via advertising revenue simply will not work with many Web Services. Exceptions are Web pages that provide a user interface for the Web Service. Such pages can inject banner ads that do not interfere with the operation of the application. However, most Web Services are all about machine-to-machine communication. Machines do not buy things. So, how do you profit financially from a Web Service? You can do this in several ways:

- Create deployable Web Services that fill a specific need in your line of business. Sell the package to be hosted on your client's own hardware.

- Charge your users based on use or the right to use.

- Reduce development costs of doing business by using a Web Service created by someone else.

- Something else...

In this chapter, we will look at existing resources that you may want to tap into and expose as Web Services. We will then look at how these might help increase your company's profitability. We will close out the chapter by explaining some of the basic things you will need to do to let people know that your Web Service exists.

Creating Services that Fill a Need

For a Web Service to be successful and make money, you have to create something for which people are willing to pay for. The most visible such family of Web Services today is .NET My Services from Microsoft. Microsoft is hoping that developers will incorporate these services into their own products, allowing Microsoft to handle Internet storage of everything from favorite Web sites and contact information to categorization details. (One of the .NET My Services is called myCategories that allows you to organize more specific items, such as myContacts.) The need they hope to fill is that of a central repository of commonly accessed data. According to the Web site, an individual company can deploy .NET My Services internally for all of its employees. At this point in time, licensing and other issues have not been announced. To stay up to date on any announcements, visit
`http://www.microsoft.com/myservices/`.

What need will your Web Service fulfill? Will your service make it easier for your customers to interact with your business? Maybe you have a large database of information that you want to allow others to use. You might have a specialized system that you host on your own hardware and allow others to access on a rental basis. Regardless of what your idea is, you have to make sure that the service fulfills a need that you believe exists.

A number of services already exist where people pay someone else to maintain data and host servers. An obvious one is Web hosting companies that provide the servers, daily backups, and Internet bandwidth to host a Web site. Another application that people farm out, where all communication is machine to machine is home and business security systems. Companies like ADT have been installing panels in homes that call into a central computer to inform operations staff about potential break-ins and other problems. Look for data or operations that specialize in hosting. Other companies might be interested in renting those capabilities from you and integrating those services into a larger application.

These are examples of where people already make conscious decisions to let someone else handle the hard problems associated with a computer-based system. How do you identify the things you own that someone else might want to rent?

Suppose you have a lot of custom libraries that you use for analysis that might be valuable to others in your industry. Exposing this code as a Web Service may make sense. For example, you may have some sophisticated simulation software. If you simulate the effect of wind on a solid structure, builders of airplanes, and buildings, other items could benefit if you figured out how to expose the application as a Web Service.

Finally, you may simply be a visionary and will know what other people will want to use as a Web Service. If you execute well on the idea and are lucky enough to be right, you may wind up a millionaire.

Decreasing Business Costs

If your Web Service decreases your cost of doing business, it can help profitability, even if you don't charge for use of the service. You could provide a service over the phone or some other medium that typically requires a lot of human interaction. For example, an insurance agent may need to track the status of a given policy. If the policy has not been approved or denied, the agent could use an application from his or her Windows laptop to access another application on the corporate mainframe and discover if the underwriter (the individual responsible for analyzing the risk associated with a given insurance policy and deciding what it will cost to cover that risk) has noted any concerns. A Web Service could be used to tie the two systems together. This improves things, because the salesperson will not have to call someone to get this information. Self-service is just one way to reduce the costs of running your business.

Alternatively, you might have some useful information that many people access for free. Examples of this type of data include census data, package tracking information, and airline flight status. Much of this information is available via Web sites already. By scaling the data down to the minimal amount needed, companies can save money on bandwidth and printing costs. For example, when UPS or FedEx shows you the tracking data for your packages, they also display a large amount of graphical data. Even sparsely populated Web pages can return 10KB of data. Contrast that with a SOAP response of a few hundred bytes and you might see some real cost savings.

Free Web Services do not need to equate to anonymous access. You can require a Passport ID or other authentication and not charge for the data. You can also require a user identity if you expose the Web Service for free to trading partners. It can also make it easier for customers to place orders. Either way, the Web Service helps you save money and become more profitable.

Revenue Models

Web Services can help your company generate income as well as save on the cost of doing business. Several different revenue models exist:

- Charge a flat fee for access to the service
- Charge based on volume of use of the service
- Creatively use the advertising model
- Use a middleman model

We will take a look at each of these models in the following sections.

Flat-Fee Access

For some Web Services, it may make sense to charge users a flat fee for use of the service, regardless of how much they actually use it. This benefits the consumers because they know exactly how much they will be charged. The downside of this for the owner of the service is that a few clients can account for the majority of the use of the service.

Flat-fee access makes the most sense when looking at renting applications for a fixed period of time. Consumers know how long they want the software, but they may have no idea how heavily they will use it. The user may rent some data analysis functionality or a full-blown application. You might provide a custom user interface that interacts with the back-end Web Service.

Volume-Based Access Fee

Use this model when you discover that users only want to pay for how they use the Web Service. You can charge users based on how much data they store at the service or on how many calls they make into it. For example, you might offer a service that provides up-to-the minute stock quotes. After analyzing the market, you discover that most individuals check their stocks ten times per day. A few users (stock brokers and day traders) may make over a thousand calls per day. To balance costs, you can set up a fee schedule that looks like the following:

- 1–50 calls/day = $0.07/call
- 51–100 calls/day = $0.06/call
- 101–500 calls/day = $0.05/call
- 501–1000 calls/day = $0.04/call
- More than 1001 calls/day = $0.03/call

To do this type of billing, you will need to audit all calls coming into the Web Service so that you can figure the costs on a day-by-day basis. This fee schedule may work for any Web Service where the revenue is based on call volume. Just make sure that your revenue is greater than your cost to provide the Web Service.

Under this model, you may also want to add a no-charge use level. Think of this as a sample that users can pay for if their needs go up. This way, you don't have to worry about charging for low use where the billing may cost more than the cost of providing the service.

So, how would you track all of this information? To correctly bill individuals, you will want to audit the Web Service access—track the identity of the caller, the date and time of the call, and the Web method that he or she called. When generating the bills, just add up the number of calls the user executed and bill appropriately. To authenticate the users, follow the recommendations in the authentication section of Chapter 6, "Security Issues with Web Services."

Creative Use of the Advertising Model

Advertising can work with Web Services. The trick is figuring out how to expose advertisements to your users. The only way to do this is to take some control of the user interface used to access the Web Service. You can do this by either creating your own user interface or by requiring licensees of the Web Service to also display ads that you provide. For applications where the primary user is a person, this model may work. Obviously, this model fails when the primary user is another machine.

A Middleman Model

Believe it or not, you can actually make money being a concentrator of information. A database of books could charge publishers for the cost of adding the books to the collection. They might charge an extra fee for particular titles to show up when specific words are searched. For example, Sams Publishing might pay such a service to prominently list the title of this book whenever a user searched for SOAP books. The Web Service could add value for the end user by showing who is selling the book for the lowest price. Why would Sams pay for this? Assuming that all booksellers pay the same price per book, Sams makes more money if all booksellers combined sell more copies.

The middleman model can work in other ways as well. You can serve as an aggregator of disparate Web Services. For example, several Web Services may exist that allow individuals to get the prices of stocks from stock markets around the globe. You could add value by aggregating these different request types and always using the provider that is currently the fastest.

In general, this model will work whenever you can add value by placing yourself in the transaction stream between the creator of the product and the end user.

Marketing the Web Service

After you have a Web Service written and you understand how you are going to make money from it, how do you get people to use it? First, you need to register the Web Service with a UDDI registry. Currently, only Microsoft and IBM have publicly shared registries. More will come online as the Web Services model takes hold. Within the registry, make sure to register your WSDL as well as information about your business, the industries it relates to, and any pertinent contact information. The good news for you is that the registries hosted by Microsoft and IBM are free. As of this writing, Microsoft and IBM intend to keep the registry free forever. The easiest way to submit a Web Service to the registry is through Visual Studio .NET. Chapter 4, "Using Attributes to Shape the WSDL and XML," has a demonstration of how to do this and details the information needed to register. For more information, go to `http://uddi.microsoft.com`.

Other than registering with UDDI, you should market the Web Service the same as you would for any other application in the industry. This means running advertisements in industry journals, sending out sales people, and direct mailing to potential customers. Make sure that you have a few samples available so that customers will know what they might be buying.

Summary

In this chapter, we took a look at how to make money from your Web Services. The first task is deciding what the Web Service will be and how it will help the business become more profitable. Then, look at how you will make money from the Web Service. You can charge for access, get paid by suppliers of data, or provide the service for free in an effort to reduce other costs. After this is all done, you need to find some way to get others to use the Web Service.

A

Additional Resources

XML General

W3 and XML: `http://www.w3.org/xml`

XML Schema: `http://www.w3.org/xml/schema`

Microsoft: `http://msdn.microsoft.com/xml/default.asp`

XML in Action, William J. Pardi, Microsoft Press, 1999 (ISBN 0735605629)

XML Bible, Elliot Rusty Harold, Hungry Minds, Inc., 1999 (ISBN 0764532367)

XML Unleashed, Michael Morrison, Sams, 1999 (ISBN 0672315149)

Professional ASP XML, Mark Baartse, et al., Wrox Press, 2000 (ISBN 1861004028)

Essential XML: Beyond Markup, Don Box, et al., Addison-Wesley, 2000 (ISBN 0201709147)

General .NET Information

Microsoft: `http://msdn.microsoft.com/net`

Got Dot Net: `http://www.gotdotnet.com`

Discussion List: `http://discuss.develop.com/dotnet.html`

"ATL Server and Visual Studio .NET: Developing High-Performance Web Applications Gets Easier," Shaun McAravey and Ben Hickman, *MSDN Magazine*, April 2001: `http://msdn.microsoft.com/library/en-us/dnmag00/html/atlserv.asp`

"C++ Attributes: Make COM Programming a Breeze with New Feature in Visual Studio .NET," Richard Grimes, *MSDN Magazine*, April 2001: `http://msdn.microsoft.com/library/en-us/dnmag01/html/attributes.asp`

You will also want to subscribe to one or more of the newsgroups located at `nntp://msnews.microsoft.com`. The following list is just a subset of the available groups:

- `microsoft.public.dotnet.general`
- `microsoft.public.dotnet.faqs`
- `microsoft.public.dotnet.framework`
- `microsoft.public.dotnet.aspnet.webservices`
- `microsoft.public.webservice`
- `microsoft.public.xml.soap`

General Web Service Information

Microsoft: `http://msdn.microsoft.com/webservices`

IBM: `http://www-106.ibm.com/developerworks/webservices/`

Web Services Resource Center: `http://soap-wrc.com`

Web Service Position Papers: `http://www.w3.org/2001/03/WSWS-popa/`

Webservices.org: `http://www.webservices.org/`

Xmethods Web Service Listing: `http://www.xmethods.org/`

Salcentral Web Services Brokerage: `http://www.salcentral.com`

SOAP Interoperability Lab: `http://www.xmethods.com/ilab`

Web Services Interoperability Organization: `http//www.ws-i.org`

SOAP/XML Protocol

Applied SOAP: Implementing .NET XML Web Services, Scribner & Stiver, Sams Publishing, 2002 (ISBN 0672321114)

SOAP: Cross Platform Web Service Development Using XML, Seely, Prentice Hall, (ISBN 0130907634)

SOAP Specification: `http://www.w3.org/TR/SOAP/`

Microsoft: `http://msdn.microsoft.com/soap`

XML Protocol: `http://www.w3.org/2000/xp/`

List of Implementations and Resources: `http://www.soapware.org/`

SOAP with Attachments: `http://www.w3.org/TR/SOAP-attachments`

"SOAP in the Microsoft .NET Framework and Visual Studio .NET":
http://msdn.microsoft.com/library/en-us/dndotnet/html/hawksoap.asp

"Fun with SOAP Extensions": http://msdn.microsoft.com/library/en-us/
dnaspnet/html/asp03222001.asp

SOAP Discussion Group: http://discuss.develop.com

SOAP Builders List: http://groups.yahoo.com/group/soapbuilders

Global XML Web Services (GXA): http://msdn.microsoft.com/library/
default.asp?url=/library/en-us/dngxa/html/gloxmlws500.asp

XML Web Services Specifications: http://msdn.microsoft.com/library/
default.asp?url=/library/en-us/dnglobspec/html/wsspecsover.asp

Remoting

"Microsoft .NET Remoting: A Technical Overview:"
http://msdn.microsoft.com/library/en-us/dndotnet/html/hawkremoting.asp

"An Introduction to Microsoft .NET Remoting Framework:"
http://msdn.microsoft.com/library/en-us/dndotnet/html/remoting.asp

UDDI

UDDI.org: http://www.uddi.org (version 1.0 and 2.0)

Microsoft: http://uddi.microsoft.com/ (includes MS UDDI SDK)

WSDL

Microsoft: http://msdn.microsoft.com/xml/general/wsdl.asp

W3: http://www.w3.org/TR/wsdl

WSDL List: http://groups.yahoo.com/group/wsdl

Transactions

"Autonomous Computing" (DAT489), Pat Helland, Microsoft TechEd 2001
(presentation)

Xaml.org: http://www.xaml.org

Principles of Transaction Processing, Bernstein and Newcomer, Morgan Kaufmann
Publishers (ISBN 1558604154)

Tools

TcpTrace: http://www.pocketsoap.com/tcpTrace

Microsoft SOAP Toolkit v2: http://msdn.microsoft.com

Security

XML Digital Signatures: http://www.w3.org/TR/SOAP-dsig/

Applied Cryptography, Bruce Schneier, John Wiley and Sons, 1995 (ISBN 0471117099)

Programming Windows Security, Keith Brown, Addison, 2000 (ISBN 0201604426)

Internet Protocol Security: http://www.microsoft.com/windows2000/techinfo/planning/security/ipsecsteps.asp

Web Service Security:
http://msdn.microsoft.com/vstudio/nextgen/technology/security.asp

The OASIS organization is working on a standard authentication and authorization specification called Security Assertion Markup Language or SAML. More information can be found at http://www.oasis-open.org/committees/security/.

ebXML

General: : http://www.ebxml.org

Specifications: http://www.ebxml.org/specs/index.htm

Sample Web Service

The sample Favorites Web Service and associated documentation can be found at the following locations:

http://msdn.microsoft.com/library/default.asp?URL=/library/techart/ssf1over.htm

http://msdn.microsoft.com/library/?url=/library/en-us/dncold/html/ssfapiref.asp?frame=true

Index